THE POLITICS OF EXILE

*The University of
North Carolina Press
Chapel Hill*

THE POLITICS OF
EXILE

Paraguay's
Febrerista
Party

Paul H. Lewis

To my parents,
 Paul and Kathryn Lewis

Acknowledgments

I should like to take this opportunity to express my gratitude to those who helped to make this study possible. To begin with, the field research was done with the support of a Fulbright-Hayes research grant. Without this opportunity to travel to Argentina to interview the Paraguayan exiles the study would never have gotten underway. Next, I must express my deepest appreciation to the exiles themselves, who gave me so much of their time and attention. I am indebted to literally hundreds of them, all of whom contributed to my understanding of *febrerismo*. Of these, I must mention especially Sr. Carlos Chávez del Valle, Sr. Elpidio Yegros, Dr. Galo Achar, Sr. José Regúnega and Sr. Ulpiano Zorrilla, all of whom extended to me the greatest help and hospitality. I am also thankful to my major professor, Dr. Federico G. Gil, who read the original manuscript, for his advice and encouragement. Finally, I must mention also the contributions of my wife, Anne, who also read the manuscript and suggested many important revisions. To all of these people my most heartfelt thanks. I hope that my ability in telling the story of the Febrerista party is worthy of their interest and help. If I fall short, the fault is mine alone.

Paul H. Lewis

New Orleans
November, 1967

Contents

ix

Introduction

Political exile is relatively common, today, as well as in the past. Banishment was often employed as a form of political retribution in the ancient world, and history is filled with accounts of political leaders, and sometimes whole populations, who were forced to abandon their homelands as a result of either domestic upheavals or conquest by a foreign power. Our own era provides notable examples: the Russian Communists during the Czarist period, the White Russians fleeing the Bolshevik Revolution, the Italian and German anti-Fascist exiles, and the thousands of Cubans and East Europeans who have taken refuge abroad from Communist regimes, to name only a few. It is strange, however, that such a common political problem has attracted so little attention from political scientists.[1]

---

1. Systematic studies of exile political organizations are so few in number that it is possible to discuss them within the space of a footnote. To this writer's knowledge, the only book-length treatment of an exile political party is Lewis J. Edinger's *German Exile Politics* (Berkeley: University of California, 1956), a study of the German Social Democrats during the Hitler period. Of course there are several books that treat exile politics as a secondary theme: E. H. Carr's biography of Bakunin, Louis Fischer's study of Lenin, and Edmund Wilson's *To the Finland Station* (Gloucester, Mass.: Peter Smith, 1959) all shed some light, for instance, upon the Russian revolutionary exiles—but only incidentally. Raymond Bauer, Alex Inkeles, and Clyde Kluckhohn base their description of Soviet politics, *How the Soviet System Works: Cultural, Psycholog-

To be sure, the study of exile politics presents the would-be researcher with a number of discouraging problems. The existing literature on this subject is scanty, and what is available is often highly impressionistic and polemical. It is difficult to obtain empirical data. Often records are either lost or were not kept, and the personal recollections of the participants are inclined to be colored by partisan emotions. This lack of "hard" data tends to leave the researcher with the problem of picking his way through a bewildering labyrinth of contradictory information, based primarily on polemical literature and interviews of varying reliability. Occasionally even these approaches are not possible. Research into exile politics is an experience that tends to make one appreciative of the conditional, tenuous nature of "facts." Men engaged in highly partisan politics seem to see what they wanted to see in the first place, and remember things in a way most convenient to justify their position. This is not to say that they do these things on purpose. To the contrary, in the experience of this writer, the sincerity of such men is not to be doubted, in most cases. Rather, we are dealing with epistemological and psychological variables whose study lies beyond the scope of this work. The possible effects that exile may have upon people's

ical, and Social Themes (Cambridge, Harvard University Press, 1956), upon interviews with Russian refugees, but again, the fact of exile is not a central concern. Closer to our subject is the study by Henry Gleitman and Joseph J. Greenbaum of the "Attitudes and Personality Patterns of Hungarian Refugees," *Public Opinion Quarterly* (Fall, 1961). However, the authors focused their attention on the perceptions and attitudes of exiles rather than on their political organization. Beyond these more scholarly studies there are, of course, journalistic works—on the Cuban exiles, for instance. There are also the personal recollections of refugees. Historical literature on the French *émigrés* is relatively ample. In the same category, the *American Political Science Review* carried a study by Michael Walzer on the English Protestant exiles under the Catholic Queen Mary (*APSR*, September, 1963). Also, we might mention Elemer Balogh's *Political Refugees in Ancient Greece* (Johannesburg: Witwatersrand U. Press, 1943). Beyond these studies, there are several works dealing with the problem of displaced persons in international politics, as well as with the process of assimilating refugee groups into new environments. All of these add to our understanding of the phenomenon of exile, but their main focus is not political. In sum, the literature on exile politics is scanty indeed.

perceptions of their environment are beyond our competence to discuss at anything but a superficial level. Such problems tend to show, however, why research in this area has been neglected.

Perhaps it will be argued by some that there is little foreseeable "pay-off" for political science in the study of exile politics. After all, the exiles are the failures in their countries' political struggles. More often than not their fate is gradual oblivion. The process is usually hastened by ugly factional squabbles, increasingly irrelevant programs based on distorted information and wishful thinking, and dissolving organizations as the exiles eventually become resigned to defeat and begin to make new homes abroad. But this is not always the case. Sometimes the exiles live to see their triumphant return. The Russian Bolsheviks are a case in point, as are the "Free French" and the German Social Democrats after World War II. The subject of this study, the Febrerista party, has spent intermittently nearly twenty-seven out of the last thirty years in exile, but it continues to be an important force in Paraguayan politics. The same could be said of the Paraguayan Liberal party. In fact, the history of Latin American politics in general suggests that exile, rather than the extermination of opponents, has usually been accepted as part of the "rules of the game." The politics of that region also affords us with numerous examples of revolutions successfully conducted from exile.

The importance of research into the area of exile politics is still more obvious if we limit our discussion to exiled political parties. By this we refer to groups that participated in their countries' politics before their expulsion, as opposed to *ad hoc* groups that form in exile. Studies of exile parties may contribute valuable insights into the workings of political parties in general. The chief assumption here is that exile parties do not constitute a genre of political organization different from other parties; they are simply required to operate under abnormal conditions. Despite the great variety that exists among political parties with respect to their particular characteristics, they seem to have certain broad concerns in common, which permit political scientists to make comparative studies. Exile parties, like other parties, have organizational structure. They are concerned with promoting internal cohesion in order to achieve control of the government. Also, to use Samuel Eldersveld's terminology, they act as task groups, communications systems, and decisional groups.[2] Finally, they have, as do other parties, problems of leadership recruitment and morale. The really important difference is the environment in which exile parties are forced to operate: their illegal and clandestine status, their removal from direct contact with their nation's political life, and the intense social and psychological pressures that are peculiar to an involuntary existence in an alien culture.

The politics of exile requires a very different approach to such matters of internal organizational structure, tactics, leadership skills, and the role of ideology in party affairs. The problem of organization becomes especially acute as the party finds its members dispersed, isolated, and demoralized. The first requirement is to somehow regroup its scattered ranks, establish contact with those who may have stayed behind in the underground, and to co-ordinate the exiles' activities with these clandestine organizations. This, in turn, raises the problem of establishing an efficient intraparty communications network—a monumental problem to face in exile.

Ideology takes on greater significance. The literature on exiles is filled with stories of bitter factional battles over doctrine, which often seem petty and futile. They divide when cohesion is required and channel hostility inward among the group instead of towards the government. To quote one writer on the results of ideological feuding among the anti-Fascist exiles: "In a real sense many of them had ceased to become politicians and had become merely political theorists."[3] Since this seems to be common among exile groups, one might assume that it constitutes a needed psychological response to the environment. These needs might be: to justify

---

2. Samuel J. Eldersveld, *Political Parties: A Behavioral Analysis* (Chicago: Rand McNally and Co., 1964).

3. Charles F. Delzell, "The Italian Anti-Fascist Emigration, 1922-1943," *Journal of Central European Affairs,* 12 (April, 1952), 20-55.

one's position despite defeat, to maintain morale and discipline for future battles, and to win control of the party apparatus.

Factionalism—the structural division of the party—usually occurs with ideological disputes. Of course, factionalism may also be traced to other causes besides ideology. A consensus on political philosophy does not preclude disputes over tactics, for instance, nor does it prevent purely personal feuds among party leaders. The old leaders are almost always put on the defensive when the party finds itself in exile. Whether or not it is justified, they must bear the onus of defeat. Moreover, should they prove unable to restore the party quickly to power, they may weaken their credibility as alternative leaders. At this point, rivals may attempt to win control of the party apparatus. The old leaders will have fewer advantages in these struggles than they would have under normal conditions. Such levers of control as patronage, prestige, and money will be either absent or severely limited.

Another important aspect of exile politics is that it is carried out in a foreign country. The attitude of the "host" country, then, is crucial. Exiles are sometimes considered as unwelcome welfare cases as well as diplomatic nuisances. Consider, for instance, the attitude of the French government towards the anti-Fascist refugees from Spain, Germany, and Italy, many of whom were put in concentration camps. On the other hand, exiles may be turned into useful weapons. Certainly the United States was well served by Castillo Armas and his band of rebels in the Guatemalan counterrevolution of 1954. Paraguayan exiles—to bring the discussion closer to the main topic—have often been employed by Argentina to install friendly governments in Asunción. In any case, the exile party is at the mercy, for the most part, of the "host" government. Its effectiveness is largely dependent upon the benevolence of those who give it refuge.

In sum, the politics of exile is abnormal politics. Nevertheless, understanding the abnormal may help to clarify our concept of what is normal. Studying exile parties may lead to a clearer understanding of the functional prerequisites for the existence of legalized parties. Finally, the exile party may shed some light upon the prevailing characteristics of the political system from which it was expelled. Exile occurs in systems undergoing severe, even violent, socio-economic strains. It also demonstrates an inability, or an unwillingness, to achieve consensus on political goals and values. If, as Eldersveld claims, parties are "merely a particular structural response . . . to the needs of a social and political system in a particular milieu," then exile parties may point to some important characteristics of the system.

With this brief discussion of reasons for studying exile parties and the outlining of some of their main characteristics, we are prepared to examine the Febrerista party of Paraguay. Before presenting the results of our research, however, let us first place the Febrerista party in its proper context by briefly describing the Paraguayan milieu.

The Paraguayan Milieu

Geography has played a crucial role in shaping the characteristics of Paraguayan society. The country is land-locked, surrounded by powerful neighbors: Brazil to the north and east; Argentina to the south and west. Bolivia, against whom Paraguay fought a bloody war from 1932 to 1935, lies to the north-west. Paraguay is relatively isolated. Its main outlet to the Atlantic Ocean is the Paraná River—a distance of about one thousand miles from Asunción, the nation's capital, and about eight hundred of these miles are through Argentine territory. The chief railroad route is, again, through Argentina. The building of new highways in Paraguay to the Brazilian border has provided an alternate route that leads to the port of Santos. However, the distance is greater and does not appear to have reduced appreciably Paraguay's heavy dependence upon Argentine good will for her economic survival.

Paraguay's location has made her a buffer state between her two giant neighbors, who have struggled for control of the Paraná—La Plata river system since colonial times. Sometimes Paraguay has been able to play the neutralist game in this contest, reaping benefits from each side. On other occasions both of the major powers have exerted pressure against

Paraguay at the same time, endangering her entire existence. The War of the Triple Alliance, from 1865 to 1870, in which Brazil and Argentina were both aligned against Paraguay, nearly liquidated her as an independent state.

As an internal factor, providing possibilities for the country's development, geography is equally important but more benevolent. Paraguay's total area is some 157,047 square miles, almost the size of California. The Paraguay River, which begins in Brazil's Mato Grosso, runs southward and divides the country into two very distinct regions. To the west lies the Chaco, which comprises roughly two-thirds of the country. This is a scrubby, desolate region, alternating between arid, rainless seasons and occasional floods from the Pilcomayo River, which forms the western border with Argentina. The only inhabitants of the Chaco are a few Mennonite colonies, nomadic Indian tribes, army outposts, jaguars, monkeys, and mosquitoes.

The eastern region provides a striking contrast. It is a rolling, red clay country, very fertile and possessing a warm, humid climate. The major portion of Paraguay's 1,875,000 people live in this region—about 70 per cent of them within a 120 mile radius of Asunción. The capital, with its 205,000 inhabitants, is by far the largest city. Other important towns are: Concepción, which lies to the north on the Paraguay River; Encarnación, the chief trading port with Argentina on the Paraná River; and Villarrica and Coronel Oviedo in the central eastern region. None of these towns has a population over 40,000.

The Paraguayan economy is predominantly agricultural, yet about 60 per cent of the agricultural population is landless. The most common forms of tenancy are sharecropping and "squatting." The country's most recent agricultural census (1956) shows the following land distribution:[4]

---

4. República del Paraguay, Ministerio de Agricultura y Ganadería, *Censo agropecuario,* 1956, (Asunción: Editorial El Arte, 1961), p. 14. The table has been collapsed for brevity.

Land Tenure in Paraguay

Size of Holdings	Number of Holdings	Percentage of Land Held
less than 10 hectares	103,666	2.3
10 to 99 hectares	41,011	5.0
100 to 499 hectares	2,802	3.6
500 to 999 hectares	589	2.4
1,000 to 2,499 hectares	687	6.4
2,500 to 4,999 hectares	328	6.8
5,000 to 9,999 hectares	259	10.7
10,000 to 19,999 hectares	130	10.6
over 20,000 hectares	145	52.2

The larger holdings, often called *latifundios,* are usually cattle ranches, *yerba mate* (Paraguayan tea) plantations, timberlands, or simply lie fallow. The smaller farms are clustered near the capital and are used mainly for subsistence farming. In either case, they do not supply the country's internal market with a sufficient quantity of food. This results in the apparent absurdity of an agrarian country importing over seven million dollars in food in 1961, nearly one-fifth of its total imports.[5] The inefficient and primitive state of Paraguayan agriculture is described by one author: "Less than one per cent of the land in Paraguay is sown to the most important field crops in the country. What land is used is by no means cultivated as intensively as it might be. The average Paraguayan farmer's equipment is an axe, a hoe, and a machete. Despite the efforts of the government to sell plows at cost, only two or three per cent of all farmers have breaking plows. The ox is the only source of power other than human."[6]

The same author states that approximately 40 per cent of the privately owned farms operate under a system of absentee-landlordism. Moreover 45.3 per cent of the farms, presumably the smaller ones, were without agricultural implements of any kind.[7]

---

5. Servicio Tecnico Interamericano de Cooperación Agrícola, *Manual estadistico del Paraguay, 1941-1961* (Asunción: STICA, 1963), p. 75.

6. Philip Raine, *Paraguay* (New Brunswick: The Scarecrow Press, 1956), p. 340.

7. *Ibid.*

In 1961 Paraguay exported a total of 30.6 millions of dollars worth of products, and imported goods totaling 30.5 millions of dollars in value. Its chief exports are: wood, *quebracho* extract (used in tanning leather), *yerba mate*, cotton, tobacco, leather and meat.

The main imports are machinery, motor vehicles, chemicals, textiles, and gasoline. Argentina is the most important customer by far, with the United States and Great Britain next in order of importance. The gross national product in 1961 was approximately $20,377,000; the annual per capita income, only a meager $119.

Industrialization is hardly noticeable in Paraguay. The most notable factors that impede it are political instability, lack of skilled labor, the shortage of electrical power, and the poor transportation system. Only some 2,892 miles of road exist, and of these only 173 miles are paved.

No systematic study has ever been made of Paraguay's social structure, with the result that we can sketch only roughly its outlines. Most observers agree that, because of the country's general impoverishment, social class lines are relatively indistinct. To quote one writer:

> Many Paraguayans who enjoyed wealth lost it in political upheavals. As is true in other Latin American countries, the great majority of Paraguayans are poor, but unlike most of those countries, Paraguay has no aristocracy of wealth. Even the upper classes are only moderately well-to-do. The basic cause, apart from internal political conditions, is that about 50 per cent of all the productive land, which is the source of the country's wealth, is foreign-owned.[8]

The Paraguayan "upper class" is quite permeable because relatively little difference in wealth separates it from the masses. As for "old families"—the aristocracy of blood—most of these were impoverished, eliminated, or egalitarianized during the first sixty years after independence, when the nation was governed under a socialist system. Therefore, the upper class may be said to be composed of the "new rich" (whose wealth is usually related to politics), the land-poor, the intellectuals, and the military and political elite. In other

8. *Ibid.,* p. 277.

words, the upper class is based on status, rather than wealth or family. Status is most easily acquired through high political or military rank, or through education and intellectual achievement. Therefore the armed forces, the political parties, and the educational system—especially the universities—are key institutions that provide for upward social mobility. Entrance to these seems easily attained.

Since education is such an important factor, it is noteworthy that the number of schools and universities is growing rapidly. Between 1951 and 1961 the number of primary schools increased 46 per cent; the number of teachers 64 per cent; and the number of students attending, 40 per cent. During the same period, the number of secondary schools more than doubled, as did the number of students. Since 1959, three new universities have been established, bringing the total to four. In 1961 there were 530 college professors and some 4,014 students. The National University in Asunción remains the most important by far; but the privately run Catholic University is growing rapidly, as are the state-operated universities in Villarrica and Concepción.[9] Illiteracy in Paraguay has been estimated at about 15 per cent in Asunción and 40 per cent in the interior.

A rough breakdown of social classes in Paraguay might result in the following categories:

The Upper-Upper Class—composed of high government officials, high military officers, the leading politicians, and *latifundio* owners;

The Upper Middle Class—intellectuals, professionals, and the more successful merchants and businessmen;

The Lower Middle Class—rural proprietors of medium-sized holdings, small merchants, school teachers, white collar workers (commerce, industry, or government). A 1948 population survey estimated this class at about 10,000 people;

The Upper-Lower Class—rural proprietors with holdings of less than ten hectares, urban labor (an estimated 40,000);

The Lower-Lower Class—agricultural labor, the rural landless.

---

9. *Manual estadístico del Paraguay*, pp. 15-21.

Paraguay's geographical position, which places it at a disadvantage with respect to its neighbors, its underdevelopment, and its heavy dependence on foreign capital have all combined to produce a high degree of nationalism. This is further accentuated by the fact that many decades of relative isolation have produced an almost racially homogeneous population of *mestizos*: a mixture of Spanish and Guaraní Indian blood. Immigration to Paraguay was never significant. Moreover, Paraguay has continued to preserve many aspects of its Indian tradition, especially in its music and language. Paraguay is a bilingual country in which almost everyone speaks both Spanish and Guaraní. This has served to reinforce the nation's feeling of uniqueness.

Moreover, Paraguay's struggle to maintain its independence and identity despite external pressure has helped to produce a politically authoritarian tradition. The country has often resembled a garrison state. Dr. José Gaspar Rodríguez de Francia, the country's first political leader after independence, sealed the country off from the outside world for the next thirty years rather than submit to Argentine pressure for unification. Francia was followed by two other dictators, Carlos Antonio López and Francisco Solano López, his son, both of whom ruled as benevolent and patriotic despots. They sought to ameliorate Francia's harsh isolation policy while at the same time they built up the nation's economic and military power. In 1865 Paraguay fought its "great war," the War of the Triple Alliance, against Argentina, Brazil, and Uruguay. According to nationalistic Paraguayan historians, this was to protect its independence against imperialistic neighbors, who were backed by British gold. From 1870 to 1876 the country was occupied by the invaders. After their withdrawal the country was ruled by the National Republican party, better known as the Colorado party, after its red banner. The dominant figure of this era was General Bernardino Caballero. Caballero made and unmade presidents until 1904, when the Liberal party, with Argentine aid, overthrew the government. A period of chaos ensued in which the Liberal party split into several warring factions that turned to violence rather than elections in order to capture the government. Only in 1928 was there more than one candidate in elections for the presidency.

Liberal rule came to an end with the revolution of February, 1936. This event, which became the genesis of the Febrerista party (the February party), did not put an end to Paraguay's authoritarian tradition. The *febreristas,* too, clamped down on the political opposition in the name of the social revolution. Their overthrow, a year and a half later by the army, was followed by another series of dictatorships, most of which were military. A brief attempt at democratization on the basis of a coalition government of military, Colorado, and *febrerista* leaders, from 1946 to 1947, ended in civil war. This was followed by a number of short-lived, unstable dictatorships until the rise to power of General Alfredo Stroessner in 1954. Stroessner's eleven-year rule is something of a record in Paraguay for the last ninety years or so.

This writer estimates that, since 1870, Paraguay has experienced some thirty-two major revolts, including the civil wars of 1921 and 1947. This is merely a rough estimate, however, and may err on the conservative side. During the same period, some twenty-five presidents were deposed. Lastly, the country has fought two major wars since independence: the War of the Triple Alliance (1865-70), which left the country devastated, and the Chaco War against Bolivia (1932-35), which gained for Paraguay the possession of the Chaco, at great cost.

Political persecution is, of course, a natural outgrowth of the violence and factionalism that have characterized Paraguay since independence. Again, Dr. Francia set the style with his relentless persecution of political opponents: exiling them, confiscating their property, and sending them to long terms in prison without any sort of judicial process. Succeeding dictatorships have been hardly less moderate. The Morínigo government, from 1940 to 1948, was notorious for its concentration camps in the Chaco and at Peña Hermosa. There is no reason to assume that similar tactics are not being employed today.

Exile, the main theme of this work, has been used as a political weapon most frequently. Before Francia became absolute dictator in 1814, he used his position as head of the governing junta to consolidate his position by exiling the Spanish loyalists and those who favored unification with Argentina. Since that time there have always been a large number of Paraguayans living outside the country, mainly in Argentina. It must be emphasized, however, that many of these emigrated for reasons other than political. Economic stagnation and lack of land or work are also powerful factors that cause this exodus. In 1895 some 14,562 Paraguayans, of a total population of about half a million, were living in Argentina. By 1914 Paraguay's population had grown to about 800,000, but the number living in Argentina had risen to over 28,000. Just before the civil war of 1947 an Argentine census estimated that some 200,000 Paraguayans were living in its northern provinces of Misiones, Chaco, and Formosa, not to mention other provinces. Juan F. Pérez Acosta, a Paraguayan writer, describes the flight of Paraguayans after the civil war in these words: "The Argentine census of 1947 was completed in May, and so its figures do not take into account the real exodus [of Paraguayan refugees] which happened in August of that year. This exodus was truly extraordinary, in terms of both quantity and duration. It took on unheard-of proportions."[10]

George Pendle, in his book, *Paraguay: A Riverside Nation*, estimated that in 1956 between 500,000 and 600,000 Paraguayans, with their families, were living in Argentina and Brazil.[11] In 1956 Paraguay's population was slightly over one and a half million, which meant that roughly one-third of the nation was living outside the country.

This, then, is the milieu within which the Febrerista party operates. In this work, we are concerned with the Febrerista party as a response to its environment and with the impact of that environment upon the internal operations of the party. The first part of this study attempts to place the Febrerista

---

10. Juan F. Pérez Acosta, *Migraciones históricas del Paraguay a la Argentina* (Buenos Aires: Talleres Gráficos Optimus, 1952), p. 17. All previous figures given on Paraguayan emigration are from this source.

11. George Pendle, *Paraguay: A Riverside Nation* (London: Royal Institute of International Affairs, 1956), p. 48.

party within the context of Paraguayan history from independence to the present, in order to delineate its antecedents in the Paraguayan political experience. In this writer's opinion, Paraguayan history can be divided into roughly three more or less distinct periods. The first can be termed the era of the Socialist State headed by Francia and the two Lópezes, a period characterized by benevolent but strong dictatorship, a high degree of political stability, economic progress, relatively little contact with foreign countries, and state-ownership of almost all land and other productive enterprises. The second period, which begins in 1870, after the War of the Triple Alliance, is characterized by the alienation of public lands, the growth of private enterprise, heavy foreign capital investment, the establishment of political parties, and a high degree of political instability. This period, which we have termed the era of the Liberal State, was brought to an end by the February Revolution of 1936.

The February Revolution, besides giving rise to the movement of social protest called *febrerismo* (which later became institutionalized in the Febrerista party) can be viewed as a rejection of the Liberal State. It would probably be an exaggeration to say that this revolution was an attempt to restore the Socialist State in every respect. Nevertheless, an attempt was made to restore the economic nationalism, the state-directed economy, and the social egalitarianism which had characterized the Socialist State. It differed from the old Socialist State in that the men who controlled the revolutionary government of 1936 based their political philosophies on such varied modern doctrines as marxism, fascism, and contemporary liberal democracy. The one underlying belief that held this motley group of revolutionaries together was their rejection of classical *laissez faire* liberalism: the belief in capitalism, liberalism, and the idea that "that government is best which governs least." Although the February Revolution was overthrown in August, 1937, its effects on the nation have proven unalterable. State economic intervention, agrarian reform, and the rights of labor to organize and bargain have become accepted as standard by most of the political parties. When seen in this context, then, the Febrerista party fits into the Paraguayan political experience. For this reason the first part of this study describes the Socialist State, the Liberal State, the February Revolution, and the process of institutionalizing the revolutionary ideal by forming the Febrerista party.

The second part of the study describes the internal workings of the Febrerista party: its ideology, its formal organization, and the patterns of relationships existing among its leaders in the top party posts. The concluding chapter discusses the research findings and their relationship to some of the more general literature on political parties.

THE POLITICS OF EXILE

1. Antecedents and Genesis
of the Febrerista Party

Some *febrerista* writers claim that Paraguay has experienced only three genuine revolutions: the Comunero Revolt, from 1720 to 1835; the Independence Revolt of May 14, 1811; and the February Revolution of 1936. The first was a colonial insurrection against the authority of the Spanish Crown. It was provoked by the power of the Jesuit Order, which had gathered most of the Guaraní Indian labor force into its missions and enjoyed a monopoly of the colony's major export product: *yerba mate,* or Paraguayan tea. Trouble arose when the colonists tried to seize the Jesuits' property, an act that resulted in an interventor being sent from the vice-regal capital of Lima to replace the colony's governor. Paraguay had been for almost two hundred years a poor, neglected colony, producing neither gold nor glory for the Crown. Such semi-isolation from the rest of the Spanish Empire had engendered strong localist feelings, and intervention was greeted with resistance. For the next fifteen years the Paraguayans, led by José de Antequera y Castro and Fernando de Mompox, successfully fought off a coalition of royal forces and Jesuit-led Indian armies, until they were finally defeated in March, 1735. The Comunero Revolt is a special source of pride to Paraguayan nationalists, who call it the first rebellion against royal authority in the Western Hemisphere. They also consider it the forerunner of other popular, nationalist revolts in Paraguay.

The Paraguayan Independence Movement of May 14, 1811, and the social transformations that followed, center around the complex personality of Dr. José Gaspar Rodríguez de Francia. A few facts concerning his personal history may clarify a number of his later actions.[1] Francia was born into the creole class: the American-born Spaniards, who were socially inferior to those born in the mother country. His father was apparently a Brazilian, a fact that led to the persistent rumor that Francia was a mulatto. He was graduated from the University of Córdoba in 1785, receiving degrees in theology and law. While at Córdoba he had also come into contact with the radical literature of the times: Rousseau, Voltaire, Montesquieu, and Diderot. It is said that he was especially influenced by the *Social Contract*. However that may be, it is certain from his later life that such thought had a greater impact upon him than the sacred learning.

Upon returning to Asunción, Francia taught Latin for a short time in the College of San Carlos but quit when he was passed over for promotion on the hidden grounds that he was a mulatto. He then took up law and earned a reputation as a lawyer for the poor, often defending them against the wealthy without charge. It appears, too, that he experienced an unhappy love affair at this time, being rejected by the girl's father, again on the basis that he was thought to be of mixed blood. As time went on, he became more withdrawn and austere in his private life and a bitter critic of the colonial system in public.

Napoleon Bonaparte's seizure of the Spanish throne for his brother Joseph, in 1808, began a chain of events that eventually brought Francia to political supremacy in Paraguay. Local juntas in Spain had formed a regency in order to resist Napoleon and had invited the colonies to send delegates to Seville to form a central government for the Empire. The colonies, however, were generally divided into two camps. On

1. The writer has depended heavily on two biographies of Francia for this section: Justo Pastor Benítez, *La vida solitaria de Dr. José Gaspar Rodríguez de Francia, dictador del Paraguay* (Buenos Aires: Editorial "El Ateneo," 1937), and Julio César Cháves, *El supremo dictador* (Buenos Aires: Ediciones Nizza, 1958).

one side were the royalists, who refused to accept the regency's pretensions to speak for the deposed King Ferdinand VII and preferred that the colonies set up their own caretaker juntas. Next there were the radicals, who wanted independence and were willing to back the royalists as the first step towards their goal. The radicals were successful in Buenos Aires, the capital of the Viceroyalty of La Plata, where the viceroy was deposed and replaced by a junta of creole leaders. These revolutionaries then requested that the various provinces comprising the viceroyalty send representatives in order to form a new government, a request that was received with mixed feelings in Paraguay. Three general currents of opinion existed there. The first was royalist and hesitant about collaborating with the revolutionaries. The second might be called *porteñista,* after the nickname applied to residents of Buenos Aires. This group favored a revolutionary federal government, to be formed out of the old viceroyalty. The capital would remain in Buenos Aires but rights would be reserved to the provinces. The third group was nationalist, demanding independence for Paraguay both from Spain and Buenos Aires, and the leader of this group was Francia.

Paraguay's reply to Buenos Aires expressed friendship but made no commitment to any political union, nor did she promise to send delegates to the junta. Meanwhile, Governor Velasco made preparations for the province's defense, in case the *porteños* should attack. An army, under the leadership of General Manuel Belgrano, was sent from Buenos Aires in December, 1810, to invade and "liberate" Paraguay, but the mission was a disaster. By the following March, Belgrano had been driven out of the province. Meanwhile, in Asunción, Governor Velasco had committed a grave blunder. In order to insure himself against another invasion from Buenos Aires, he had entered into negotiations with the Portuguese, requesting Brazilian troops for help. When this became known, the leaders of the colonial militia were determined to revolt. Among the civilian leaders involved in the plot was Francia, who, some of the other plotters say, actually directed

the rebellion.[2] On May 14 the country fell into the hands of
the revolutionaries as the Asunción barracks revolted and
forced Velasco to capitulate. All negotiations for Brazilian
troops were terminated abruptly. Velasco was forced to accept
participation in a governing triumvirate. This was short lived
and soon replaced by a junta elected by a General Congress
convened in June, 1811.

The struggle now centered around the question of federation with Buenos Aires. Francia soon showed his political
astuteness by joining with the Spanish royalists to block any
porteñistas from being included in the junta. Nonetheless,
Francia's intransigence towards Buenos Aires was too extreme
for the other members of the junta who were willing at least
to negotiate. He resigned his position but was soon asked to
return. With the Buenos Aires diplomatic delegation on its
way to Asunción, it was felt that he should represent Paraguay, since he was the only educated person among the political leaders. Francia's return to the junta was bought at the
price of giving him a free hand to deal with the *porteñistas*.
By the time the Buenos Aires delegation arrived in Paraguay,
all of their known sympathizers had been arrested and sent
into exile—the first of a long series of similar measures taken
against opposition groups in Paraguay.

The outcome of Francia's negotiations with the *porteños*
was a diplomatic triumph for him. The Treaty of September
12 expressed Buenos Aires' recognition of Paraguayan independence in return for only vague declarations of Paraguay's
desire for some future federation. Upon reading it, the junta
back in Buenos Aires refused to accept it.

Meanwhile, Francia found himself once again at odds with
the two other leaders of the junta, Fulgencio Yegros and
Pedro Juan Caballero. Yegros and Caballero were uneducated, almost illiterate military leaders who had helped to
overthrow Governor Velasco but were incapable of running a
government. With Francia's second withdrawal from the
junta the political situation soon became chaotic again.
Banditry was rife in the countryside and undisciplined troops

2. Cháves, *El supremo dictador*, pp. 96-100.

pillaged the towns. Moreover, there was external pressure from Buenos Aires, which was threatening to close off the La Plata River to Paraguayan trade. After almost ten months of near anarchy, Yegros and Caballero pleaded with Francia to return. This time, however, his terms were even harsher: he was to have his own army and one-half of the country's total arms and munitions. In desperation, the junta agreed.[3]

Once back in the junta, Francia assumed the role of popular tribune. He broadened the suffrage to include all male Paraguayans, even the illiterate and propertyless. Then he convoked the Congress of September 30, 1813, whose representation favored the peasants. This Congress dissolved the junta and replaced it with the consul system, under which Francia and Yegros were to alternate as chief consuls for terms of ten months. While Francia devoted most of his time to building up his private army, Yegros took little interest in governing and expressed the desire to be allowed to retire from public life. One year later he was granted his wish. A new Congress scrapped the consul system and gave Francia temporary dictatorial powers.

Francia began his dictatorship by purging the army, now wholly under his authority, of any elements suspected of being disloyal. Internal order was restored as banditry was quickly suppressed by this new, tightly disciplined military. The most severe measures were reserved for the foreign-born Spaniards, who were accused of royalist plotting. They were compelled to register with the government, and heavy taxes were levied against them. Worst of all, they were to be eventually eliminated forever as a social class with pretensions to aristocracy by a law forbidding their men to marry white women. This must have been delicious revenge for the man whom they had so often accused of being a mulatto.

The temporary dictatorship lasted until June, 1816, when a new Congress, again heavily representative of the peasants and impressed by Francia's success in imposing order and stability, voted to grant him perpetual dictatorial powers. By congressional act, then, Francia was made dictator for life,

3. *Ibid.*, p. 138.

with the title of "El Supremo." In this manner the revolutionary dictatorship was launched.

The Socialist State

Francia's rule proved to be revolutionary in many ways. Not only was Spanish royal authority overthrown and *porteño* domination warded off, but far-reaching social and economic changes were instituted. Individuals and groups suspected of being sympathetic towards foreign powers were either imprisoned or driven into exile. Spies and informers were employed to help root out political dissidents, and Francia's personal army was strong enough to suppress internal rebellions. Politics became a monopoly of "El Supremo."

One of Francia's most effective techniques for destroying actual or potential opposition was to confiscate the property of all foreign-born residents and Paraguayans suspected of disloyalty. Within a short time most of the country's land belonged to the state and was worked by peasants under the system of emphyteusis, the leasing of land from the state. Along with this, the state tightly regulated production and trade, and it also claimed a monopoly in certain industries.

Social distinctions soon disappeared under such a rigid, puritanical, collectivist system. In the place of the hierarchical structure of colonial society, with its subtle social distinctions, there evolved an egalitarian society based on a state-directed economy and a regime of terror. While it may be overdrawing the similarity somewhat to compare this regime to Stalinist Russia, it is nonetheless accurate to call it the Socialist State as does Anselmo Jover Peralta, a pro-Marxist *febrerista* writer. Although socialist doctrine was probably unheard of at this time in Paraguay, Francia's revolution was undoubtedly socialist in its program.

Francia's political and economic policies grew out of one basic principle: that Paraguay must maintain her independence at all cost. On the other hand, Buenos Aires had closed off the La Plata River to Paraguay in an attempt to starve the latter into submitting to union. Francia's answer to this blockade was to close the country's frontiers and build up its military and economic strength. His diplomatic policy was strict neutrality—nonintervention—so as not to squander the nation's scarce resources on foreign wars.

Isolation meant that Paraguay would have to pursue a policy of economic autarchy. This, in turn, required a state-controlled economy. As one Paraguayan historian has put it:

> The attempt at autarchy implied and demanded a directed economy. And Paraguay lived a quarter of a century under full economic control. The state intervened in all economic life. It fomented the production of wealth, regulated its distribution, assured its proper investment, enjoyed its profits, and prohibited the excessive enrichment of individuals. The state imposed its interests, control, and direction on the nation's economy. Private interests were relegated to a secondary position or disappeared.[4]

Since Paraguay was an agricultural nation, the state had to focus most of its economic planning on the countryside and regulate agricultural production. Planting and harvesting were controlled. Each proprietor was told which crops to plant and how much land was to be allotted for each type of crop. The state's economic plan forced a more varied production. Cotton and wheat, which had been imported before, were now planted by order of the state. The result was that the country was soon self-sufficient in these. Food crops replaced the traditional export crops of *yerba mate* and tobacco in importance. As with planting, so with harvesting. When the 1819 harvest was destroyed by a plague of locusts, Francia ordered a second planting. The experiment was a success, and since that time Paraguay has had two harvests each season. Production almost doubled, giving the regime a more solid economic base.

The state also owned its own farms, forty-five altogether, which were staffed by army personnel for the purpose of raising cattle, horses, and mules. The success of these farms can be judged by the fact that they produced such a surplus that cattle were given away to peasants. Isolation also meant that Paraguay would have to supply its own manufactured goods. Accordingly, the state fostered and regulated such small in-

---

4. *Ibid.*, p. 271.

dustries as cloth, leather, lumber, iron, dyes, and various handicrafts.

Paraguay was never totally isolated, however, and total self-sufficiency was never achieved. In 1823 a pact was signed with Brazil to open up commercial relations between the two nations, a trade to be closely regulated by the Paraguayan government. Brazilian goods could enter only through the port of Itapuá, and all merchants and their goods were checked and registered. The prices of imports and exports were fixed, and no commerce was permitted on credit. Only those Paraguayans with government permits were permitted to trade. These same regulations also applied to the port of Pilar, which was later opened to trade with the Argentine province of Corrientes. Payments were made with currency at first. Later, the Brazilian merchants secured the right to extract gold and silver, but they abused this right to the point that Francia placed those metals under a government monopoly and forbade their export.

The state's income was derived from several sources: there were import and export duties, as well as sales taxes and turnover taxes on all domestic goods; the state had monopolies on the sale and export of wood and *yerba mate;* and heavy fines and confiscations were applied against political opponents. The state also reserved the right to inherit all property belonging to foreigners who died without Paraguayan-born heirs. As a result, it became the largest and richest landowner. Francia personally attended to the administration of the state's holdings in a manner in keeping with his own character: austere, parsimonious, and scrupulous. At the time of his death, the state's treasury reserves were almost double the amount held in 1811.[5]

One of Francia's main concerns was the army, since it was essential to Paraguay's continuing independence as well as to his own position. Not only was it purged from time to time, but all of the military heroes of the independence period were eliminated as potential threats. Fulgencio Yegros was executed in 1821 in connection with an alleged plot to over-

---

5. *Ibid.,* p. 277.

throw Francia. Pedro Juan Caballero, who had also been accused of complicity in that plot, committed suicide in prison. Other military leaders were either executed or withdrew to discreet retirement.

Military expenditures comprised a large percentage of the government's modest budget. Most of these went to buying arms, for Francia was never successful in his attempts to establish an armaments industry. So concerned was he to insure a constant flow of imported arms and munitions that he exempted armaments merchants from the prohibition on the extraction of gold and silver from the country.

In sum, Francia's dictatorship insured the independence of Paraguay, brought a measure of stability and prosperity, and established a strong army to defend those gains. On the other hand, the price for these was the surrender of individual liberties by the citizens. The dictatorship was absolute, severe, and often arbitrary. No public meetings were allowed, all mail was censored, no newspapers or books could be published, and no one was allowed to enter or leave the country, or travel within it, without a permit. Francia's opponents were hounded into exile, ruined economically, put before the firing squad, or sent to prison, where they stayed for years, frequently without ever knowing why. Francia *was* the state, and his suspicions, whether accurate or unfounded, were sufficient cause for persecution.

Francia died of natural causes on September 20, 1840. Today, more than a century later, he is still a controversial figure. One biographer, noting "El Supremo's" taste for Rousseauian philosophy, compares him to Robespierre:

> Both pursued a political goal. Robespierre dreamed, like Saint-Just, of a happy collectivity, of a Europe redeemed by the Revolution, ruled by the Social Contract, with the aristocracy humbled. Francia wished to found a State, and to this end he subordinated everything: religion, commerce, education, institutions, government. He was a totalitarian. . . .
>
> But if they differed in the spirit in which they acted . . . they are co-disciples in doctrine; both were agents of social transformation. Robespierre theorized in order to castigate; Dr. Francia was a pragmatist, a realist. The first arrived at his Thermidor; he fell. The other lasted in the government a

quarter of a century. The fiery turmoil devoured the first; but it helped the other, devouring his enemies.[6]

The Era of the Lópezes / Francia's death left the country in a temporary state of confusion. "El Supremo" had monopolized the decision-making power, permitting no other figure to rise to share responsibilities. Only the decision of the army to form a provisional junta prevented chaos. The junta was followed shortly by a consul system, with power shared between the army's commander-in-chief, Mariano Roque Alonzo, and Carlos Antonio López, a lawyer. As in the case of the consul system in 1813, the civilian was the better educated, more dynamic, and more imaginative of the two. In 1844 a General Congress replaced the consul system with a presidential system and elected Carlos Antonio López to the presidency. Although López was supposed to share his power with a congress and a judiciary, he was a *de facto* dictator.

López's rule, however, was considerably more relaxed than Francia's had been. During his term as consul he showed his liberal inclinations by freeing the political prisoners and entering into commercial negotiations with neighboring countries in order to break down Paraguay's isolation. Whereas Francia had prevented most foreigners from entering the country, López welcomed contacts from abroad as a means to enrich the national culture. Moreover, López recognized that while Francia's policies of isolation and self-sufficiency might have been necessary at one time, they could be maintained only by keeping Paraguay at a primitive economic level. López's chief goal was economic development, and to promote this he began an ambitious program of internal improvements and commercial expansion. By 1857 Paraguay had 408 public schools attended by 16,755 pupils, as well as a normal school and schools of law, mathematics, and philosophy at the college level. By the time he died, five years later, López had added another 27 schools serving 8,000 additional students. Several graduates of these public schools were granted government scholarships to continue their education in Europe. A sign of the growing literacy rate was the establishment of

6. Benítez, *Francia*, pp. 74-75.

the country's first newspaper, *El Paraguay Independiente*, in 1845.[7]

Progress was even more impressive in the area of economic development. López contracted foreign technicians to build the first railroad (1861) and the first telegraph line (1864) in South America. British engineers built Paraguay's first iron factory in 1850, which in turn fostered industries for the production of agricultural implements and armaments, an accomplishment that Francia had never been able to realize. Other important industries that were initiated during this period included paper, porcelain, ink, sulphur, lime, nitrate and gunpowder.[8] This was the era, too, in which most of Asunción's large public buildings were constructed.

While Paraguay was building internally, López also worked to increase commerce. Dockyards for the construction and repair of vessels signaled the country's growing naval strength. By 1862 its river fleet counted eleven steamships—including the 226-ton *Iporá*—and about fifty sailing vessels. The port of Encarnación was built to serve the Upper Paraná River; today it is Paraguay's second largest city. One Argentine historian comments: "All this greatly increased activity in the port of Asunción. Normally, up until 1853, some 125 schooners, of between 30 and 85 tons, arrived at that port. This figure climbed rapidly to an average of some 330 ships annually, and by 1861 the number had reached 420. At he same time, the value of such international commerce grew from 1,097,000 gold pesos in 1853, to 3,740,000 in 1859."[9] In short, López had tripled Paraguay's commerce in six years.

López's development program was financed from several sources. Commercial expansion provided much of the government's income in the form of import and export duties and trade licenses. Moreover, such expansion was backed by a sound financial situation. As a result of Francia's careful ad-

7. Juan F. Pérez Acosta, *Carlos Antonio López, "obrero maximo"* (Asunción: Editorial Guaraniá, 1948), Chapters 11, 16, and 17; also, Atilio Garcia Mellid, *Proceso a los falsificadores de la historia del Paraguay* (Buenos Aires: Ediciones Theoria, 1964), I, 272.

8. Pérez Acosta, *Carlos Antonio López*, Chapters 1-6; Garcia Mellid, *Los falsificadores*, I, 281.

9. Garcia Mellid, *Los falsificadores*, I, 275.

ministration, the López government inherited treasury holdings amounting to 224,881 gold pesos, a large sum for those
times. Second, López continued Francia's system of state socialism, with its state-owned farms and its monopoly on the
export of wood and *yerba mate*. Third, López also followed
Francia's policy of prohibiting the export of precious metals;
for according to the economic theories of the day, large gold
and silver reserves were necessary for a country's currency
stability. The country's financial soundness was indicated by
López's message to Congress in 1847 in which he requested
authority to print 200,000 pesos worth of paper currency:
"The only formerly Spanish country that can undertake this
operation is the Republic of Paraguay, because it is the only
one that has existing capital, great and valuable properties,
and no internal or external debt."[10]

This was further confirmed in a study by Dr. Ramón Zubi-
zarreta for the Buenos Aires daily, *La Prensa:*

> One has to do justice to the government of Don Carlos
> Antonio López which, while it prohibited the exportation of
> metallic currency, issued inconvertable paper money in propor-
> tion equal to silver, decreeing that in all payments the creditor
> might receive half in one specie and half in another kind. With
> this method, so simple and efficient, the government was able
> to double the coinage of the Republic in order to facilitate
> transactions and negotiations without losing the confidence of
> holders of paper money that it was as sound as gold and
> silver.[11]

López also continued Francia's system of state socialism with
respect to land tenure, on the basis of emphyteusis: the granting of public lands in temporary usufruct to private tenants.
The state granted the use of the land for a period of eight
years, and the grant was renewable indefinitely, but sub-letting
was prohibited. The concessionaire was obliged to settle on his
land and cultivate it personally. In return, the state received
its rent in the form of a 5 per cent tax on the land's value.[12]

---

10. *Ibid.,* I, 276.
11. *Ibid.,* I, 277.
12. Anselmo Jover Peralta, *El Paraguay revolucionario* (Buenos
Aires: Editorial Tupá, 1946), II, 44.

This system of emphyteusis was employed in Paraguay so widely that in 1856 the British engineer, F. W. Morgenstern, estimated that, of the country's 16,590 square leagues of land, 16,329 were public property, leaving only 261 square leagues in private hands.[13]

When Carlos Antonio López died in 1862, his son, Francisco Solano López, was elected to succeed him. The younger López inherited the serious diplomatic problems that had been forming during his father's regime—pressure from the Brazilian Empire on one side and pressure from Buenos Aires on the other. Brazil presented the major threat. For her, Paraguay's economic, political, and military strength was dangerous to the control of Brazil over her western provinces. Brazil was continually plagued by the problem of national unification in a highly regionalized system. The provinces of Mato Grosso and Rio Grande do Sul, lying on the western frontier, were difficult for the central government in Rio de Janeiro to control. The Paraguay and Paraná rivers, which have their origins in the Mato Grosso, flow westward through Paraguay, with the result that Mato Grosso's trade is oriented in that direction. Geographically, then, Mato Grosso and Paraguay belong to the same system; so a strong Paraguayan state constituted a potentially dangerous factor to the Brazilian Emperor. Moreover, Brazil was interested in controlling Paraguay for expansionist reasons. Control over Paraguay would give Brazil access to eastern Bolivia by way of the Bermejo and Pilcomayo rivers, which are navigable northward to the Bolivian province of Santa Cruz. Control over Paraguay would also mean access to the Argentine provinces of Corrientes and Entre Ríos.[14]

Argentina's interest in dominating Paraguay was also a question of regionalism. Until the battle of Pavón, in 1862,

---

13. *Ibid.*, II, 54; also, Garcia Mellid, *Los falsificadores,* II, 476. For the reader's convenience, one square league is equal to nine square miles.

14. See Juan Bautista Alberdi, *História de la guerra del Paraguay* (Buenos Aires: Ediciones de la Patria Grande, 1962), pp. 102-4; and Carlos Pereira, *Solano López y su drama* (Buenos Aires: Ediciones de la Patria Grande, 1962), pp. 7-25.

Argentina had been at war almost constantly as the provinces of the interior fought the attempts of Buenos Aires to impose political, economic, and cultural hegemony over them. Since Buenos Aires controlled the La Plata estuary, and hence the chief river outlet to the sea, Carlos Antonio López had supported the provinces' struggle to achieve free navigation rights. Although the battle of Pavón had apparently united the country under the presidency of Bartolomé Mitre, in reality the spirit of provincial autonomy was still strong. Therefore, Mitre's policy was to remove the strong Paraguayan state as a potential ally of future provincial revolts.[15]

The move that triggered the war was Brazil's invasion of Uruguay in 1865 to eliminate a government that was sympathetic to Paraguay and the Argentine provinces. Francisco Solano López responded by declaring war on Brazil and sending an invasion force to the Matto Grosso. He then mobilized an army of some forty thousand troops on the Argentine frontier and asked the Argentine government for permission to cross the territory of Misiones so that he might attack Rio Grande do Sul. When Mitre refused permission, López crossed anyway, and Argentina declared war on him as an invader.

On May 1, 1865, Brazil, Argentina, and Uruguay signed a treaty in Buenos Aires pledging a united effort to defeat Solano López. The War of the Triple Alliance lasted five years and, despite Paraguay's heroic resistance against the two major countries of South America, ended in total disaster for her. After the battle of Paraguarí, the allies sacked Asunción, following a mass exodus of Paraguayans. A new capital was built in the north, and the war carried on until March 1, 1870, when Solano López was finally killed at the battle of Cerro Corá. This war marked the end of Paraguay as a power in South America. The country lay ruined and prostrate. Its sacrifice can be comprehended by the following figures which, if they are not exact, still give a clear picture of desolation: at the beginning of the war Paraguay had had a population estimated at 1,337,000, and at the war's close only 221,079

15. Alberdi, *La guerra,* pp. 87-98 and 128-47; also Garcia Mellid, *Los falcificadores,* Vol. II, Chapter 9, especially pp. 174-78.

were left. Of the survivors, almost all were women, old men, and young children.[16]

Paraguay's defeat also signaled the end of the Socialist State. Military occupation brought an end to economic independence. To the victors went the spoils: Paraguay's lands and wealth. In the following section, we shall discuss the meaning of the Liberal State for Paraguay and suggest reasons for the reaction against liberalism which brought about the February Revolution.

The Liberal State

While the last remnants of Solano López' army were fighting in the north, the allied armies occupying Asunción installed a provisional government, a triumvirate composed of Paraguayan "legionnaires" who had openly supported the invaders. The "Paraguayan Legion" had been formed shortly before the war by political exiles living in Buenos Aires, with the purpose of enlisting exiles in the allied armies in order to help "liberate" their country from the dictatorship. Although their actual participation in the fighting was minimal, their zeal in dismantling the old system was so great that they proved handy to the allies. Indeed, they were so pliable to the allies' purposes that in Paraguay today the word "legionnaire" is practically synonymous with "traitor."

The war was brought to a definite end with the death of Solano López on March 1, 1870. Soon after, an assembly was called to approve a new constitution for the country and to elect a president and a vice-president. This assembly became a type of barometer that measured which of the allies, Brazil or Argentina, was more effective in dominating the new government. Argentina's participation in the war had been relatively ineffectual because, despite its outward appearance of unity, the country was still divided. Revolts and mutinies had broken out in the northern provinces of Corrientes and Entre Ríos, where many people refused to support a war whose chief purpose was to strengthen Buenos Aires. Therefore, Brazil had borne the brunt of most of the fighting, and the

---

16. Manuel Cibils, *Anarquía y revolución en el Paraguay: Vórtice y asíntota* (Buenos Aires: Editorial Americalee, 1957), p. 24; also García Mellid, *Las falcificadores*, II, 391.

war's close found the Brazilians almost alone as the occupation force. However, since the easiest access to Paraguay was by way of the La Plata, Argentina had the geographical advantage. This balancing off of the two powers was perhaps the main reason that Paraguay did not disappear altogether as an independent nation. Nonetheless, the victors satisfied themselves by stripping Paraguay of nearly 160,000 square kilometers of territory and saddling her with a war debt of nearly 19,000,000 gold pesos. Only Uruguay eventually renounced any intention of collecting her debts.[17]

Since most of the constituent assembly delegates were legionnaires, and since the Paraguayan Legion had been formed largely under Argentine auspices, it followed that the assembly would be sympathetic towards Argentina. However, when it elected Facundo Machain, a pro-Argentine, to the presidency on August 30, 1870, Brazilian troops soon ejected him and put pro-Brazilian, Cirilo A. Rivarola in office.

While the allies were struggling to control the situation, the legionnaires, too, were beginning to split apart. Two main groups appeared: the "Club del Pueblo" and the "*Gran* Club del Pueblo." The first centered around Candido Barreiros, a former commercial representative for Solano López in Europe. Barreiros, along with other officials and students returning from abroad, formed their "Club" in opposition to the legionnaire government, and they were soon joined by dissident legionnaires who, for one reason or another, felt cheated of their due. The Club del Pueblo gained considerable prestige by having as one of its members General Bernardino Caballero, one of Solano López' officers who had fought by him to the last and who had recently been released from a Brazilian prisoner-of-war camp.

The Gran Club del Pueblo, on the other hand, was formed by legionnaires who were affiliated with the government. Among them were Captain Benigno Ferreira, Salvador de Jovellanos, and José Segundo Decoud. The bitter rivalry of these two groups led to the eventual expulsion of the Club del Pueblo from the country. As a result, under General

---

17. Teodosio González, *Infortunios del Paraguay* (Buenos Aires: Talleres Graficos L. J. Rosso, 1931), pp. 32-34.

Caballero's leadership, they turned to armed revolts to express their opposition.

This was a difficult policy to carry out with Brazilian troops still guaranteeing the existing regime. Moreover, the government had been reorganized. Salvador de Jovellanos, the new president, had the backing of Benigno Ferreira, the "strong man" behind the government. Caballero's first attempt, in March, 1873, to overthrow the government was quelled, but in January of the following year, he defeated the government's troops. However, because of Brazilian intervention, he was forced to accept a compromise: Jovellanos would remain as president while Caballero was given the post of minister of interior and Candido Barreiros was named minister of foreign affairs. This compromise did not last long. In the following month President Jovellanos staged a *coup d'état* and removed Caballero and Barreiros. The reaction of the ousted men's supporters was quick and violent. Jovellanos and his collaborators had to take refuge in the Brazilian embassy. Once again Brazil intervened. Jovellanos was reinstated and Caballero returned to the cabinet. Barreiros, however, refused any further collaboration.

The climax to this era of violence came with the assassination of President Juan Bautista Gill, who had been elected in 1874 and was murdered three years later during an unsuccessful revolution attempted by former presidents Rivarola and Machain. Both of these culprits were later murdered themselves. One other notable event of this period was the withdrawal of Brazilian troops in 1876.

The final victory of Candido Barreiros' Club del Pueblo, now renamed "Club Libertad," was achieved with his election to the presidency in 1878. His sudden death, two years later, provoked General Caballero's *coup d'état* in order to prevent the presidency from being turned over to Vice-President Adolfo Saguier, who represented the opposition. It was Caballero who ruled as the real power in Paraguay for the next quarter of a century, making and unmaking presidents.[18]

---

18. Presidents up to 1904: Bernardino Caballero, 1880-81, 1881-86; Patricio Escobar, 1886-90; Juan González, 1890-92 (overthrown); General Juan B. Egurzquiza, 1894-98; Emilio Aceval, 1898-1902 (overthrown); Colonel Juan Antonio Ezcurra, 1902-4 (overthrown).

The most important political development during this period was the formation of Paraguay's two major parties: the Liberals and the Colorados. The Liberal party's roots extend back to the Gran Club del Pueblo of the legionnaires in power. Since the 1874 revolution this group had lost much of its influence and had become the opposition, renamed the "Club Democrático." Because the Club Democrático was unable to combat Caballero's strong rule effectively from within Paraguay, it depended heavily upon the support of exiles within Argentina and upon the tacit support of the Argentine government. One month after the founding of the Club Democrático in July, 1887, Caballero organized an assembly of political friends and aides to form the "Asociación Nacional Republicana" as the government's official party. Caballero was elected the party's president, and it was from this post that he controlled the selection of official candidates. Since the Club Democrático chose blue for its political banner, Caballero chose red for the Asociación Nacional Republicana. This gave rise to the party's popular nickname, the Colorados. While it is true that the two parties did adopt different political poses, it is this author's opinion that they were little more than two opportunistic groups. The Colorados claimed to be the political heirs of Solano López, waved the bloody shirt, and accused their opponents of being legionnaires. The Liberals, on the other hand, followed a more philosophical creed, derived from the writings of John Locke, Adam Smith, and the utilitarian philosophers. They professed to believe in free elections, representative government, the rights of private property, and a minimum of state intervention in the economic order. They loathed the memory of Solano López and the authoritarian Socialist State he had led.

Nevertheless, these ideological differences should not be taken too seriously. To begin with, the membership of the two parties did not differ greatly. Legionnaires could be found in the directorate of the Colorado party, and former López officers in the Liberal party. Also, the Colorados followed economic policies just as liberal as those advocated by the Liberals. In addition, neither practiced liberalism in its political sense. Both were personalist parties, given to violence, electoral manipulation, and opportunism. In the last analysis, it was simply a case of the "ins" *versus* the "outs."

The Colorados' political dominance was brought to an end in 1904 by an invasion of Liberal exiles, backed by the Argentine government. The head of the revolution was none other than Captain Benigno Ferreira, the president of the Liberal party, who had been collecting for some time a cache of arms and munitions for an invasion. His opportunity came when the commander of the Paraguayan merchant ship "Sajonia" turned the vessel over to Ferreira. The ship, now heavily armed, made its way back north, capturing another ship along the way, despite the Paraguayan government's pleas that it be intercepted by the Argentine navy. Instead, Argentine warships appeared in Asunción's harbor, under the pretext of "protecting Argentine nationals" during the forthcoming invasion. Colonel Juan Ezcurra, the Paraguayan president, realized now that Argentina was supporting the revolution, as did the members of his cabinet, many of whom now defected. Faced with a losing cause, Ezcurra capitulated. On December 12, 1904, aboard the Argentine gunboat "El Plata," he signed the Pact of Pilcomayo, which handed over the government to Benigno Ferreira.

Bankruptcy and the A l i e n a t i o n of Public Lands / In general, the period from 1870 to 1936 was one of economic collapse and financial fraud. As we have already noted, the war cost Paraguay more than three-fourths of her population. The task of rebuilding was to be difficult in any case, but the cynical manipulations of the post-war politicians only deepened the crisis. Economic difficulties began early, with the floating of two loans. The first loan was made by a British banking firm, Baring Brothers, for one million pounds sterling at 8 per cent interest. The bonds were issued at 80 per cent of their quoted price. Then, a 16 per cent commission was charged by Baring Brothers, and the Paraguayan agent in London, D. Máximo Terrero, simply pocketed another 237,000 pounds. Other deductions were made for amortization, remuneration expenses, stamps, and miscellaneous items. At the end of all this, the government received not more than 403,000 pounds of the original one million contracted for.[19]

This financial disaster was followed by another that was even worse just a year later. In 1872 the government negotiated another loan—incredibly enough—from the same source, Baring Brothers, in conjunction with Robinson Fleming and Company. When all of the deductions had been made from the one million pounds, the Paraguayan government received some 562,000 pounds, of which 125,000 were dispatched immediately from London on Paraguay's urgent request. This sum never reached the treasury. On the night of its arrival, it was secretly taken from the ship and, it is alleged, divided among President Jovellanos and his ministers. In short, out of two million pounds in loans, only about 840,000 pounds ever reached the treasury. The manner in which this money was spent was only slightly less scandalous. Thirteen years later the country was as bankrupt as ever. In fact it was necessary to put public lands up for sale in order to cover the payment due on the loans of 1871 and 1872. The total debt, including the amortization and the unpaid interest, had climbed to some three million pounds.[20]

The alienation of the public lands was a final blow to the legacy of the Socialist State. Actually, the process had begun back in 1869, as soon as the legionnaires had taken office. At that time a law was passed allowing cattle raisers to occupy public lands and granting them provisional titles to those areas. A second law, entitled "Civil Procedures," passed in 1873, allowed owners who had lost their property titles to receive new ones simply by appearing, with witnesses to their claims, before a justice of the peace. The predictable result was that many lands were turned over on the basis of false testimony and bribery. In 1874 President Jovellanos sold the railroad built by Carlos Antonio López to an Argentine-Brazilian company for one million pesos. This money was soon squandered, and the following year saw public lands put up for sale. Another large sale of lands came in 1876. Little by little the vast tracts of public property accumulated by

19. Teodosio González, *Infortunios*, pp. 108-9.
20. *Ibid.*, pp. 112-13, 121.

Francia and the two Lópezes were being taken over by private owners, most of whom were Argentines and Brazilians.[21]

The coming to power of the supposedly nationalistic Bernardino Caballero and Candido Barreiros did nothing to halt this process. To the contrary, it reached its climax with the "Law of the Sale of Public Lands" in 1885. This law divided the nation's public lands into five categories, according to their quality, and offered them for sale at these bargain prices:

Prime Quality Lands	1,200 pesos @ square league
2nd. Quality Lands	800 pesos @ square league
3rd. Quality Lands	300 pesos @ square league
4th. Quality Lands	200 pesos @ square league
5th. Quality Lands	100 pesos @ square league

In order to discourage small buyers the law prohibited the sale of tracts smaller than one-half of a square league.[22]

Enactment of this law was followed by a wave of speculation. Many people borrowed money from the National Bank to make the first payment and then sold their titles immediately to foreign investors. Because of the bank's lack of caution in making these loans, many borrowers failed to repay them, and the bank soon went out of business. Meanwhile, foreign companies snapped up the cheap fertile lands, forming huge domains. By 1935 it was estimated that the nineteen largest companies together owned over one-half of the country's land, in the following proportions:[23]

Carlos Casado, Inc.	1,640
La Industrial Paraguaya	1,140
Compañía Richard	486
Compañía Barthe	412
Sociedad de Tierras y Maderas	250
International Products Co.	200
Frahenheim	180
American Quebracho Co.	178

21. *Ibid.,* pp. 145, 149-50; also, Garcia Mellid, *Los falcificadores,* II, 477.

22. Carlos A. Caroni, *Sintesis histórica del problema agrario en el Paraguay* (Buenos Aires: Editorial Tupá), p. 19.

23. Garcia Mellid, *Los falsificadores,* II, 484.

Victor Bence	175
La Rural Argentina-Paraguaya	170
Enrique Astengo	170
Smeid and Oswald	156
Quebrachales Paraguayos	152
Compañía Argentina de Maderas	120
Campos y Quebrachales Puerto Sastre	120
River Plate Quebracho	100
Liebigs Extract of Meat Co., Ltd.	100
Estancias y Quebrachales Puerto Galileo	100
Suc. de Eloy Palacio	100

TOTAL   5,949 square leagues

Territory left to Paraguay after
the war   9,737 square leagues

The favoring of private over public ownership might have been excusable had it enriched the country. However, as we have seen, the revenue from the sale of the public domain was either stolen or squandered, and every year the country went further into debt. Moreover, the sale of public lands fostered the establishment of *latifundios,* immense tracts of privately owned land, much of which may not be rationally exploited. This system still prevails in Paraguay. According to the nation's latest agricultural census (1956), the 145 largest landowners own slightly more than one-half of the total land area.

It is to the Liberal party's credit that it suspended the sale of the public lands after throwing the Colorados out of power in 1904. Nevertheless, the Liberals did little to change the miserable working conditions on the *latifundios.* The law of forced peonage, passed in 1871, was not rescinded—a law that tied the peon to the *latifundio* and forbade him to leave without permission. If he ran away, he would be pursued. If caught he would be carried forcibly back to his work, besides being fined for the cost of capturing him. Indeed, the *latifundios* were like feudal domains, owning their own ports, running their own railroads, founding their own towns, and

printing their own money. As one bitter anti-Liberal described it:

> Travelers going up the Alto Paraguay know that for hun-
> dreds of leagues of Chaco litoral, between Villa Hayes and
> Fuerte Olimpo, there exist neither ports nor populations which
> are not under private dominion. Anyone disembarking is in the
> hands of *latifundistas*. Towns and colonies have been formed
> on their lands. The ports are private property, with access
> prohibited to the public.
> When someone dares to disembark at them without previous
> permission of the administrators, he is put on board the next
> passing vessel, be it to the north or south. In nearly 500 kilo-
> meters of litoral there is not a port nor a public road giving
> free access to the Chaco. This phenomenon is distressing and
> irritating. Along the Alto Paraná the same thing occurs. Every-
> thing falls under the caprice of the landowners.[24]

In 1931 the Liberal writer, Teodosio González, stated that
only 5 per cent of the population owned its own land. In a
rural country, where land is the chief means of production
and subsistence, this meant that many people would turn to
using the land of others—"squatting" with the result of occasional clashes between squatters and the large landlords, who
were backed by the rural police.

The financial record of the government of the Liberal
party was no better than that of the Colorado's, and two
loans were floated in 1912. The first was from the French
Bank of the Río de La Plata for the sum of 500,000 gold
pesos. The money was squandered, and the government had
to sell off part of its river fleet to repay the loan. The second
loan was probably the most scandalous in the country's history. In 1911 Eduardo Schaerer obtained a loan of 250,000
gold pesos from Manuel Rodríguez, a Portuguese money-
lender, to finance the revolution that brought him to power
the following year. Once in the presidency, Schaerer formally
proclaimed the government's obligation to pay off the debt.
Since the risks of revolution are high, so was the interest on
the loan. By the time Schaerer was in power the debt had
mounted to 2,219,247 pesos. Indeed, the many revolutions

---

24. Juan Stefanich, *Renovación y liberación: La obra del
gobierno de febrero* (Buenos Aires: Editorial El Mundo Nuevo, 1946), p. 88.

that followed the Liberal party's coming to power proved so costly that by 1931 Teodosio González calculated the country's total debt to be in the neighborhood of 17,000,000 gold pesos.[25]

It would require numerous pages to describe all of the revolutions that took place after 1904; however, a brief account of the fortunes of Liberal presidents from 1904 to 1932 may serve to give some picture of this chaotic period. Juan B. Gaona was named provisional president after the 1904 revolution, but he was deposed a year later and replaced by Cecilio Báez, the party's leading intellectual. Benigno Ferreira was elected president in 1906, but the old "strong-man" lasted only two years before being ousted in favor of Emiliano González. González finished out his term, but during that time he had to suppress a bloody revolt by the Colorados and a faction of the Liberal party called the *cívicos*. Manuel Gondra was elected in 1910 but lasted only two months before being overthrown by Colonel Albino Jara. Jara suppressed one major revolt and executed its leader, Adolfo Riquelme, but was finally toppled in July, 1911. Liberato Rojas now filled the presidency, but he lasted only eight months before being overthrown by a Colorado revolt that brought Pedro Peña to power. Peña lasted only twenty days before the Liberals recaptured the government and installed Emiliano González in the presidency for a second time. González put down revolts by the *cívicos* and Colonel Jara, during which the latter was killed, but in August, 1912, he was dislodged by Eduardo Schaerer in a bloody revolt. Schaerer was ousted for a few days in 1915 by the *cívicos*, led by Gómez and Luis Freire Esteves, before a counterrevolution reinstated him. Manuel Franco was elected in 1916 but died of a heart attack two years later, and José P. Montero finished out his term.

Manuel Gondra was elected to the presidency for a second time in 1920 but stepped down after five months in favor of Eusebio Ayala, the man who later was to be overthrown by the February Revolution. Ayala was intended to be a compromise between two hostile wings of the Liberal party: the

---

25. Teodosio González, *Infortunios*, pp. 124-28, 166.

followers of Gondra and the followers of Schaerer. According to the Liberal historian, Efraím Cardozo, the cause of the feud lay in Schaerer's insistence that the party become centralized and disciplined, with a hierarchical structure, presumably with himself at the top.[26] Although he was apparently in the minority, Schaerer had a large enough backing to cause a serious split in the party ranks and force Gondra to appease him by placing *schaereristas* in his cabinet, but this was not enough. Supported by part of the army led by Colonel Adolfo Chirife as well as by the Colorado party, he pressured Gondra into resigning. Eusebio Ayala, who was not openly committed to either Gondra or Schaerer, was named provisional president by Congress until elections could be held at the end of the year. As election time drew near, it became evident that Colonel Chirife, who was backed by the *schaereristas* and the Colorados, would probably become the next president. At this point President Ayala showed his *gondrista* sympathies by canceling the elections. Colonel Chirife declared that the constitution had been violated, and, with part of the army behind him, he marched on the capital. Ayala quickly withdrew his veto, but it was too late. The country was plunged into a civil war that was to last for two years and divided the Liberal party for several years to come.

Eusebio Ayala resigned from the presidency during the civil war and was replaced by Eligio Ayala (no relation), who prosecuted the war to a successful conclusion. During the period of relative peace and stability that followed, his government emphasized order and honesty, in contrast to the preceding chaos and corruption. To secure order, he cultivated the military and surrounded himself with loyal officers, chief among whom was José Felix Estigarribia—a future Liberal leader in his own right. Cardozo states that Ayala might have continued in the presidency indefinitely, supported by bayonets, if he had so wished. Instead, he stepped down in 1928 to permit José P. Guggiari to take office.

The Guggiari administration proved to be a turning point

---

26. Efraím Cardozo, *23 de octubre: una página de história contemporanea del Paraguay* (Buenos Aires: Editorial Guayrá, 1956), pp. 19-25.

in Paraguay's political history, for it led to a rapid and definitive split between the Liberals who were in control of the government and all other political parties and factions. In fact, Guggiari began his administration with his own party badly divided into three main factions: his own faction, inherited from Manuel Gondra, which had been in control of the government since the 1921 revolution; the *schaereristas*; and the "dissident" Liberals, the party's "young radicals," among whom such men as Anselmo Jover Peralta, Roque Gaona, and Salvador Garcia Melgarejo were later to become leading *febreristas*. The dissident Liberals' opposition to the government stemmed from the existing electoral laws, which provided that: (1) representation in Congress was to be proportional but limited to only those two parties receiving the most votes; (2) the voter had to vote a straight party ticket and could neither substitute names for those on the list nor change their official order. Since the dissidents were a small faction, this left them without chance for representation.[27]

The Colorado party was also split. The "abstentionist" Colorados refused to participate in elections, preferring to conspire for the government's violent overthrow. The *infiltrista* Colorados (those who favored collaboration with the Liberals) felt that, abstention, in practice since 1904, had proven to be a sterile position. After previous negotiations with Guggiari, they entered candidates in the 1928 elections and formed the minority bloc in Congress.

It was during this period that certain groups and individuals reached prominence who were to bring about the February Revolution of 1936 and later create the Febrerista party. Most important of all for the history of *febrerismo* was the Liga Nacional Independiente, headed by Adriano Irala and Juan Stefanich. The Liga began in 1928 as a political club formed by university intellectuals who advocated broad social and economic reforms, without regard to party politics. Although small in numbers, the Liga exercised considerable influence through its newspaper, *La Nación*, and through the prestige of its leaders. Both Irala and Stefanich were noted professors at the National University. The latter had already

---

27. *Ibid.*, p. 90.

written three well-known books, in addition to being a corresponding member of the League of Nations Secretariat.

Guggiari's administration began under ominous conditions. Despite the participation of the *infiltrista* Colorados, only 76,500 of the 165,000 registered voters cast ballots for one of the two lists; the rest either abstained or turned in blank ballots.[28] The *schaereristas,* the dissident Liberals, and the abstentionist Colorados claimed from the very beginning that Guggiari represented a minority government.

Faced by such opposition, Guggiari was in a bad position to confront the crises that were forming. Chief among these was the growing threat of war with Bolivia over conflicting claims to the Chaco, the vast stretch of barren land that lay between the two countries. The boundary lines between Paraguay and Bolivia had never been definitely fixed, principally because neither country had ever shown much interest in populating the inhospitable Chaco. However, when Bolivia lost her outlet to the Pacific Ocean as a result of a war with Chile in 1879, the necessity for an outlet to the sea turned her attention to the east. There the Paraguay and Pilcomayo rivers, flowing through the Chaco, connect with the Paraná—La Plata river system, making possible a route from the Bolivian province of Santa Cruz all the way to the Atlantic Ocean. Thus, Bolivia began to take interest in the Chaco, which brought her into conflict with Paraguayan claims to that area. Several treaties attempting to fix the boundaries were signed, but none was ever ratified. Meanwhile, Bolivia kept building military outposts in the Chaco. By 1913 it became clear to the Paraguayan government that her claims were in danger, and Eusebio Ayala was sent to negotiate a new treaty. The result was the Ayala-Mujía Treaty, which provided for arbitration of the boundary claims.[29] One key phrase that was to haunt Ayala later stated that neither country had modified its positions in the Chaco

---

28. Enrique Volta Gaona, *23 de octubre: Caireles de sangre en alma de la patria paraguaya* (Asunción: El Arte, 1957), p. 31.

29. See Republica Argentina, Ministerio de Relaciones Exteriores y Culto, *La politica argentina en la guerra del Chaco* (Buenos Aires: Guillermo Kraft Ltd., 1937), I, pp. 6-7 (for text of the treaty) and pp. 29, 39.

since the Pinella-Soler Treaty of 1907. This was blatantly untrue because Bolivia had built forts far beyond those earlier lines. In fact, Mujía later insisted that he had shown those forts to Ayala before the treaty was signed, claiming that they had been built in 1906. By accepting the presence of these forts in the arbitral zone and claiming that there had been no modification of positions, Ayala was to open himself to charges of treason from Paraguayan nationalists. In any case, Paraguay could scarcely confront Bolivia at this time. Bolivia was preparing a large, well-equipped, German-trained army to back up her diplomatic claims, while Paraguay was almost totally unprepared to fight.

This growing crisis was inherited by President Guggiari. Its seriousness was brought home with full force by the Fort Vanguardia incident in December, 1928. The Bolivians had continued to advance their positions to the upper Paraguay river, where they constructed Fort Vanguardia, and this gradual take-over of the Chaco had been watched with great misgivings by many Paraguayan military officers. They felt frustrated by the refusal of the government to take action. One such officer was Major Rafael Franco, who was in charge of the garrison at Bahía Negra, a short distance to the south of Vanguardia. On December 5, acting without orders, he attacked Vanguardia and destroyed it—a deed that produced alarming repercussions. The Bolivians replied promptly by taking the Paraguayan forts of Boquerón and Mariscal López. Both countries ordered partial mobilization, and this mobilization produced a scandal in Paraguay. The reserve officers and troops reported to the barracks only to find that there were no arms, no munitions, no food, no clothes, and no medical supplies. There was barely enough in the way of supplies for the small number of regular army men.[30] Morale sank and criticism soared against the government's lack of preparations. It was the perfect opportunity for the *schaereristas,* the dissident Liberals, and the abstentionist Colorados to attack Guggiari, but the strongest criticism came from the Liga Nacional Independiente. *La Nación* demanded

---

30. Antonio E. González, *Preparación del Paraguay para la guerra del Chaco* (Asunción: Editorial El Grafico, 1957), I, 363-64.

to know: "What has been done? If there is no organization, nor sanitation, nor administration, nor chiefs, nor officials, nor arms, nor equipment, nor horses, nor material, nor soldiers: What is there? What *has* been done?"[31]

The answer is that very little had been done. Liberal party apologists, such as Policarpo Artaza, claim that Guggiari had been building up the nation's fighting capacity in secret because he was afraid that, should such preparations be revealed, the League of Nations might brand Paraguay as the aggressor and that Bolivia might launch a full attack before Paraguay was ready.[32] If this is true, such preparations were so well hidden that they were a secret even to the Chief of Staff, General José Felix Estigarribia. In his memoirs Estigarribia says of the Fort Vanguardia crisis: "The Vanguardia crisis passed, incidentally demonstrating the appalling disorganization in which Paraguay found herself from a military point of view."[33]

Guggiari tried to pacify his critics by setting up a National Defense Council in which all of the parties and factions would be represented, but the council was a failure almost from the first meeting. According to Juan Stefanich of the Liga Nacional Independiente, Guggiari informed the council members that Paraguay was unable and unprepared to fight a war, a confession of the government's failure to provide for the national defense. Policarpo Artaza, a Liberal journalist, defended Guggiari by saying that Stefanich presented an impossibly ambitious program for the acquisition of war materials. Stefanich answered by saying that he based his statement on estimates supplied by Colonel Camilo Recalde, head of the Military College, and that these recommendations were ignored by Guggiari because he felt the economy would not support such a heavy expenditure for defense.[34] Even the arms

31. Juan Stefanich, *El 23 de octubre de 1931* (Buenos Aires: Editorial Febrero, 1958), p. 105.

32. Policarpo Artaza, *Ayala, Estigarribia y el Partido Liberal* (Buenos Aires: Editorial Ayacucho, 1946), Chapter 3, pp. 33-39.

33. José Felix Estigarribia, *The Epic of the Chaco: Marshal Estigarribia's Memoirs of the Chaco War, 1932-1935,* translated and edited by Pablo Max Insfran (Austin: University of Texas, 1950), p. 7.

34. Artaza, *Ayala, Estigarribia,* and Stefanich, *El 23 de octubre de 1931,* pp. 106-14.

that had been purchased before by the Liberal government gave rise to strong criticism. Ten thousand Spanish rifles had been bought in 1925. Upon being fired, they often exploded, creating the ignominy of the *metaparaguayos*: "Paraguayan killers."[35]

The National Defense Council did not enjoy a long life. The Guggiari government wanted conciliation in the Chaco, and to this end it agreed to a Pan-American Peace Conference in Washington for the settlement of the Vanguardia issue. The opposition, led by Stefanich and the Liga Nacional Independiente, called this appeasement. The government lost face even further when it accepted a clause in the protocol that implied that Paraguay had been the aggressor. Unwilling to condone this, the Liga Nacional Independiente, the dissident Liberals, and both sectors of the Colorado party withdrew from the National Defense Council. Meanwhile, the Pan-American Peace Conference ordered Paraguay to rebuild Fort Vanguardia and return it to the Bolivians. This was done, to the humiliation of the Guggiari administration. As for Major Franco, who had touched off the incident, he was removed from his command in the Chaco and assigned to another post.

War had been averted for the time being, but the situation remained unchanged, and the Bolivians continued to advance while the Paraguayan government vacillated. The opposition increased its criticism, and Major Franco continued to be a thorn in the government's side. He was now the commander of the important Campo Grande garrison, just outside of the capital, and was sought out by desperate opposition leaders who hoped to get his support for a *coup d'état*. After much cautious negotiation, Franco and Major Arturo Bray agreed to lead a revolt. Early in the morning of March 19, 1831, Franco began to march his troops towards the capital, but the plot was betrayed by Major Bray at the last moment. The government acted quickly. Franco received news that the Bolivians had begun a major attack and that all commanders

---

35. See, Antonio E. González, *Preparación del Paraguay*, I, 304-15; Juan Stefanich, *El Paraguay en febrero de 1936* (Buenos Aires: Editorial El Mundo Nuevo, 1946), pp. 123-35. For a defense of the Liberal government, Policarpo Artaza, *Ayala, Estigarribia*, pp. 39-42.

were to report to the Chaco immediately. He was completely fooled by this ploy. Following orders, he left his troops and reported to the Chaco command at Puerto Casado, where he was given new orders to report to Asunción. There he was arrested and relieved of his command.[36] However, since Franco enjoyed great popularity throughout the army, the government tried to shunt him aside gently by offering him a grant to Europe to study military tactics. His indignant refusal left no other choice but to remove him from the army.

The nadir of Liberal party rule was reached on October 23, 1931, when government troops fired upon student demonstrators in front of the Presidential Palace, killing eleven persons.[37] Colorados and *febreristas* have pointed to this still-infamous "23rd. of October" as showing the total moral bankruptcy of the Liberal party. On the other hand, Liberals such as Efraím Cardozo and Policarpo Artaza have long tried to minimize its importance and have alleged that the government was only trying to protect itself against an attempted revolt by Communists, Fascists, and the Liga Nacional Independiente. Cardozo claims that the demonstrators were not led by students, that the incident was not a massacre as opponents allege, and that the soldiers who turned their machine guns on the crowd did so only out of self-defense. It is impossible to recreate with objectivity an event that is still discussed as passionately as this, but out of the conflicting and polemical literature written, it seems possible to establish a few facts.

The "23rd. of October" was preceded by a series of events that had built up tension, all of them connected with the worsening of Paraguay's position in the Chaco before Bolivia's continuing advance. Despite Guggiari's claims that he was building up the country's fighting strength, it appears that Paraguay was even less prepared to confront the enemy in 1931 than it had been at the time of the Vanguardia crisis.

---

36. Antonio E. González, *Preparación del Paraguay*, I, 151.
37. Works consulted about this event: Artaza, *Ayala, Estigarribia,* pp. 53-63; Cardozo, *23 de octubre,* pp. 229-349; Volta Gaona, *23 de octubre,* 154-303; Stefanich, *El 23 de octubre de 1931,* pp. 5-23; Justo Prieto, *Llenese los claros* (Buenos Aires: Talleres Graficos Luciana, 1957); Antonio E. González, *Preparación de Paraguay,* I, 151-64.

This is confirmed by Estigarribia, who describes his trip to the Chaco as inspector general in June, 1931: "In my new journeys to the interior of the country I witnessed the pitiful negligence in which everything had been left since 1928. The telegraph lines lay on the ground. The Bolivian penetration had made enormous progress."[38]

On September 7 the Bolivians seized the Paraguayan fort of Samaklay, an outpost that Estigarribia had found in wretched condition only three months earlier. The news of this incident was censored by the Guggiari government. Almost four weeks passed before the story became public knowledge through the Bolivian radio station, letters from troops serving in the Chaco, and the stories that leaked out from the hospitals where the wounded were brought. When the news of Samaklay did become known, however, it produced a new store of criticism, especially on the part of the university students, who began organizing demonstrations to agitate for a forceful stand in the Chaco. Government attempts to stifle this criticism through pressure on the university administration only led to a general strike by the students, bringing their protest demonstrations onto the street. A few days previous to October 23, a band of students appeared during the night before the rector of the School of Medicine, a Guggiari appointee, to demand his resignation. Despite the presence of the police, order broke down and several windows of the rector's house were smashed. On the night of October 22, students broke into the office of the progovernment daily, *El Liberal*, destroying and burning much of the equipment. The demonstrators then moved on to President Guggiari's house, where they found themselves confronted by troops. One of the students hurled a paving stone that struck a soldier. At this, the entire detachment charged with fixed bayonets and dispersed the demonstrators.

The Plaza Uruguaya, a park in downtown Asunción, was filled the next day with hundreds of students who had come to hear speeches castigating the government for not defending the Chaco and for using violence the previous night against the students. Among the major speakers was Dr. Stefanich,

38. Estigarribia, *Epic of the Chaco*, pp. 8-9.

who exorted the crowd to demand redress from the government. The demonstrators then moved on to the Presidential Palace. Guggiari took refuge in the Military College, turning over control of the situation to Major Arturo Bray, who commanded the capital's military garrison. When the crowd learned of Guggiari's whereabouts, they went to the Military College, but were prevented from entering by Major Bray's troops. According to the demonstration's student leaders, Marcos Fuster and César Garay, the protest broke up at this point and most of the participants went home; the events that followed had not been planned.

The demonstrators went next to the home of Major Rafael Franco to demand that he lead the antigovernment forces. Franco spoke briefly and reminded them of the grave situation in the Chaco but participated no further in the demonstration. Next, the Plaza Independencia, the city's central park, was occupied. Speeches by Anselmo Jover Peralta, a dissident Liberal, and Juan Natalicio González, a Colorado leader, exhorted the listeners to demand action from Guggiari. The crowd then left the plaza and went to the home of President Guggiari, where it was again met by troops. There are at least five written descriptions of what happened next. Policarpo Artaza, Efraím Cardozo, and Guggiari say that the crowd tried to enter the house forcibly and that a pistol was fired at the soldiers. On the other hand, Enrique Volta Gaona, a Colorado, and Juan Stefanich claim that the demonstrators were almost all students, that they were unarmed, and that there was no attempt to break into the house, although stones were thrown. It is incontestable, however, that soldiers on the rooftop suddenly began to open fire with their machine guns. The crowd broke and fled, leaving ten students and one unidentified woman dead on the street. Another twenty-nine people were wounded, of whom all but five were students. No soldiers were reported hurt by the demonstrators.

The "23rd. of October" left the "officialist" Liberals with a definitely minority government. Although Guggiari finished out his term and was peacefully succeeded by Eusebio Ayala, both sectors of the Colorado party, the dissident Liberals, and the Liga Nacional Independiente abstained from the 1932 elections. However, President Ayala did manage to unite, in appearance at least, the "officialist" and the *schaererista* wings of the party. Moreover, with his old friend, Estigarribia, in the post of commander-in-chief of the army, his position seemed firm.

The outbreak of war in the Chaco in July, 1932, following Bolivia's seizure of Fort Pitiantuta, seemed to promote a surge of national unity. The military reservists were called up to strengthen the regular army, which was forced to retreat before the Bolivian offensive. Rafael Franco was not only called back to active duty but was promoted to the rank of colonel and given command of the Second Army. Despite its superiority in men and arms, the Bolivian army's advance was checked by the Paraguayans, who counted upon superior knowledge of the terrain, morale, and shorter supply lines. The Paraguayan army won a series of bloody victories and began to take the offensive. Meanwhile, the appearance of national unity was deceiving. Even while they were prosecuting the war, many officers and subalterns were preparing for a postwar revolution.[39]

Indeed, rather than promoting unity among parties, the Chaco War might be viewed as a catalyst bringing together the opposition as well as those classes, the peasants and workers, who would be potential material for a social revolution. Within the corps of regular army officers there were many who sympathized with Rafael Franco's criticism of the government's prewar diplomacy and who remembered the diplomatic solution to the Vanguardia incident as a national disgrace. Franco himself was rapidly becoming a national hero through his dashing and successful tactics in the war. Moreover, his concern for the welfare of the troops won him their almost fanatical loyalty. Another critical factor that served as a link of sorts between the regular officers and the soldiers was the reserve corps, which consisted mainly of university students who had taken some military training. It was through them that bitter memories of the "23rd. of October" were to find an outlet for revenge against the Liberal party government. As one *febrerista* writer puts it: "The social con-

39. Antonio E. González, *Preparación del Paraguay*, II, 346.

tact produced between the peasant and the university student, between the student converted into a reserve officer and the plantation workers from La Industrial and the mill workers of the Alto Paraná, bore fruit. . . ."[40]

The conduct of the war also produced critics. By December, 1933, a year after the war had begun, the Paraguayan army had won back most of the Chaco through a series of spectacular victories. However, just when it seemed that the Bolivians were on the verge of surrender, President Ayala proposed an armistice. Liberal writers defend the Truce of Campo Vía as a device to gain time to strengthen the Paraguayan army's over-extended lines and to regroup for a renewed attack. Opponents charge that the truce was treasonous because it allowed the exhausted Bolivians time to regroup as well and to carry on the war for another year and a half. Some anti-Liberals allege that the truce was the result of a temporary split in the government between the "officialist" and *schaererista* Liberals, involving Estigarribia and other army officers. Others say that it was simply one more instance of inept Liberal diplomacy and unwillingness to fight.

The final armistice came on June 12, 1935. The Paraguayan army occupied all of the disputed territory, save for a narrow strip in the west. The two armies were deadlocked at this point: the Bolivians had been driven from the Chaco, and the Paraguayans had been unable to push beyond into the Andean foothills or to the province of Santa Cruz. While a Chaco Peace Commission met in Buenos Aires to negotiate a definite end to the war, most of the soldiers were sent home, leaving only regular army troops to patrol the truce line.

The Overthrow of the Liberal Government

The February Revolution came as a surprise to almost everyone but the plotters. The Ayala government had just brought the country through a successful war. The nation had doubled the size of its undisputed territory and had gained a certain measure of prestige besides. Moreover, Estigarribia, now promoted to the rank of field marshal, was a loyal Ayala supporter. Nevertheless, the opposition forces

---

40. Cibils, *Anarquía y revolución,* p. 33.

had coalesced and, with the war now ended, were free to turn their complete attention to the overthrow of the Liberal government. Colonel Rafael Franco headed a war veterans' association, the Asociación Nacional de Ex-Combatientes (National Veterans' Association), which claimed a membership of over 100,000 and posed a formidable threat to the government.[41]

Postwar social dislocation as well as shortsighted governmental policies only fed the growing ferment. Contact with the university-trained reserve officers had instilled discontent among peasants and workers towards the country's social and economic conditions, among the most backward in South America. The terrible costs of the Chaco War in terms of human casualties were also charged to bungling Liberal diplomacy both before and during the war. On its side, the Ayala government ended the war with a treasury so exhausted that the Liberal-dominated Congress voted down pensions for disabled war veterans. At the same time, however, Congress promoted General Estigarribia to the rank of field marshal (a rank not held since Francisco Solano López) and gave him an annual pension of 1,500 gold pesos for life.[42] This contrast in treatment between Estigarribia and the common soldiers led to many bitter jokes about "the General's fifteen hundred pesos" and greatly diminished Estigarribia's prestige with his troops as well as with fellow officers, many of whom had received neither promotions nor higher wages. In addition, rumors were rife that Ayala was planning to change the constitution to permit his re-election in 1936.[43] This led to the fear that he and Estigarribia were going to establish an out-and-out dictatorship.

The revolutionary plot that developed in the early weeks of 1936 seems to have been almost completely sponsored by the military. Some civilians have been mentioned by writers in connection with the plot: Juan Stefanich, Felipe Molas López, and Bernardino Caballero (grandson of the famous general) of the Colorado party; Facundo Recalde (a journal-

---

41. *Ibid.*, p. 50; also, Stefanich, *Renovación y liberación*, p. 273; and Artaza, *Ayala, Estigarribia*, pp. 112-13.

42. Artaza, *Ayala, Estigarribia*, pp. 72-73, 99-103.

43. Cibils, *Anarquía y revolución*, 45-46.

ist), the brothers Gómez and Luis Freire Esteves, old *cívico* Liberals. In this writer's opinion, they played marginal roles. More central to the decision-making concerning the projected revolt were Colonels Rafael Franco and Camilo Recalde, Major Juan Martincich, Captains Federico Jara Troche, Federico Varela, Pablo Jiménez y Nuñez, and Juan Speratti.[44]

It appears as though the plot was not a well-kept secret. Policarpo Artaza claims that President Ayala knew of these activities but refrained from taking action because no peace treaty with Bolivia had been signed yet, and he wished to avoid publicizing any political divisions within the country. Nonetheless, Colonel Franco was arrested and exiled to Argentina on February 6 because of an antigovernment speech he had given the night before at the Military College. Franco's exile robbed the conspirators of their leader and threw them into momentary confusion. The *coup d'état* needed a prestigious military leader in order to win army support. Colonel Aristides Rivas Ortellado was approached first because he was known to be critical of the government. He refused. Meanwhile, the government seemed to have learned that Franco's exile had not been enough to snuff out the conspiracy. The arrest of Colonel Camilo Recalde was ordered, whereupon he was taken to the military hospital—so as not to arouse suspicion—and kept under surveillance. At this point the revolutionaries turned to Colonel Federico Weddell Smith, the commander of the Campo Grande garrison. In a letter written some ten years later, Colonel Smith claims that he was first approached by Facundo Recalde, brother of Colonel Camilo Recalde, on February 16.[45] Smith goes on to say that he agreed to lead the revolt, on three conditions: (1) that the new president be a civilian, (2) that Colonel Recalde be made minister of war, and that (3) he, Smith, be allowed to retire from the army. These conditions accepted, Smith met that evening with the other military

---

44. Policarpo Artaza gives more importance to the civilians' role in the plot. Antonio E. González emphasizes its military character (*Preparación del Paraguay*, I, 321-57). Interviews with Colonel Federico Jara Troche and Elpidio Yegros, both *febreristas*, have led this writer to favor the view that the plot was essentially a military enterprise.
45. See Artaza, *Ayala, Estigarribia*, pp. 238-40.

plotters at the home of Facundo Recalde's sisters, in a suburb of Asunción. At 10:30 P.M. they went to Campo Grande to begin the revolt. Smith then repeated his conditions, this time specifically naming Gómez Freire Esteves for the presidency. These were accepted, he says, by the unanimous consent of everyone present.

Now the revolutionaries moved quickly. By 3:00 A.M. they were in control of the barracks and the armory, and they had released Colonel Camilo Recalde from his confinement. The rebel troops arrived by railroad to the capital just before dawn and took up positions in the Plaza Uruguaya. President Ayala, advised of the sudden, unauthorized presence of troops in the city, barely managed to escape arrest at his home. His car was fired upon as he fled to take refuge in the police station, the main point of resistance to the revolt. Facundo Recalde, Captain Jara Troche, and Captain Juan Speratti were sent there to demand his resignation. He refused. The revolutionaries now began to blast the police station with mortar fire, forcing the defenders to retire to positions in the post office and the naval ministry. These places became untenable in turn, and Ayala was taken to a navy gunboat anchored in the harbor. The gunboat exchanged fire with the revolutionaries for a few hours, until Ayala realized the situation was hopeless and surrendered.

The rapidity with which the revolt had taken place made it impossible for Estigarribia, who was in the Chaco, to do anything about salvaging the government. He flew back to Asunción and surrendered.[46] Only a few hours had sufficed to bring three decades of Liberal party rule to an end.

The February Revolution

Once the Liberal government had been overthrown, the revolutionaries evidently felt the need to justify their

---

46. Ayala and Estigarribia were held for six months while a plan was considered to create special tribunals to try them. Both were accused of treason for the Armistice of Campo Vía. The tribunals were never set up. Instead, the new Supreme Court, headed by Dr. Pedro P. Sarmaniego, ordered the two men released under a writ of habeas corpus. Estigarribia's pension was reduced from 1,500 gold pesos annually to 25,000 pesos in currency monthly. Upon their release from prison both opted for exile. (See *Febrero de 1936*), pp. 76-79.

action, for they quickly issued a proclamation to inform the public of the reasons for the revolt. This proclamation is essential for an understanding of the February Revolution, for it places that event in relation to both the Liberal and Socialist States. The heroes of the latter are eulogized while the misdeeds of the former are amplified. As we shall see, the initial stages of the February Revolution attracted diverse elements to its ranks: Marxists, reformist moderates, and Fascists. The only bond that held these people together, temporarily, was their shared hatred of the Liberals, and as the revolution proceeded to develop its own ideas, many of its former adherents became opponents. Nevertheless, the revolt of February 17, 1936, might not have taken place at all had it not been for the vague, widespread, anti-Liberal sentiments such as the ones expressed in the following proclamation:

PROCLAMATION OF THE LIBERATING ARMY[47]

PARAGUAYANS!
ILLUSTRIOUS NATION OF ANTEQUERA, OF RODRÍGUEZ DE FRANCIA AND OF THE LÓPEZES!

Your soldiers in arms have assumed the honor of protecting the national colors, our sacred soil and the immortality of the Fatherland.

We announce to you that . . .

We have heard the mandate of the solemn deeds in our nation's history
    . . . as in the armed plebiscite of Antequera's militia, which established the creed for the spiritual formation of the Republic;
    . . . as in the summons of the army on May 14, 1811, which gave us our sovereignty;
    . . . as in the support of those same troops for José Gaspar Rodríguez de Francia, affirming the collective oath to continue as an inviolable and independent nation in the Río de la Plata throughout the centuries to come;
    . . . as in the Juntas of the Asunción militia in 1842, which engendered by their swords the best governed nation on earth under their united idealism and its faithful interpreter, don Carlos Antonio López;

---

47. República del Paraguay, *La revolución paraguaya* (Asunción: 1937), pp. 345-49.

. . . as in the Plebiscite of the Armies in 1865, at the beginning of the great national epic, to triumph or die at the side of
Marshal don Francisco Solano López—preserving on this earth
the principle of nonintervention as the only norm of international law for America and insuring all free, civilized nations
the right to live together in peace;

. . . so is the pledge of your armies, which have just finished
three years of battle, defending our inviolable Chaco from one
end to the other, sweeping before them remnants of hordes
fallen on our open plains—having invaded us with the intention of snatching the inheritance that has been ours since Ñuflo
de Chávez and his soldiers arrived at Parapati from our glorious Villa de Asunción.[48]

Now we come, in our turn, to speak for all the men and
women who love this land, to voice the indignant protest of the
entire Republic against a regime of frock-coated bandits and
cold-blooded assassins who, after many decades of violent
domination, have ended by becoming the infectious force for
even greater crimes, both within and outside the country—
crimes which may never be righted, and which now threaten to
destroy the nation's moral and material welfare.

That group of declassed politicians' long hegemony, which
has brought this nation to the brink of disaster, can only be
explained by the fact that the Fatherland scarcely existed: only
special interests, always conspiring against the general welfare.

The whole nation knows about the shameless dictatorship
and politics-as-a-business that the Paraguayan government has
practised since it fell into the hands of that group of treasonous politicians of that party which the military arm of the
people has now cast from power.

We need not repeat this charge for the present, except to
offer some concrete examples.

President Eusebio Ayala built a tissue of criminality that
offered to public opinion the limitless audacity of his all-
powerful mafia.

In 1913, in connivance with the leading politicans and their
agents, he signed the Treaty of April 5, establishing with the
Seal of the Republic the lie that Bolivia was confining herself
to those possessions she had held in 1907—knowing all the
while that this was false.

Later, he proclaimed the country's disarmament as the
desideratum of so-called Paraguayan pacifism, while in the
meantime Bolivia pursued her systematic advance toward the
Río Paraguay.

He did not have to wait long for his reward for this defeatist

---

48. Ñuflo de Chávez, an early Spanish explorer.

doctrine. The negotiator of that faithless treaty soon appeared vested with the job of high representative of the same foreign interests who were supporting the Bolivian invasion. He became the steward of foreign companies and a fifteenth-century slave trader at their service, strangling the Paraguayan workers and buying up the highest political offices.

The corruption of that negotiator, who was bribed by foreign gold, gradually caught on in all the leading circles of the regime. Defeatism and surrender became not just the seraphic-pacifistic theories of he who signed the Ayala-Mujía Treaty, but the very program of that party to which he was the Word Incarnate.

And then came the expatiation of that horrible crime of conspiring against the external security of his own land.

The savage war broke loose over our people, who were manacled by the satrapy of Puerto Pinasco and its occult machinations.

Through the irony of fate, he was the president and commander-in-chief of the nation's armies, whose men went off to leave their bones in the blood-stained fields of the Chaco, already the home of enemy machine guns. And then not a day passed when the compromised agent of foreign bosses did not try to diminish by every means in his power the miraculous victories of a Paraguay revived.

We will omit the innumerable examples of his deceit. But there was one unmistakable gesture, the proof of treason carried to its maximum: the offering of an armistice to Bolivia after the victory of Campo Vía, in order to prevent the capture of the remainder of the invading army.

All that he did afterwards, including the ridiculous protocol of Buenos Aires, is nothing but the crowning of the continuous crime of hurting his country, which begins with the Treaty of April 5, 1913, and ends with the final diplomatic machinations of said president, who will pass into history with the notoriety of a trafficker in the blood and patrimony of his countrymen.

If such is the worth of that mafia chief in international affairs, what should be said of his impudence in domestic matters—he who fought in 1922, with his famous veto, the law to convoke presidential elections, so as to remain in office. And the entire Republic has been a witness to his recent attempts to have himself re-elected.

Here is a specimen of born traitor to his country—he who managed to corrupt with gold the Paraguayan general who helped him achieve the armistice of Campo Vía, in order to convert the army's high command into his palace guards. And he dared buy off this general so that he could imprison and proscribe from the soil of the Fatherland *our only authentic leader: Colonel Don Rafael Franco,* living symbol and mirror of the highest virtues that live within the ranks of our Liberating Army![49]

As a result, President Ayala cast himself into the arms of his political cronies, the political assassins of the "23rd. of October," the criminals responsible for the massacre of students. He planned the destruction of the Liberating Army in order to replace it with a prison guard.

We will not mention the people's anguish and desperation, which the vampires dwelling in the presidential circle sharpen day by day in order to enslave them. Hunger strikes every home. Thirty-thousand Paraguayans died in the Chaco, thousands of millions of pesos have been spent, yet in the postwar period they casually debate the most urgent problems and ramifications of this international catastrophe brought upon the country by the regime.

And they speculate in hunger with impunity, while the people curse the criminals who burn the sugar fields in order to raise the price of sugar and speculate with the rising price of food.

There is no chance to protest through the press, for it is in the exclusive service of the government. All constitutional guarantees are ended. Outside of the governing clique all Paraguayans are pariahs, without the right to publicize their ideas, nor to assemble, nor to enjoy the rights of citizenship.

But all this might have been sufferable had it not been for new plans by the people's unfaithful president and his accomplices to pare down the Republic's territorial sovereignty and to irredemiably frustrate all the victories of our armies in the Chaco War.

We shall not lend ourselves to this. One more day of inaction on our part would have been a desertion of our urgent duty to assert the sovereignty of the Paraguayan people and provide the vital necessities for their organization and security.

And on these grounds we declare to the world, in the name of the people, that we take for our guiding principle the finest justification that contemporary Europe affords: "No State can be sovereign over itself and compromise its future for the benefit of another State."

We decree, therefore, that the President of the Republic, Doctor Eusebio Ayala, and all the personnel of his administration in the three branches of government, cease in the performance of their official functions.

---

49. Italics added.

PARAGUAYANS!

Your soldiers in arms swear to comply with their mission. The Nation will be restored to the level of its past history in the Río de la Plata, to the free dominion over its soil, and to the grandeur of its future.

ASUNCIÓN, FEBRUARY 17, 1936
Lt. Col. don F. W. Smith
Lt. Col. don Camilo Recalde

Although the author of this document was Gómez Freire Esteves, the revolt was essentially military in character. Paraguay had not experienced military rule for some twenty-five years, since the brief dictatorship of Albino Jara in 1911. Therefore, this made it all the more necessary for the military to justify its overthrow of a civilian government. The Proclamation of the Liberating Army delineated a tradition of patriotic military participation in politics by identifying the military with national heroes. It also emphasized Paraguay's historical debt to the military: (1) Antequera's militia gave the country its creed for its "spiritual formation," (2) the army secured the country's independence on May 14, 1811, and helped to maintain that independence by supporting Francia; (3) the army's idealism engendered "the best governed nation on earth" under Carlos Antonio López; (4) the army had stayed to "triumph or die" at the side of Francisco Solano López in the nation's great war to preserve its sovereignty; (5) Ñuflo de Chávez *and* his soldiers gave Paraguay the patrimony of the Chaco; and (6) the present-day army had just fought a bloody war to defend that patrimony.

The Liberal party—personified in Eusebio Ayala—was the antithesis of such patriotism, according to the proclamation. To select only a few points: (1) it threatened the extinction of the country's "moral and material welfare;" (2) it conspired against the nation's collective welfare and external security; (3) it had disarmed the country and, while Bolivia continued her "systematic advance," had denied that such an advance was taking place; (4) it had committed further treason during the Chaco War when it offered Bolivia the Truce of Campo Vía, just when the Bolivian army was about to be captured; (5) it was in the pay of foreign companies, referring especially to Eusebio Ayala, who was a lawyer for Puerto Pinasco, a quebracho company in the Chaco; (6) Ayala himself was guilty of trying to establish a personalistic dictatorship on two occasions; (7) it exploited the people economically and deprived them of their constitutional rights; (8) it was guilty of the massacre of students on "the 23rd. of October;" and (9) it had bribed Estigarribia and tried to convert the army's high command into "hired guards," an affront to military patriotism, in addition to trying to purge patriots from the military by trying to destroy the Liberating Army.

Given this situation, the military "assumed the honor of protecting the national colors, our sacred soil and the immortal life of the Fatherland." Its right of intervention was based on these points: (1) the Fatherland owes its existence in large part to the military in the first place, for its support of Francia and the Lópezes; (2) the military had just finished defending the existence of the Fatherland, once again, in the Chaco; (3) if the military's duty is to defend the nation against its external enemies, then it can be assumed that the military can intervene against "treasonous politicians" who conspire with the nation's external enemies; and (4) the army speaks for the people, who cannot protest against the regime, publicize their ideas, assemble, or enjoy any rights of citizenship. Therefore, the army proclaims "the highest protest of the entire Republic," hears the "commanding mandate of the solemn deeds of the nation's history," is the "military arm of the people," and has the "urgent duty to assert the sovereignty of the Paraguayan people" and to provide the vital necessities for their organization and security.

The Proclamation of the Liberating Army also contains ideological ramifications that hint at future policies of the revolutionary government. Such ideological cues must, of course, be tested against the actual behavior of the revolutionary government. However, taking them at face value for the moment, they may be said to be:

1. *Nationalism*—Ayala was accused of preparing to surrender all or part of the Chaco to Bolivia at the Peace Talks

in Buenos Aires. The Liberating Army promised a firm, nationalistic stand. Moreover, Ayala was accused of being in the pay of foreign companies, who "strangle the Paraguayan workers." This implies a possible antiforeign bias and probably economic nationalism.

2. *Socialism*—It is interesting to note that all of the historical figures used as patriotic symbols are from either the colonial period or from the era of the Socialist State. Not one figure from the post-1870 period (with the exception of Rafael Franco) is mentioned as a hero, not even the supposedly nationalistic and pro-López Bernardino Caballero. The "long hegemony of declassed politicians" and the "shameless dictatorship and politics-as-a-business that the Paraguayan government has practised since it fell to a group of treasonous politicians" must certainly refer to the "legionnaires," who were the founders of the Liberal party and the Liberal State. The army promised to restore the nation to the level of its past history. This calling upon the memory of the nationalistic socialism of the Francia-López era signals a desire to rebuild along lines similar to the socioeconomic structure of that period.

3. *Democracy*—The proclamation is not clear as to whether the new government was to be based on free elections, with representation open to the opposition. It is clear, as we have seen, that the army identified itself with the nation and "the people." Moreover, the abridging of constitutional guarantees by the Liberal government aroused the army's indignation. On the other hand, the army declared its "mission" to restore the nation to its past glory. Missions presumably were not to be sidetracked either by permitting a relentless opposition to thwart them nor by permitting them to be submitted to the vagaries of public opinion.

It is also important to note the phrase in the proclamation which reads: "our only authentic leader, Colonel Don Rafael Franco." One of the first steps the revolutionaries took was to wire Franco, who was living in Buenos Aires, asking him to return immediately. Franco arrived in Asunción on February 19 to take command and to form a new government. A con-

troversy still exists over Franco's right to do this. The reader
will recall that Colonel Smith said in his letter that Gómez
Freire Esteves had been the revolutionaries' choice for the
presidency. Smith then went on to say that when Franco arrived at the capital he was taken to the Presidential Palace to
participate in the discussions over forming a new government.
Franco was invited to preside over these discussions, an invitation which he took to mean that he was to assume the
presidency of the revolutionary government. Gómez Freire
Esteves made no objection, and the other participants accepted this new development as an accomplished fact.[50]

Franco's version of the event is that before the discussions
had begun Colonel Smith himself offered him the presidency
and that he had been led to the presidential chair by Gómez
Freire Esteves.[51] While it is possible that Franco may have
misunderstood Smith's offer, the weight of testimony is
against Smith's assertion that Gómez Freire Esteves, not
Franco, had been the revolutionaries' choice for the presidency. Felipe Molas López, a Colorado participant and no
friend of Franco's, claims in a letter written in reply to
Smith's that from the beginning the revolutionaries had in
mind a government presided over by Franco.[52] Moreover, as
we have seen, the Proclamation of the Liberating Army, written by Gómez Freire Esteves, states that Franco was the "only
authentic leader."

In any case, Franco's presidency was confirmed the same
day by the army's "Plebiscitory Decree."[53] Besides naming
Franco president, the decree outlined a set of directives for
the provisional government to follow. Chief among these was
to prepare a constitutional convention to revise the Constitution of 1870. Meanwhile, the rights guaranteed by the old
constitution would be respected until a new document could
be prepared. Franco swore allegiance to this decree on the
following day, and the new revolutionary government, based

---

50. Letter of Colonel Federico Weddell Smith to J. Rodolfo
Bordón, quoted in Artaza, *Ayala, Estigarribia*, p. 240.
51. Letter of Rafael Franco to Juan Stefanich (June 9, 1946),
quoted in Stefanich, *Renovación y liberacion*, pp. 307-8.
52. Artaza, *Ayala, Estrigarribia*, pp. 243-44.
53. *La revolución paraguaya*, pp. 5-6.

on a mandate from the military, was launched.[54]

Franco's first act as provisional president was to form a cabinet. Gómez Freire Esteves was appointed minister of interior, and his brother Luis was named minister of the treasury. Both were strong nationalists and alleged admirers of Mussolini's corporate state. Bernardino Caballero, grandson of the founder of the Colorado party, was made minister of agriculture. Caballero had resided some twenty years in Germany and was said to be an admirer of Adolf Hitler. The "left" was represented by Anselmo Jover Peralta, a dissident Liberal and partisan of *aprismo,* the Peruvian social revolutionary movement. Jover Peralta held the posts of minister of justice and minister of education and culture. Juan Stefanich, the minister of foreign affairs, was the "moderate center" of the cabinet. Stefanich had written many laudatory articles about Woodrow Wilson and held to a line of progressive liberalism. He was for social reform but was opposed to what he considered the extremist position of Jover Peralta. At the same time he was a nationalist, favoring a tough stand at the Peace Talks, but was opposed to the authoritarian tendencies of Caballero and the Freire Esteves brothers.[55]

At the first cabinet meeting, February 20, the ministers unanimously agreed on two basic points: that the revolution would emphasize Paraguayan nationalism and that there would be no attacks against the Roman Catholic church, the country's dominant religion.[56]

One means used by the revolutionary government to promote nationalism was to revive the figure of Francisco Solano López as a patriotic symbol, in contrast to the policies of the

54. At this point three principal actors disappear from the main story of the revolution. Colonel Federico Weddell Smith refused any post in the new government. Colonel Camilo Recalde was named ambassador to Chile, where he died some years later. The fact that he never returned to Paraguay can probably be attributed to the fall of Franco's government in 1937. Policarpo Artaza's account of Colonel Recalde's reasons for leaving—a personal grudge against former President Ayala had been satisfied, so he had no reason to stay—(see Artaza, *Ayala, Estigarribia,* p. 127) does not seem convincing. Facundo Recalde went on to edit the newspaper of the Asociación Nacional de Ex-Combatientes, *Verde Olivo,* but played no major role in the revolution.

55. Stefanich, *Febrero de 1936,* pp. 15-16.

56. *Ibid.,* p. 16.

Liberals. The latter had proscribed both López and his descendants in 1870, and since then they had attempted to promote the image of him in the schools as a symbol of the supposedly brutal and unenlightened era of the Socialist State. Now he was proclaimed a national hero, and a commission was appointed to locate his lost, unmarked grave. The marshal's remains were found, exhumed, and carried to Asunción, where they were placed in the "Pantheon of Heroes," the remodeled downtown chapel build by Carlos Antonio López.[57]

The new government quickly began far more important projects as well. Perhaps the most basic of all, for such a predominantly rural nation, was the Agrarian Reform Law of May 5, 1936.[58] Drafted by Bernardino Caballero, it represented the first serious attempt since 1870 to place land in the hands of the peasants. The statement of the law began with an interesting summary of the existing problems, claiming that the property-holding class did not exceed 5 per cent of the population and that such a situation had led to continuing emigration of Paraguayans to other countries where conditions were more favorable. Thus, the purpose of the law was a re-structuring of the land tenure system to encourage the growth of a number of small and medium-sized holdings. Ideologically, the revolution accepted neither collectivism nor the concept that the rights of private property are absolute. Private property should be respected, but it also should have a social function.

This law provided for the expropriation of lands up to a total of two million hectares (about 4.5 million acres), which would be divided into farms of between ten and one hundred hectares. The old owners would be indemnified for the property taken, and the new owners would be sold, not given, the land with fifteen years to pay for it. Those already occupying the designated lands—sharecroppers and/or squatters—would be given the first option to buy. The new owners would have

---

57. Juan Stefanich, *La restauración histórica del Paraguay* (Buenos Aires: Editorial El Mundo Nuevo, 1946).

58. For the text of this law, see R. P., *La revolución paraguaya,* pp. 147-54.

to live on their new holdings and work them personally, and they would not be able to sell, sublet, or alienate them in any other way.

Programs for agricultural education and rural finance were also planned. Regional agricultural schools were to be created, and classes in farming were to be obligatory in all schools. Military farms were to be created, as in the days of the Socialist State, and were to function as agricultural experimental stations. An Agrarian Bank was to be set up to provide loans to farmers and to encourage rural co-operatives. The entire program was to be financed by issuing bonds at 5 per cent interest, through export taxes and a head tax on cattle. According to Juan Stefanich, between May 5, 1936, and August 13, 1937, more than 200,000 hectares had been expropriated, and titles to new farms given out to some 10,000 families.[59]

Another crucial measure was the decree law that created the Labor Department and a Labor Code.[60] The Labor Department was to function under the minister of interior. Its chief functions were to enforce the Labor Code, to offer its services in the arbitration or conciliation of labor disputes, to inspect working conditions in the shops and factories, and to foster producer and consumer co-operatives. This law also gave the Labor Department tremendous potential power, for it required labor unions and business associations to register with the department and authorized the department to "study, revise, and approve the statutes of these organizations."

The Labor Code was moderately progressive. Among other things, it provided for an eight-hour day with Sundays free, the right of workers to unionize and to demand a just wage, paid annual vacations, and payment in national currency. This last point was aimed at the practice of some *latifundio* owners of paying their workers in script, which could be exchanged only at company stores.

Despite these attempts to better the lot of the worker, the

---

59. Stefanich, *Renovación y liberación*, p. 39.
60. Decree Law #2303, June 24, 1936. See R. P., *La revolución paraguaya*, pp. 276-82, for the text of this law.

revolutionary government was beset from the first by labor agitation. Radical orators and organizers, buoyed up by revolutionary euphoria, urged the workers to take direct control of the government, and marches were organized in which workers paraded through the streets bearing red flags. Writers such as J. Rodolfo Bordón and Arnaldo Valdovinos attacked the government from their respective newspapers, *Paraguay* and *El Diario,* calling it vacillating and "pseudo-revolutionary."[61] Labor strikes became more violent, and clashes occurred in the streets between workers and the police. The Argentine Embassy was attacked during one of these demonstrations, leading to a tense diplomatic situation. The chaotic atmosphere of those times is described by Stefanich:

> Those were the first days of the February government, and one lived in times of anxiety and agitation. It was extremely difficult to get co-ordinated action or to canalize the popular and individual activities that had been unleashed on all sides. Meetings, assemblies, and improvised debates heated the atmosphere; the most divergent opinions were expounded in the streets; labor unions acted tumultuously at the service of their own ends; the ranks of the army were incited by these trends, while the students found themselves laboring for the most disparate and antagonistic doctrines.
>
> This anarchy sapped our strength, and it became necessary to give direction, definition, and organization to the popular forces of the revolution. Delegations of unknown origin were appearing in the towns and cities of the interior, sowing discord with their exalted discourse. Orators with suspicious affiliations became self-appointed tribunes and announced drastic revolutionary measures: the division of land, the confiscation of property, factories, and industries; and announced extremist programs behind the backs of the authorities.[62]

In short, the revolutionary government was not so revolutionary that it intended to acquiesce to these radical programs. Indeed, the entire cabinet, with the exception of Jover Peralta, was in favor of curbing the revolutionary ebullience. Franco intervened personally in the workers' demonstrations, forbidding the display of any flag other than the national

61. For a leftist critique of the February government, see J. Rodolfo Bordón, *La revolución del Paraguay de febrero* (Buenos Aires: Editorial Claridad, 1937).

62. Stefanich, *Febrero de 1936,* p. 42.

colors. The more extremist labor leaders were jailed. Bordón and Valdovinos had their newspapers closed down, and both went into exile.

The political and social goals of the revolution had been outlined by President Franco shortly after he had come to power in a public address entitled "The Structure of the New Paraguayan State."[63] It was stated that the purpose of the revolution was to establish a "natural democracy" based on peasants and workers. Such a transformation would be based on national realities, and therefore the revolution eschewed the transplanting of any foreign system, whether Communist, Fascist, or "racist." Nor was any sort of "constitutional dictatorship" planned. While the provisional government reserved the right to act forcibly, given the urgency of the situation, the ultimate goal was the establishment of a representative democracy. A constitutional convention would be called as soon as the revolution was consolidated. Meanwhile, even though the provisional government felt that Paraguay's traditional parties had completed their missions, they would not be dissolved forcibly.

Despite such assurances, the gravity of the situation and the insecurity felt by the new government led to some harsh attempts to suppress dissent. One such measure was the notorious Decree Law 152, passed on March 10, 1936.[64] This law was drafted by Gómez Freire Esteves and clearly mirrored the pro-Fascist sympathies of its author. Its preamble identified the state with the liberating revolution and declared that the revolution was of the "same type as the totalitarian social transformations of contemporary Europe," a direct repudiation of Franco's earlier statements against importing foreign ideologies. This law abolished for one year all labor unions, business organizations, political parties, and all types of political activity not emanating directly from the state. A "committee of civil mobilization" was to be created and placed under the minister of interior. It is not clear what duties were planned for such a committee, but presumably it would in-

63. For the text of this speech, see R. P., *La revolución paraguaya*, pp. 13-14.
64. For the text of this law, see Artaza, *Ayala, Estigarribia*, pp. 155-57.

volve broad powers of national planning and control over both labor and business, and it also might possibly have broadened its functions to include secret police duties—internal security being one of the functions customarily exercised by the minister of interior.

Decree Law 152 caused an immediate storm of protest from the Asociación Nacional de Ex-Combatientes, the Liga Nacional Independiente, the Federation of University Students, and several labor unions. Although it carried the signatures of all the cabinet ministers and that of President Franco's, all but the Freire Esteves resigned their posts in the face of such widespread resentment against the decree. Franco removed Gómez and Luis Freire Esteves on the following day and invited the other ministers to return to the cabinet. Germán Soler became the new minister of interior and Emilio Gardel took over as minister of the treasury. Since both were members of the Liga Nacional Independiente, that organization now controlled three of the five cabinet seats. As for Decree Law 152, it remained on the books but was not enforced.

Soler's appointment as minister of interior initiated a more constructive stage in government-labor relations. It was he who set up the Department of Labor and drafted the Labor Code. Moreover, he began to implement that code vigorously. Five months after taking office, Soler could report that the department had settled some seventeen strikes and labor disputes and that seventy-three new unions had been formed representing a total membership of 7,320.[65] The next step was to combine all of the unions under one big national union, the Confederación Paraguaya de Trabajadores (Paraguayan Workers' Confederation), which was responsible to the Labor Department. Requiring governmental recogniton before they could legally bargain or strike deprived the unions of much of their freedom of action, fitting them into a paternalistic, corporative system, but it also welded them into a bloc. Considering the government's prolabor sympathies, this gave them greater power vis-à-vis the employers. Soler also undertook the pacification of anarchic conditions in the countryside

---

65. R. P. *La revolución paraguaya*, p. 288.

by turning the Asociación Nacional de Ex-Combatientes into a rural police. The country was divided into ten districts, each under the supervision of a veteran officer.[66]

The revolution was becoming organized and channeled. The right wing of the cabinet had been seriously weakened with the ousting of the Freire Esteves brothers. Now with the moderates of the Liga Nacional Independiente holding a majority of the cabinet posts and with the labor situation brought under control, pressure was brought to bear on the left. Although the more radical revolutionaries had been exiled during the government's crackdown on labor agitation, the left still had cabinet representation in Anselmo Jover Peralta. They also had an influential political vehicle in the Club 17 Febrero, an organization of intellectuals, students, and workers. Given the broad popular appeal of these radicals in their emphasis on social and economic reforms and their position as the revolutionary "vanguard," it appears that Liga cabinet members preferred to launch an oblique, rather than a direct, attack on Jover Peralta, who claimed that he was the victim of "conservative opinion" and "an agile maneuver by the reactionaries."[67] According to some sources, Jover Peralta was referring to strong pressure placed on Franco by the army and the Asociación Nacional de Ex-Combatientes. In addition to his outspoken socialist position and his longtime reputation as a popular agitator, the fact that he had been a pacifist during the Chaco War earned him the antagonism of the military. By June, 1936, he had been pressured into resigning. He was still connected with the revolutionary government, however, through his appointment as ambassador to Mexico. Still, such a faraway post stripped him of any weight in the inner circles of the government. His cabinet positions were taken over by Crescencio Lezcano, another member of the Liga Nacional Independiente.

Now the only remaining member of the original cabinet, other than Stefanich, was Bernardino Caballero. Although, like Jover Peralta, he was outvoted by the Liga members, his

66. *Ibid.*, pp. 289-90.
67. Jover Peralta, *El Paraguay revolucionario,* I, 30. Also, Antonio E. Gonzalez, *La rebelión de Concepción* (Buenos Aires: Editorial Guaranía, 1947), p. 36.

position was much stronger. He was supported by the Colorado party, one of the country's two major parties and the only one still permitted to function openly. The Colorados also held other offices: Felipe Molas López was the mayor of Asunción, J. Isidro Ramírez represented Paraguay at the Chaco Peace Conference, Juan O'Leary was the ambassador to France and Italy, and Juan Natalicio González and Victor Morínigo had been appointed to a special commission whose purpose was to travel in neighboring countries spreading favorable propaganda concerning the new government.

Stefanich's project to integrate the various revolutionary groups under a new political party brought the government into conflict with the Colorados, but there were other strong supporters of the revolutionary government at that time. In probable order of importance these were:

1. *The Asociación Nacional de Ex-Combatientes* (National Veterans' Association). Claiming some 106,000 members, it was the largest single group. Since it was also the national police force, its organization extended to all parts of the country, with the exception of the Chaco, which was still under military occupation. Being armed, it was the only group capable of forcibly opposing any attempted *coup d'état*. Its strong loyalty to Franco made it all the more reliable. Guided by its acting-president, Elpidio Yegros, it was truly the backbone of the revolutionary government.

2. *The Liga Nacional Independiente* (National Independent League). Although this was a small group, it exercised influence out of proportion to its numbers through its domination of the cabinet and its position as the revolution's "Brain Trust." Its influence was also based largely on ties of close personal friendship existing among Juan Stefanich, President Franco, and Elpidio Yegros. Yegros had been a student of Stefanich's at the university in the days of the "23rd of October," and it was largely through his support that Stefanich had been able to pressure his opponents out of the cabinet.[68]

3. *Confederación Paraguaya de Trabajadores* (Paraguayan

---

68. Stefanich, *Renovación y liberación,* p. 277, and Cardozo, *23 de octubre,* p. 121.

Workers' Confederation). This was the government's official national labor organization. It is difficult to gauge the intensity of enthusiasm that the workers may have had for the government itself, but there is little doubt that they were committed to the revolution and would be against a conservative counterrevolution. Organized as it was under one national directorate supported by the government, labor could also be mobilized more effectively to defend the revolution.

4. *Club 17 Febrero.* This group of radicals differed from the Liga Nacional Independiente in that its membership included revolutionaries outside of the intellectual class. Its commitment to socialism was also more pronounced.

5. *Dissident Liberals.* These were the radical Liberals, who had broken formally with the parent party after the "23rd. of October." They were to hold important positions in the new party and in all other *febrerista* organizations thereafter.

6. *The Federación Universitaria.* This was the university students' organization, which was strongly behind the revolution. There seems to have been a considerable number of these students represented in the Club 17 Febrero as well.

These, then, were the groups that Stefanich hoped to weld into a new political party, but to do so he would have to run counter to the wishes of the Colorado party chiefs. Moreover, he would have to be careful to keep the army at least benevolently neutral for, in the final analysis, the army was the most important factor of all in keeping the revolution in power. Indeed, Policarpo Artaza claims that during the Chaco Peace Conference, Stefanich told Spruille Braden, the American representative, that "Franco's government rests on bayonets."[69] Although Stefanich denies having said this, the fact remains that the army, if united against the regime, did have the power to unseat Franco. The army was still in the field for, since peace had not been declared, it was necessary to keep it ready to fight at any moment. This made unfeasible any attempt at purges at the time which might weaken morale. The result was that many pro-Liberal and pro-Colorado officers still held high positions. One of these was Colonel Ramón Paredes, the commander of the Chaco forces, a Liberal who

---

69. Artaza, *Ayala, Estigarribia*, p. 186.

had received this post because he was President Franco's *compadre,* godfather to his son. Paredes was actively conspiring against the revolution in conjunction with Colonel Damaso Sosa Valdés, the head of the cavalry, and these two managed to foment dissatisfaction among the troops by seeing to it that supplies sent by the government were held up in Puerto Casado, the main point of entry to the Chaco.[70] Criticism spread among the soldiers over supposed government unconcern and negligence, creating the very attitudes that Paredes and the Liberals hoped to exploit.

Meanwhile, Stefanich's plan to create a new political party to generate support for the revolution was reaching fulfillment. The grand assembly for the founding of the Unión Nacional Revolucionaria (National Revolutionary Union) met in the National Theatre on November 15, 1936. A "Declaration of Principles" was adopted which advocated representative democracy, a unitary form of government, the socialization of property and industries that might be essential for public welfare, and the protection of the rights of workers and peasants.[71] A directorate composed of thirty-two members was elected, with Stefanich as president. After the founding of the UNR, the Liga Nacional Independiente announced that it was dissolving itself and merging completely with the new party. According to Stefanich, the UNR had accepted 38,000 members by August, 1937.[72] Still, one may suspect that it may have been an artificial party, for it did not survive the fall of the revolutionary government as it might have had it established deeper roots. Perhaps, as some critics imply, the UNR was nothing more than the Liga Nacional Independiente's absorption of all other revolutionary factions.[73] On the other hand, Stefanich claims that only five of the thirty-two men on the directorate were Liga members.

The founding of the UNR led to Bernardino Caballero's

---

70. Interviews with Colonels Federico Jara Troche (April 16, 1964) and Francisco Chávez del Valle (April 20, 1964); also interview with Elpidio Yegros (May 4, 1964).

71. R.P., *La revolución paraguaya,* pp. 385-405.

72. Stefanich, *Renovación y liberación,* p. 275.

73. For critical views of the U.N.R., see Artaza, *Ayala, Estigarribia,* pp. 169-72; and Bordón *La revolución,* pp. 9-10.

resignation from the cabinet, and his place was taken by Guillermo Tell Bertoni, a Liga member. A firm Colorado, Caballero would not join the new party and protested the government's almost inseparable identification with it. He and Felipe Molas López were arrested a few days later and accused of plotting against the government.[74] Elpidio Yegros took over as mayor of Asunción; and most Colorados holding government posts were soon separated from their jobs. This left the government with both of the nation's major parties in opposition to it. The revolution could survive only if the UNR could win over the peasantry and the intellectuals from their habitual allegiance to their traditional parties—a difficult and time-consuming task. One indication of the unwillingness of most people to leave their old parties can be seen in the case of the Asociación Nacional de Ex-Combatientes. The ANEC claimed 106,000 members; the UNR only 38,000, of whom many were from groups other than the ANEC. We can take this to mean that, despite the great loyalty that the ANEC members had for Rafael Franco personally, not more than one-third could have joined the UNR.

The UNR might have developed into a great mass party had the revolution lasted longer. However, nine months after it was formed the counterrevolution overthrew the revolutionary government and dealt a fatal blow to all attempts to make the UNR a permanent institution. The fall of the revolutionary government was caused ostensibly by its alleged diplomatic failure at the Chaco Peace Conference. The actual cause, however, was that Colonels Paredes and Sosa Valdés, in conjunction with the Liberal party exiles, were able to stir up enough discontent within the army for it to intervene against a government that was pictured as inept and irresponsible. It must be emphasized that the counterrevolutionary conspirators never attacked President Franco; he was still too much of a popular figure. Instead, criticism was directed against Franco's cabinet; the counterrevolution came in the name of "saving" Franco from "bad advisors." The issue that gave these conspirators their excuse to strike was the Treaty of January 9, 1937.

---

74. Stefanich, *Febrero de 1936*, pp. 104-5, 155-56.

The Chaco War had ended with Paraguayan troops in control of most of the Chaco, including the road connecting the Bolivian villages of Villa Montes and Boyuibe, which had cut off communications between the Bolivian armies. This road also ran near the oilfields that Bolivia had leased to Standard Oil. In order to dislodge the Paraguayans from this sector, the Bolivians pressed hard at the Peace Conference for the creation of a neutral zone there. Paraguay was firmly opposed to any step that might weaken her control of this strategic position, but she could count on little support at the Peace Conference. The Argentine government was sympathetic towards Paraguay but lent her only lukewarm support, and Brazil stood closer to the Bolivian position. Another bad sign for Paraguay was the appointment of Spruille Braden as the American delegate to the Peace Conference. Braden had first obtained the oil concessions from Bolivia back in 1921 and had sublet them to Standard Oil. Stefanich and Isidro Ramírez tried throughout the year to break what appeared to be a hostile phalanx by negotiating treaties with Argentina and Brazil to study trade problems. Nevertheless, acting upon agreements made with the Liberal government before its overthrow, the Peace Conference announced that it would create a neutral zone along the Villa Montes—Boyuibe Road and would send a Neutral Military Commission to police it.[75]

Isidro Ramírez informed the conference on the following day that his government was absolutely opposed to any such move. The formal but harsh note delivered by Ramírez stated the Paraguayan government's "energetic opposition to any innovation or modification of the *de facto* situation" and denied that the Conference had a right to create such a neutral zone or a Neutral Military Commission to police it.[76] This note led to many tense and heated conversations, during which the Paraguayan delegates refused any compromise. The revolutionary government was particularly opposed to the power the Neutral Military Commission would have over the

75. *La revolución paraguaya*, pp. 443-44; also, Juan Stefanich, *La diplomacia de la revolución* (Buenos Aires: Editorial El Mundo Nuevo, 1946), p. 68.

76. R. P., *La revolución paraguaya*, pp. 449-57; and, Stefanich, *La diplomacia de la revolución*, pp. 69-70.

number of arms and troops the belligerents were maintaining and its power to intervene in the mobilization of fresh troops or the acquisition of new arms.[77]

Finally, on October 29, the conference delivered an ultimatum to Paraguay that it name its delegates to the Neutral Military Commission by November 2. Paraguay refused. Her army was alerted, as though she were preparing to resume the war, but November 2 passed without an incident or with any move on the part of the conference.[78]

An impasse had been reached in the peace negotiations, and Stefanich received an invitation in December to hold talks in Buenos Aires with the American, Argentine, Brazilian, and Chilean delegates. It was during these conversations that Stefanich was supposed to have told Spruille Braden that the Franco government was supported by bayonets. According to Stefanich, his actual words were: "In Paraguay, no government could last twenty-four hours if it consented to even the most minor retreat in the Chaco."[79] In any case, the conference decided that the only way out of the deadlock would be to confer with the military chiefs of the two belligerent powers. A commission was sent to the Chaco where, from December 23 to 25 it negotiated with Colonel Paredes. Paredes finally consented to a preliminary agreement that would: (1) permit free commercial transit on the Villa Montes—Boyuibe road, (2) permit transit of no more than five trucks at one time, (3) prohibit the transit of any troops or war materials, (4) allow the troops of both sides to pull back in order to minimize the possibility of renewed violence, and (5) allow the establishment of a joint Paraguayan-Bolivian gendarmery to police the route.[80]

Neither the Paraguayan nor the Bolivian foreign ministries would accept this agreement at first, which led to new and heated debates. At last the conference agreed to the following changes demanded by Stefanich: that the present positions of the two armies be maintained, instead of pulling back; that

77. R. P., *La revolución paraguaya*, p. 448.
78. R. P., *La revolución paraguaya*, p. 467; Stefanich, *La diplomacia de la revolución*, pp. 79-80.
79. Stefanich, *La diplomacia de la revolución*, p. 89.
80. *Ibid.*, pp. 93-94.

no withdrawal of troops or commands could be effected without the prior approval of their governments; and that the expense of maintaining the road would be borne by Bolivia. The treaty was finally signed on January 9, 1937.[81]

Criticism of the treaty, from both friends and enemies of the government, began to build up in Paraguay as soon as the agreement was made public. To these critics, even the limited use of the road allowed to Bolivia seemed like appeasement. A three-hour public address by Stefanich on June 10 in the National Theatre failed to convince many that the treaty provided for no withdrawal of the army, no neutral zone, nor any disclaimer of sovereignty over all of the Chaco. Ill feeling was especially widespread in the army, as supplies were still being held up in Puerto Casado while Paredes and Sosa Valdés were fomenting discontent. The scars left on the government from the previous cabinet in-fighting had given many people a bad impression and lent some credibility to the charge that President Franco was surrounded by untrustworthy politicians who were bungling the revolution and selling out Paraguay's interests in the Chaco. Such criticism, of course, stemmed in no small measure from Liberal propaganda.

On August 12, Captain Francisco Chávez del Valle, an officer in the Military College, informed Franco of a rumor that a military revolt was brewing and could be headed off only by a change in the cabinet, presumably Stefanich's dismissal.[82] Captain Federico Jara Troche had also heard such rumors and had moved his artillery unit from Villa Hayes across the Paraguay River, where he took up a position in front of Asunción to ward off any invasion that might come by way of the river. However, when word came to him that the revolt had been called off, he returned to Villa Hayes.[83] Meanwhile, Franco refused to believe that Paredes, his *compadre,* would betray him, and no official action was taken to protect the government.

---

81. *Ibid.,* pp. 98-99; and, *La revolución paraguaya,* pp. 471-72. For a critical view of this treaty, see Artaza, *Ayala, Estigarribia,* pp. 253-57.

82. Interview with Francisco Chávez del Valle (April 20, 1964).

83. Interview with Federico Jara Troche (April 16, 1964).

During this time, Paredes had begun moving his troops towards Asunción and was soon joined by the Concepción garrison. On the morning of August 13, three gunboats took up threatening positions in the harbor, and Paredes' troops entered the capital. A crowd of veterans from the ANEC went to the armory to demand weapons to defend the revolution, but the pro-Franco commander, Major Joel Estigarribia (no relation to General Estigarribia), was already a prisoner and the armory was in the hands of the counterrevolution.[84]

While Paredes' troops were taking their positions, Franco's entire cabinet presented itself at the Presidential Palace to offer their resignations: Juan Stefanich, minister of foreign affairs; Germán Soler, minister of interior; Crescencio Lezcano, minister of education; Emilio Gardel, minister of finance; Guillermo Tell Bertoni, minister of agriculture; Pedro Duarte Ortellado, minister of public health; and Colonel Arístides Rivas Ortellado, minister of defense. The counterrevolution had accomplished its stated purpose. Paredes arrived at the Presidential Palace soon after and took charge, announcing by radio that Franco would remain as president and that a new cabinet would be formed. Franco, however, refused to continue under such pressure or to accept orders from Paredes, so he was arrested on the following day and placed in a cell at the naval base.[85]

The February Revolution was over.

---

84. *Ibid.*
85. Stefanich, *Renovación y liberación,* pp. 291-95.

2. The Revolutionary Purpose
Institutionalized

The revolutionary government was followed by a provisional government headed by Felix Paiva, a professor of constitutional law at the National University. Colonel Paredes took over the Ministry of Interior, from which post he could control the police. Paiva's administration was wracked by a series of revolts by the ousted revolutionaries, who had been deposed without a fight because they had been taken by surprise, more or less. Now they were determined not to relinquish the revolution. On September 7, 1937—less than a month after Paredes' coup—Major Juan Martincich raised part of the army against Paiva. Colonel Franco flew back from exile to lend his support, but the revolt had been crushed by the time he arrived in Asunción. A second revolt was attempted on November 2, when Major Vicente Quiños and Captain Cicancio López led the Concepción garrison against the government, but they were put down quickly by troops arriving from the Chaco. On December 21 Major Joel Estigarribia, the former commander of the armory, slipped back into Paraguay from exile and, with a few army friends and a portion of the navy, seized the armory. However, before any concerted action could be taken, Major Joel Estigarribia was shot by one of his soldiers and the revolt collapsed.

The most important action taken by the Paiva government was the signing of the peace treaty of July 21, 1938, formally ending the Chaco War. This treaty was criticized severely by the exiled revolutionaries, who pointed out that it surrendered some 110,000 square kilometers that Paraguay had claimed originally and that the final settlement fixed the boundaries somewhat behind the final battle lines of the Paraguayan army. With much justice, then, the revolutionaries contrasted their own hard diplomacy, which had opposed any withdrawal of troops from the armistice line, to what they labeled "Liberal appeasement." On the other hand, the Liberals claimed that it was to Paraguay's advantage to secure a definite boundary settlement rather than allow the question to remain unresolved, giving cause for future conflict. Moreover, Paraguay still had received the lion's share of the Chaco. It is interesting to note, though, that the pulling back of the Chaco troops and the surrendering of land to the Bolivians by the Liberals did not provoke an army revolt.[1]

Marshal José Félix Estigarribia had returned to Paraguay as preparations were being made to hold elections in 1939. The Liberal party needed a prestigious figure who would "stand above factionalism" to unite itself, and so nominated the marshal. Since the Colorados had returned to their old policy of electoral abstention, Estigarribia won without opposition and was inaugurated on August 15, 1939.

Estigarribia was caught from the beginning between two violently opposed forces. On one side were the Old Guard Liberals who pressured for a return to the prerevolutionary order; opposed to them were the students, workers, and veterans who demanded that the social changes initiated by the February Revolution be pursued. The revolutionary attitudes of these latter groups made for an unstable *status quo*. At the same time, Estigarribia was handicapped by the reactionary majority of the party supporting him, but within that party

---

1. The treaty also provided for a guarantee of free transit for Bolivia through the port of Puerto Casado, where she might also establish a customs zone, depots, and warehouses. In Paraguay the treaty was ratified by a plebescite. The results: 135,385 in favor; 13,204 against. (See, David H. Zook, Jr., *The Conduct of the Chaco War*, New Haven: Bookman Associates, 1960, p. 253.) Critics of the treaty note that at that time many of its opponents were in exile. Nor was the plebiscite preceded by a free, public debate. (See, Marco Antonio Laconich, *La Paz del Chaco: Un pueblo traicionado*, Montevideo: Editorial Paraguay, 1939, pp. 151-52.)

was a clique of so-called "New Liberals" who were determined to put the Liberal party at the head of the February Revolution, rather than against it. Sensing the urgency of the situation, Estigarribia gathered the New Liberals around him and formed his cabinet from their ranks.[2] Even with this, the Old Liberals still controlled the Congress and could stalemate the president's program. The opportunity to break this deadlock came when the Old Liberals, hoping to stabilize the *status quo,* negotiated a compromise with the Colorados: Congress would dissolve itself, call new elections, and base the new Congress on proportional representation.[3] On February 17, 1940, the Liberal Congress decreed its own dissolution. Estigarribia made his coup on the following day, declaring himself absolute dictator with these words:

> I assert that it is no longer possible to defend the peace and future of the nation by the present constitutional means. Events go beyond their limits. We need new juridical norms and new bonds of solidarity in order to eliminate anarchy and secure the country's progress in accord with the purest nationalism and within the framework of a new realistic and reformist democracy. . . . In view of the Congress' collective resignation, basing my belief in the powers lent me by the nation with devout conviction, inspired in my conscience as a loyal soldier and citizen, and placing my acts before the judgement of Almighty God, I assume as of today total responsibility over political power for the time necessary to insure the Paraguayan nation stability and peace and to make possible its prosperity and grandeur.[4]

The president clamped down quickly. Using the February Revolution's notorious Decree Law 152 as a precedent, he prohibited all political activity not sanctioned by the state. Meetings, assemblies, political speeches, and political publications were forbidden, and the government assumed the right of press censorship.[5]

----

2. Among the most prominent of the New Liberals were: (1) Justo Pastor Benitez, minister of finance; (2) Alejandro Marin Iglesias, minister of government and labor; (3) Pablo Max Insfran, minister of public works; and (4) Efraim Cardozo, ambassador to Argentina.

3. Policarpo Artaza, *Ayala, Estigarribia y el Partido Liberal* (Buenos Aires: Editorial Ayacucho, 1946), pp. 195-96.

4. O. Bárcena Echeveste, *Concepcion, 1947* (Buenos Aires: Juan Pellegrini Belgrano, 1948), pp. 18-19.

5. *Ibid.,* pp. 21-23.

Perhaps the major accomplishment of Estigarribia's administration was the Constitution of 1940, which is still in effect. This was drawn up by a team of New Liberal jurists, headed by Justo Pastor Benítez, and published on July 10. It was ratified by a popular plebiscite on August 4 and promulgated by Estigarribia eleven days later.

The new constitution incorporated the concepts of the February Revolution concerning property rights and individualism.[6] The section entitled "General Declarations" decreed that (1) "in no case will private interests prevail over the general interests of the nation"; (2) "all citizens are obliged to collaborate for the good of the state and nation"; and (3) the powers of state regulation are broadened to include the entire economy, as well as education, labor contracts, working conditions, and social insurance.

The section entitled "Rights, Obligations, and Duties" declares that (1) "the exploitation of man by man is forbidden"; (2) private property is to be respected but the state has the right of eminent domain; (3) the maximum amount of land that a single individual or corporation may hold can be limited by the state; (4) every Paraguayan home must be situated on its own piece of land—to discourage squatting; and (5) the state's powers to suppress dissent extend to the supervision and regulation of books, pamphlets, and periodicals (none of which may be published anonymously), as well as "the organization, functioning, and activities of groups or bodies of a public character."

The Congress, as effected in 1940 and as it exists today, is unicameral, directly elected every five years, and meets every year from April through August. It is definitely overshadowed by the president, who may dissolve Congress and call for new elections within two months. Projects sent to Congress by the president must be acted upon during that year's session or they become laws without such action. While Congress is adjourned the president can issue decrees having the force of law, and he may also exercise state of seige powers during a national crisis. The constitution also provides for a Council

6. Amos J. Peaslee, *Constitutions of Nations* (The Hague: Martinus Nijoff, 1956), II, 111-31.

of State, an advisory body to the president that is composed of the members of the cabinet, the rector of the National University, the Archbishop of Paraguay, one representative of the commercial interests, one from the utilities, the president of the Bank of the Republic, and one each from the army and navy.

The New Liberals' day in the sun was a short one. President Estigarribia was killed in an airplane accident on September 7, less than a month after promulgating the new constitution. The New Liberals were defenseless now, unable either to profit from the prestige of their former leader or to find support among the majority of their own party. Once again Colonels Paredes and Sosa Valdés stepped forward to decide the situation, and Higinio Morínigo, the minister of defense, was picked to succeed Estigarribia. At the same time, the New Liberals in the cabinet were removed and either sent into exile or to Peña Hermosa, a prison camp in the north.

It is alleged by some writers that Morínigo was put in the presidency because Paredes and the Old Liberals felt him to be a colorless, unimaginative figure who would be easily manipulated while they worked to stop the movement towards social reform begun by the February Revolution and Estigarribia. If this is so, they were mistaken. Morínigo quickly took advantage of a quarrel between Paredes and Sosa Valdés, which had arisen during the discussion over Estigarribia's successor, to exile Sosa Valdés. As for Paredes, he was "promoted" to minister of interior, which removed him from his command of the Campo Grande garrison. Two months later he was suddenly ousted and exiled.[7]

Now Morínigo turned on the Old Liberals. In 1940 the Argentine Foreign Ministry published a book of documents called *The Chaco Peace Conference, 1935-1939*. In it there was a report by Spruille Braden in which he commented that on December 19, 1936, a group of Paraguayan exiles had approached the Bolivian minister, Enrique Finot, to solicit Bolivian aid in overthrowing the Franco government. Since at that time the Liberals had been the main exile group, they

7. Harris Gaylord Warren, *Paraguay: An Informal History* (Norman: University of Oklahoma Press, 1949), pp. 331-32.

became the target of the scandal that followed this publication. Although the Liberals secured a letter from Finot stating that the men who approached him were merely "extremist elements" not identifiable with the Liberal party, the Liberals' "legionnaire" origins were recalled by their opponents. Morínigo took this opportunity to crush this last remnant of opposition to him. The Liberal party was outlawed by decree on April 25, 1942, and most Liberal politicians went into exile.[8]

Febrerismo: In the Underground and in Exile

While all this was going on, the *febreristas*—as the supporters of the February Revolution were now being called—were trying to reorganize their ranks, but with little success. Rafael Franco headed a faction of the Asociación Nacional de Ex-Combatientes but had quarreled with Juan Martincich, one of his major supporters. Anselmo Jover Peralta formed a leftist party called the Partido Revolucionario Paraguayo but was never able to increase its size beyond a handful of members. Juan Stefanich was no more successful with his Unión Nacional Revolucionaria and spent most of his time writing a five-volume defense of the February Revolution and several books dealing with a political philosophy of his own creation, *solidarismo*.

Perhaps greater *esprit de corps* existed within Paraguay, where the February Revolution was strongly supported by the university students, who formed an organization called the Comando de la Juventud Revolucionaria and began to work towards an understanding with Morínigo. The first step was to collaborate with a group of Christian Socialists called the *tiempistas,* after their newspaper *El Tiempo.* Led by Luis Argaña, the *tiempistas* were furnishing Morínigo with the only, albeit tiny, civilian support that he had in an otherwise purely military dictatorship. The *febrerista* students' connections with the *tiempistas* won them permission to organize

8. The anti-Liberal argument is presented in Bárcena Echeveste, *Concepción, 1947,* pp. 57-62; and Juan Stefanich, *El 23 de octubre de 1931* (Buenos Aires: Editorial Febrero, 1958), pp. 238-43. A defense of the Liberals is to be found in Artaza, *Ayala, Estigarribia,* pp. 205-9.

openly within the university and the labor unions. Nevertheless, this was a fundamentally unstable arrangement, for the students of the Comando were far more radical than Morínigo was prepared to accept in the end. Encouraged by the students, the Confederación Paraguaya de Trabajadores called a general strike in January, 1941, to demand better working conditions for the unions, more autonomy from government supervision, and the return of Rafael Franco. Morínigo's answer was to dissolve the CPT. More than two hundred persons were arrested, and union leaders were sent to Peña Hermosa.[9]

Meanwhile, the Comando had formed a plot with *febrerista* sympathizers in the Military College and the navy, and the revolt broke out on April 17. Morínigo asked for a truce and offered to negotiate. However, while the two sides were conversing, troops loyal to the president arrived in Asunción and the revolt was defeated. The Comando students were exiled and the military conspirators joined other political prisoners at Peña Hermosa.

The military base upon which Morínigo's dictatorship rested was divided. The most influential group, from 1941 to 1945, was called the Frente de Guerra and was headed by a triumvirate of colonels: Victoriano Benítez, the chief of staff and head of the Campo Grande garrison; Bernardo Aranda; and Pablo Stagni. This group was noted for its sympathy with the Axis cause during World War II—one of the main reasons that Paraguay not only remained neutral during most of the war but also became a haven for Nazi sympathizers.[10] When Dr. Argaña, the *tiempista* leader, openly supported the Allies, the Frente de Guerra pressured Morínigo into removing him from his post as minister of foreign affairs. With Argaña's departure, Morínigo was left without any organized civilian support whatsoever. The more liberal military faction was represented in Morínigo's cabinet by General Amancio Pampliega, the minister of interior, and General Vicente Machuca, the minister of defense. As events were to show, this faction was a majority within the military, even

---

9. Warren, *Paraguay*, p. 340.
10. *Ibid.*, 339-40, 348-48.

though the Frente de Guerra commanded enough key posts to exercise more influence for the time being.

Meanwhile, the *febrerista* movement had continued to evolve. Most of its activity continued to come from student political clubs within Paraguay, the most notable of which were the clubs Fermín Franco Delgado and Pedro P. Sarmaniego. The latter was the more important by far. Its founding went back to May, 1941, just after the abortive revolt of that year. During the crackdown on the *febreristas*, Morínigo had ordered the dismissal of all teachers and professors of known *febrerista* sympathies. This violated the Law of University Autonomy, which guaranteed the universities against state intervention. Silvio Báez, the president of the University Student Federation, called for a general strike of university and secondary school students to protest this. He soon received backing from some of the labor unions, most notably the Railway Workers' Union, represented by Carlos Chávez del Valle. Small protest groups were formed in each ward of the capital, as well as in the towns of the interior, and a census of their members was taken. Although this strike failed, the organization was kept intact and was to become transformed into a permanent revolutionary network.[11] It was called the club Pedro P. Sarmaniego after the Chief Justice of the Supreme Court under the Franco government, who had died in exile. A Declaration of Principles identified the club with the February Revolution. Its goals were representative democracy, greater opportunities for peasants and workers, anti-imperialism, economic nationalism, the separation of church and state, and state economic planning. The club accepted the theory of class struggle but viewed itself as the co-ordinator of the combined efforts of the peasants, workers, and middle class to overthrow the old regime of land barons, commercial oligarchs, and foreign interests.[12]

The clubs Fermín Franco Delgado and Pedro P. Sarmaniego were to become the primary building blocks for a larger coalition of *febrerista* revolutionary groups. In July,

11. Interview with Carlos Chávez del Valle (March 12, 1964).
12. *Declaración de principios del Club Revolucionario "Pedro P. Sarmaniego"* (Montevideo: Charrua, 1945).

1944, Elpidio Yegros, the former acting president of the ANEC and mayor of Asunción under Franco, obtained a temporary permit to re-enter Paraguay. While there, he and Roque Gaona, the former secretary-general of the UNR, sought to contact former members of the now-suppressed ANEC and the leaders of the revolutionary clubs. Intensive conversations held among these groups during the next week resulted in the formation of the Committee of Revolutionary Organization (COR, Comité de Organización Revolucionaria). Two representatives from each of the three groups would comprise an executive committee to co-ordinate revolutionary activity among the exiles as well. José Soljancic was named president of this committee, and Germán Soler became the vice-president.[13]

The next step was to form an even more cohesive organization. A convention was held in Montevideo, Uruguay, in October, 1945, for the purpose of founding a political party. Each *febrerista* group sent delegates. All had an equal voice and veto in the debates. The outcome was the formation of the Concentración Revolucionaria Febrerista, a federation of revolutionary groups rather than a true political party. The Act of Montevideo, which announced the Concentración's formation, stated that it would respect "the organic structures already voted on by the revolutionary citizenry without passing judgement upon them." "The definitive decision on the permanent and stable organization of the *febrerista* forces" would be postponed until a National Revolutionary Febrerista Convention could be held.[14] The constitution of the Concentración also emphasized the federative and unfinished nature of the organization.[15] Article 1 stated that the Concentración was only the *provisional* organic expression of the revolution, and Article 10 instructed the National Executive Committee to prepare a National Convention for the purpose of resolving the organization's structure.

---

13. Interview with Elpidio Yegros (August 20, 1964).

14. Concentración Revolucionaria Febrerista, *Documentos políticos* (Asunción: Departamentos de Prensa y Propaganda, 1946), pp. 6-7.

15. For the text of the constitution, see Concentración Revolucionaria Febrerista, Comité de Resistencia, *Construyendo el febrerismo* (Buenos Aires: Alea, 1951), pp. 81-87.

The Concentración's loosely knit nature was reflected in other ways too. The constitution provided for two presidents —a concession to Juan Stefanich, who would share the highest executive power with Rafael Franco. Those sectors operating within Paraguay and having to face the political struggle directly were given special consideration. A separate chapter of the constitution dealt with the Resistance Committee, the underground organization. Although the secretary general of this committee had to be a member of the National Executive Committee (hereafter referred to as the CEN, Comité Ejecutivo Nacional), he was given considerable autonomy in applying the CEN's directives to the realities of the situation. The chapter entitled "Organic Co-ordination" showed the CEN's problem of promoting co-ordinated decision-making while at the same time having to respect the autonomy of the Concentración's various member groups. Article 47 stated: "The CEN will be connected directly with all the party's organizations within the country and in exile. . . . Correspondence will be exchanged directly with the presidents of the committees and will be signed by the corresponding authorities of the CEN. No other form of contact will have official validity. . . . Also, official correspondence from the exile committees and the Resistance committee must be directed to the proper organs of the CEN."

The Concentración was meant to be a vehicle for militant, revolutionary action. The function of the Resistance Committee was subversion, and its primary organs were cells, to which orders would flow down from the CEN. The cells would elect chiefs to represent them on the local or town committees; the local committees then elected presidents, who would form the regional committees; and the secretary of the CEN had direct jurisdiction over the local and regional committees. The duties of the CEN, composed of twenty-five members and five substitutes, were divided among several executive departments, whose over-all supervision was in the hands of a secretary general. A Political Committee, headed by the first president of the CEN, was to "attend the relations of the Concentración Revolucionario Febrerista with the public power and its diverse branches and with the other political parties." The Department of Foreign Relations was to connect *febrerismo* with like-minded political movements in other parts of Latin America. Other departments carried on the functions of finance, press, culture, and propaganda. Since the Concentración was only an intermediate step in the process towards the final formation of a true revolutionary political party, it does not seem necessary to go further into its organization. Let it be enough to describe the gradual coalescing of *febrerista* forces and the building of a more institutionalized organization. The federative nature of the Concentración, arising out of this process, was to have an important effect on the internal politics of the Concentración's successor, the Partido Revolucionario Febrerista.

In the meantime, important changes had taken place within the Morínigo regime. The pro-Fascist Frente de Guerra had been purged in favor of the more moderate military sector. It is not clear just why this had taken place, but the most probable explanation is that by 1944 the Axis powers were definitely losing the war. As a consequence, Morínigo began paying greater attention to pressure from the State Department of the United States to liberalize his government and to lend more support to the Allies. Colonel Benítez Vera was sent to Buenos Aires, ostensibly to attend the presidential inauguration of Juan Perón. Once the leader of the Frente de Guerra was out of the country, Morínigo announced that he had been removed from his command of Campo Grande. Benítez Vera returned immediately in an Argentine military plane, rallied Colonels Aranda and Stagni around him, and attempted a revolt. Morínigo, however, found support from the bulk of the army, and the Frente de Guerra was defeated and forced into exile.[16]

Morínigo now began to negotiate with both the Colorado party and the Concentración Revolucionaria Febrerista, with a view towards liberalizing his government even further. The Committee of Revolutionary Organization, which had preceded the Concentración, had been in close contact with many military leaders, especially General Machuca. When

16. Interview with Elpidio Yegros (August 20, 1964); also, Warren, *Paraguay*, pp. 348-49.

Morínigo suggested that they participate in a coalition government with the Colorados and representatives from the military, they accepted with the following conditions: (1) a declaration of amnesty for all parties, including the Liberal party, (2) the derogation of all laws restricting political groups, labor organizations, and the press, (3) the calling of a national constitutional assembly to draft a new basic law, and (4) the right of the Concentración Revolucionaria Febrerista, not Morínigo, to name its cabinet ministers.[17]

Morínigo met these demands. Laws censoring the press and banning political activity were abolished in January, 1946; labor was allowed to reorganize under a new national confederation called the National Workers' Council; and December 25, 1947, was set as the date for the holding of a constitutional convention. Lastly, the *febreristas* could name their own ministers.

The Concentración's decision to participate in Morínigo's government was not made without much heated discussion beforehand. The idea of collaborating with the old archenemy caused the majority of the CEN to reject the proffered pact on the first vote among its members. Only the persuasiveness of Arnaldo Valdovinos and José Soljancic, the COR chief, made the CEN change its mind, and then by only one vote.[18]

The coalition government was formed in June, 1946, with three cabinet posts going to the *febreristas*, three to the Colorados, and two to the military.[19]

Coalition Government and Civil War

The era of the coalition government proved to be short and stormy. From the very beginning, the Liberal party

17. Concentración Revolucionaria Febrerista, *Documentos políticos,* p. 28.

18. Interview with Elpidio Yegros (August 20, 1964) and interview with Arnaldo Valdovinos (October 30, 1964).

19. *Febreristas:* Arnaldo Valdovinos, minister of agriculture and minister of industry and commerce; Miguel Angel Soler (padre), minister of foreign relations; José Soljancic, minister of public health. *Colorados:* Federico Cháves, minister of public works; Juan Natalicio González, minister of finance; and G. E. Velloso, minister of education. *Military:* General A. Pampliega, minister of interior; General Vicente Machuca, minister of defense.

carried on a bitter campaign of criticism against Morínigo from its daily, *El País,* calling for military intervention to guarantee free elections. The Colorados, fearful of the Liberals' potential electoral strength, were determined to keep them disenfranchised. In this they had the backing of Morínigo himself. Meanwhile, the Colorados were feuding among themselves. The moderate sector, led by Federico Cháves, had promoted the coalition government from the beginning and had agreed to an equal division of cabinet seats with the *febreristas.* However, the extremist sector, which followed Juan Natalicio González, wanted complete Colorado domination of the cabinet.[20] To achieve this González formed a type of "shock corps" called the Guión Rojo (Red Banner), which attempted to control the streets and intimidate the opposition.

The *febreristas* followed their own political plan, which consisted of two basic options: (1) to go to the countryside and attempt to increase their support among the peasants before the elections, and (2) establish close contacts with the military chiefs in the event that violent tactics should become necessary. Their hopes for success in both these areas were raised by the large and enthusiastic reception Rafael Franco received upon his return to Asunción on August 4.[21]

Dissension soon broke out within the cabinet between the Colorados and the *febreristas.* According to the Colorados, the *febreristas,* backed by General Machuca, demanded a fourth cabinet post, which would have given them one more than the Colorados. Morínigo refused. The *febreristas,* on the other hand, claimed that they broke with Morínigo over his refusal to curb the Guión Rojo and that he and Natalicio González were planning a coup.[22] In any case, a conference of *febrerista* leaders met on January 10, 1947, and decided to propose that both the Colorado and *febrerista* ministers resign and that Morínigo form an all-military cabinet. Arnaldo

---

20. Juan Natalicio González, *Como se construye una nación* (Buenos Aires: Editorial Guaranía, 1949), p. 134.

21. Warren, *Paraguay,* p. 350.

22. O. Bárcena Echeveste, *Concepción, 1947,* p. 150; Manual Cibils, *Anarquía y revolución en el Paraguay: Vórtice y asíntota* (Buenos Aires: Editorial Americalee, 1957), p. 58; Philip Raine, *Paraguay* (New Brunswick: The Scarecrow Press, 1958), p. 263.

Valdovinos, the *febrerista* minister of agriculture and commerce, fought this idea, arguing that to resign from the cabinet would be to quit important positions of power. When the CEN rejected his argument, he walked out of the meeting. The CEN had a point, however, as both the *febreristas* and the Liberals had many sympathizers within the military, whereas the Colorados did not. Presumably, then, an all-military cabinet would work in favor of both the *febreristas* and Liberals.

Before they could communicate this proposal to Morínigo, however, the *febreristas* found that he had removed them from the government, dividing the eight cabinet seats equally between the Colorados and the military. A number of arrests were made of *febrerista,* Communists, and pro-*febrerista* military leaders. On March 7, 1947, the *febreristas* replied with an attack on the Asunción police station. This ill-planned *coup d'état* was repulsed, but on the following day the military garrison at Concepción rebelled, and they were joined a few days later by the Chaco garrison. The military rebels called for Morínigo's resignation, and it seemed as though he had no other choice but to comply. Within a few days nearly all of the regular army had gone over to the side of the revolution. The rebels, led by Colonels César Aguirre and Alfredo Galeano, could count on the support of almost the entire officer corps, five thousand or so troops from the Chaco and Concepción garrisons, as well as the civilians of the *febrerista,* Liberal, and Communist parties. Against this, Morínigo had only some two thousand troops from Campo Grande and so few officers that Colonel Federico Weddell Smith was called out of retirement to head the government's army.

Nevertheless, Morínigo had other, more important resources. The first of these was the Colorado party, which in turn had some fifteen thousand *py nandi* ("barefoot ones"). These were its peasants, whose habitual loyalty to the party would make them follow fanatically their political leaders, and from them Morínigo was able to build a new army.[23] It is

---

23. Antonio E. González, *La rebelión de Concepción* (Buenos Aires: Editorial Guanaría, 1947), pp. 109-11.

widely believed that Morínigo had still another crucial source of support, the Argentine dictator, Juan Perón. The *febreristas* and Liberals claim that Perón sent Morínigo large supplies of guns, ammunition, and trucks, which would explain why Morínigo was able to equip his new peasant army with such speed and to enjoy such a superiority of fire-power over the regular army, even though the latter began the revolt with most of the country's military supplies in its possession.[24]

The rebellion now became a civil war. According to one Colorado colonel, had the rebels attacked at once they would have won easily. Instead, they inexplicably chose to defend the area around Concepción, giving the government time to mobilize the *py nandí* and to train its new army. During the first few months, neither side could gain a clear advantage. Then, on April 26, the navy revolted in Asunción, nearly putting an end to the government. However, Morínigo held out for four days until mobs of *py nandí* could be rushed to the capital to brutally crush the rebels. It was at this point that Colonel Federico W. Smith resigned as head of Morínigo's army, denouncing alleged Argentine intervention in the civil war.

A strong government offensive was launched in July which finally, on July 31, took Concepción. But the rebels had already abandoned the city and were heading down the Paraguay River in a fleet of small boats for a surprise assault on the capital. Once again Morínigo had to hold on until his out-maneuvered troops could be rushed back to his support.

---

24. This charge is denied by Bárcena Echeveste, *Concepción, 1947*, pp. 255-58. However, Liberals, *febreristas*, and other sources insist that such intervention did take place. See Policarpo Artaza, *Que hizo el Partido Liberal en la oposición y en el gobierno* (Buenos Aires: Lucania, 1961), pp. 68-69; Cibils, *Anarquía y revolución*, p. 58; the statement of General J. A. Flores of the Brazilian general staff, quoted in Warren, *Paraguay*, p. 353; and the statements of Federico Weddell Smith and Rafael Franco, quoted in Bárcena Echeveste, *Concepción, 1947*, pp. 255-57. Also, the laudatory remarks made about Perón in *El País*, the Liberal newspaper taken over by the Colorados after the revolt, in an article entitled "El *py nandí*" (May 30, 1947), quoted in *ibid.*, pp. 178-80, tend to support the idea that the Perón and Morínigo governments were on extremely cordial terms.

25. Juan F. Pérez Acosta, *Migraciones históricas del Paraguay a la Argentina* (Buenos Aires: Talleres Gráficos Optimus, 1952), p. 17.

The rebel attack reached the suburbs of Asunción but got no further. By August 20 they had been overcome by superior forces and collapsed, retreating to exile. It is estimated that some 400,000 people left Paraguay over the next few months.

The Resistance Committee

As we saw earlier, the constitution of the Concentración Revolucionaria Febrerista provided for an underground organization. Clandestine activities had been carried on previously by the Committee on Revolutionary Organization, but these had been suspended during the period of the coalition government. The outbreak of civil war in 1947 provided the impulse to form the Resistance Committee, whose purposes were to engage in subversion and to provide the rebel army with information. Although the war was lost the Resistance Committee continued to function, doing its best to reorganize the shattered party within Paraguay. As might be expected, the violence of civil war was followed by an era of revenge and "terror." *Febreristas* claim that no fewer than four thousand political prisoners were held in Asunción alone.[26] Colorado civil guards were organized in the countryside to rout out political suspects.

The civil war had left Morínigo at the mercy of the Colorados and their *py nandí* army. Now that they were the masters of the situation, the Colorados apparently decided that they should have the presidency as well. Morínigo had already proven many times his ability to outmaneuver his competitors, but this time he was given no opportunity to do so. He was removed from office by a coup on June 3, 1948, and Juan Manuel Frutos, a Colorado leader, was named provisional president.

As for the Colorados, their earlier split between Federico Cháves' moderates and the Guión Rojo was carried into their general party convention in November, 1947. Elections had been set for August, 1948, and it had been assumed that Cháves, the party's president, would be the official candidate. Instead, armed bands of Guión Rojo men descended upon the convention and forced the delegates to accept Juan

---

26. Cibils, *Anarquía y revolución*, p. 59.

Natalicio González. Cháves and his second-in-command, Eulogio Estigarribia, were arrested and exiled. Major Vicente González, an influential Cháves supporter in the military, was arrested and executed. His fate was shared by other opposition leaders such as Alberto Candia, the general secretary of the Communist party (died April 16, 1948), and Humberto Garcete, the general secretary of the Concentración Revolucionaria Febrerista (died May 1, 1948).[27]

The atmosphere of those days was one of terror for political opponents of the Colorados, and the massive exodus of Liberals and *febreristas* from the country seriously weakened all attempts to form an effective opposition to the Colorados. The *febrerista* Resistance Committee led a precarious underground existence, with its members spending the first months of the Colorado terror attempting to stay out of the hands of the police and to reorganize the party's shattered ranks. Its problems, as described in the following report to the party's CEN, in exile give a rather vivid picture of the nature of those times.[28]

December 18, 1948
Asunción

To the President of the CEN of the
Concentración Revolucionaria Febrerista,
Sr. General don Rafael Franco
Buenos Aires, Argentina

[The introductory greeting has been omitted]
*Historical Review of the Activities of
the Resistance Committee*

Contents:

1. Origin and Development of the Resistance Committee
2. Function of the Resistance Committee
3. Structure and Organization of the Resistance Committee
4. Conclusions

ORIGIN AND FUNCTION OF THE RESISTANCE COMMITTEE

When, on the 27th of April, 1947, the military defeat of the insurrectionist movement in the navy was certain, the last ac-

27. These events set forth in *Ibid.*, pp. 59-60, 65-68.
28. The full text of this document is to be found in Concentración Revolucionaria Febrerista, Comité de Resistencia, *Construyendo el febrerismo*, pp. 45-49.

tivist member of the CEN abandoned the Capital. A few days later three known leaders—not members of the CEN—formed the Resistance Committee. . . . This Committee was composed of three members: Raimundo Careaga, Carlos Schaerer, and Humberto Garcete; later it was increased to include Victor Ojeda. The first-named acted as General Secretary. Due to the arrest of *compañero* Garcete, Carlos Chávez del Valle joined the Committee, occupying the post of Secretary of Organization. Later, Schaerer replaced Careaga as General Secretary [October, 1947] and was replaced in turn by José Huidobro [May, 1948].

[other changes have been omitted]

FUNCTION OF THE RESISTANCE COMMITTEE

The functions exercised by the Resistance Committee correspond to the following revolutionary stages:

Stage 1: Civil War [April to August, 1947]

(a) Reorganization of the party's ranks of activists in the Capital and principal centers;

(b) Collaboration in every possible way with the movement in Concepción;

(c) Extending the organization of the Resistance, insofar as possible, to the country's Interior.

In pursuance of these objectives, a plan was developed to foment and organize party underground teams and extend these to other democratic sectors for the purpose of weakening the dictatorship from within by organized sabotage, provocation of revolts, and the obtaining of information and economic and medical supplies of all kinds. During this stage the Resistance Committee formed a part of the Democratic Resistance Committee made up of Liberals and Communists as well, presided over by a military officer. This organization lasted until August 20, when it was voluntarily disbanded.

Stage 2: From the termination of the armed conflict to the 1947 Colorado Convention [August 20, 1947, to November 16]

After August 20, the Resistance Committee continued acting in accordance with the party and national objectives already sketched. With the end of the armed conflict, the country was almost deserted by responsible members. This period was hard and difficult. The jails were filled with patriots, the exodus of citizens seemed interminable, families lived in fear of the vandalistic terrorism which respected neither modesty nor interest. Just as the problems mounted, the party's forces were reduced to a minimum. The Committee then formulated the following emergency plan:

Internally:

(a) Seek the unification of all dispersed members, with the main idea being to aid the political prisoners;

(b) Constitute small nuclei of resistance;

(c) Attempt to contain the demoralization caused by the exodus of *febrerista* families to the exterior;

(d) Exhort the Paraguayan people to struggle against the dictatorship;

Externally:

(a) Seek contact with other popular sectors who coincide with our objectives;

(b) Foment division within the officialist ranks, divided into Guions and "democrats," organize infiltrations, and propagandize within the army.

By the end of this stage some strong nuclei of resistance had been formed through primary organizations. The Department of Labor [of the party] had been reorganized and clandestine papers were being published.

Stage 3: The Morínigo-Guionist Government [November 10 to June 3, 1948]

With the division of the Colorado Party, the people regained their awareness of their degrading situation, and therefore the resistance against the dictatorship became stronger. Our organization broadened and some important Commissions were formed to attend party affairs. It is necessary to say that many *compañeros*, for the most part professional men, refused to collaborate in active militancy with the Resistance Committee.

Parallel to the organic broadening of the party, the Committee continued intensifying its propaganda and trying to open breaches in the governmental front. One result of the antagonism of rival [Colorado] groups was the coup of June 3, at which time the group headed by Molas López, called "La Peña," came to the fore.

The short period from June to August, under the presidency of Dr. Frutos, is not worthy of consideration, for during these months the Resistance Committee continued with the same tasks as before. In this period numerous *febreristas* returned from exile and reincorporated themselves into the movement, giving greater impulse to the underground. Moreover, they caused readjustments in the Committee and in the party's primary organizations.

By the end of this stage the resistance movement had acquired roots throughout the country. Whenever circumstances demand it, the Resistance Committee held conventions, both consultive and exploratory, with other sectors of the opposition, including the "democratic" Colorados.

Stage 4: The Natalicio González Government

The party is preparing for any political or military contingency but mainly is structuring its organization for future civil struggles. It has faith in its own forces and very few illusions about "coup-ism." At this time the organization is being strengthened and broadened everywhere, finding the *febrerista* masses' morale heightened.

The ascension to the presidency of J. Natalicio González has not surprised the resistance movement; rather, it was foreseen. Many incidents have occured already during the four months of "constitutional" government, and despite the present chaos, this dictatorship may continue for a more or less lengthy period.

STRUCTURE AND ORGANIZATION OF THE COMMITTEE

The system or structure of the Resistance Committee is a type of secretariat, and the party organization is based on the cell system, in the Capital and in the interior of the country, according to the rules agreed to.

The state of the party's organization is still incomplete and can be described in the following way: satisfactory with respect to the condition of the party after the civil war; precarious and weak with respect to what it might be as a vanguard of our oppressed people. Nevertheless, something has been done, and much is being done at the present to invigorate the party's primary groups—so much so that the organization now extends to all of the principal towns of the Republic, and most of all in the Capital.

The Capital is divided into zones and districts; the countryside into zones and regions. [Here follows a listing of towns in which cells have been organized.]

Specific organizations, for workers, women, students, Civil Defence, etc., are progressing, which broadens the party's basic organization. The feminine movement has been reorganized recently and its development is still shaky, but meritorious women have acted and are acting in party tasks along with the men. Student activity is reduced, despite our having formed cells in the schools and colleges. In the Department of Labor, the most advanced organization, due to more favorable conditions, is that of the Commercial and Industrial Employees. The sector of manual laborers has been stalled and retarded due to the policies of O.R.O. [the Colorado labor confederation] and the police; but many cells exist and their Directing Committee functions in the secretariat, regularly publishing its newspaper, "Avance."

Up to the present, the professional people have been remiss in the organization, with the exception of some who collaborate responsibly with the party.

After this there follows a set of recommendations and points of view on party organization which will be reserved for discussion in later chapters dealing with factionalism and intraparty communications.

This description of the evolution of Paraguay's political milieu might be brought to a close with a brief summary events since 1947. Since that time the Colorado party has remained in power, supported by the army. Juan Natalicio González became president in a one-party election in August, 1948, but was ousted by a military-"democratic" Colorado coup in January of the following year. General Raimundo Rolón then assumed power but fell the following month when the Colorados reunited temporarily in order to prevent a purely military government. Felipe Molas López then became president but lasted only until September when he was replaced by Federico Cháves. Cháves' administration showed a marked increase in Argentine influence in Paraguayan politics and economic affairs. A customs union was established between the two countries which seemed to indicate that the Perón regime was taking positive steps toward bringing Paraguay more firmly within the Argentine sphere of influence.

Chaves was overthrown in May, 1954, by a military coup led by General Alfredo Stroessner. Tomás Romero Pereira was made the provisional president until Stroessner took over formally in August, 1955. He is still president.

Stroessner's regime appears to be more militarily based than Colorado, but he is officially the Colorado leader. His regime appears to be by far the most stable since Morínigo's, and his ability to stay in power some eleven years is something of a record for contemporary Paraguay. He seems to enjoy at least the tacit support of the great bulk of the military. Some dissident elements have attempted revolts from time to time, but these have been isolated and without importance. The regime also has the support of the "officialist" Colorados—the former Guión Rojo faction—with its mass of *py nandi*. Although there have been rumors that the Colorados are dissatisfied with their apparent de-emphasis in favor of the military sector, they were instrumental in aiding the regime in December, 1959, when the *py nandi* were called out to help the army suppress guerrilla invasions in the interior.

Stroessner, through his foreign minister, Raúl Sapena Pastor, has also been adept in diplomatic relations. Argentine influence has been lessened somewhat by the building of new roads connecting Paraguay to the Brazilian highway and railway system, which allows Paraguay to play a neutralist game between those two competitors. This has also been used to persuade those neighboring countries to keep a check on insurrectionist activities by the exiles. The regime has also been able to count on continued foreign aid by the United States and the International Monetary Fund. Despite its authoritarian nature, Stroessner's government has impressed these foreign financial sources with its attempts to install fiscal responsibility and to make some modest reforms in the land tenure system. An Agrarian Reform Law passed in 1961 provides for the expropriation of all lands not rationally exploited, lands whose improvements do not represent 50 per cent of the fiscal value of the land. According to an economic survey made by the Organization of American States, some 25,000 families received titles to new lands in 1962, and another 11,253 were given small to medium-sized farms in the first half of 1963.[29] The new owners have fifteen years in which to pay, and credit and technical aid are supposedly provided, although the opposition claims that they are not.

Less progress has been made in liberalizing the political situation. It has been estimated that some one-half million people—nearly one-third of the country's population—are expatriates. It is difficult to estimate, of course, how many of these live abroad for political reasons. Political amnesties have been granted occasionally but never for long duration.

---

29. Organization of American States, *Economic Survey of Latin America, 1962* (Baltimore: Johns Hopkins Press, 1964), pp. 220-21, 224-25.

One faction of the Liberal party has been permitted to participate in elections and to form an opposition bloc in Congress, but it is branded by the other sectors of the opposition as a "tame" opposition.

Nevertheless, political amnesty was extended to the *febreristas* in August, 1964, and they accepted it. Most of the National Executive Committee, including General Franco, returned to Paraguay and began to prepare for the municipal elections scheduled for October, 1965. Meanwhile, the party began to issue a weekly newspaper, *El Pueblo,* whose columns carried strong but responsible criticism of the government. The *febreristas* presented an "open" list at the municipal elections, inviting Liberals and Christian Democrats to run under the *febrerista* banner when the party lacked candidates of its own in certain localities. Unfortunately, the elections were marred by the fraudulent practices of many local officials. In some cases the open list was declared illegal because of the presence of non-*febreristas* on the ballot. In other towns the local officials did not permit *febrerista* observers to be present at the counting of the votes. This is not to say that the Colorado party might not have won in any case, but it is disappointing that the country's first opportunity in many years to begin institutionalizing democratic practices ended on such a sour note. At the same time, the majority of the Liberal party, the "democratic" Colorados (Movimiento Popular Colorado), and the Christian Democrats are still outside the country's normal political life. Political prisoners—notably, Juan Speratti, the *febrerista* secretary general—are still being held, labor unions have been "intervened" by the Colorado party, and the universities are controlled by "good conduct" laws that can remove a student for antigovernment activities.

This brief description may give the reader an idea of the contemporary situation within which the Febrerista party must operate. With this, we have finished the story of *febrerismo's* antecedents, genesis, and evolution. Now we shall focus on the party's organization and internal problems, considering the major facets of its structure and operation, as well as the behavior of its different factions.

3. The Ideology and Organization
of the Febrerista Party

From the very beginning the Concentración Revolucionaria Febrerista was considered by its founders to be only a temporary organization. Article 10 of its constitution instructed the National Executive Committee to "prepare the convocation of a Grand National Assembly for the purpose of resolving the definite organization of the Febrerista Party." The unsettled period of coalition government, civil war, and exile caused the fulfillment of this duty to be postponed until December, 1951. On that date delegates from all the local and regional committees met in Buenos Aires to give the party a new constitution, which would settle the question of its structure. No less important was the task of defining its ideology and drawing up a practical economic, social, and political program for the party to follow should it come to power.

Ideology

The political ideas of *febrerismo* have been clarified since the Revolution of 1936. The reader will recall the deep ideological disputes of that era, during which fascism, socialism, and liberal democracy competed for primacy within the government. As is the case with many Latin American thinkers, the intellectuals of the February Revolution tended to look abroad, to Europe or the United States, for political inspiration. Bernardino Caballero, for instance, had resided in Germany, where he had been impressed by Hitler. Gómez and Luis Freire Esteves were alleged admirers of Mussolini's Fascist state. Anselmo Jover Peralta looked to the Peruvian Aprista party's brand of socialism as a guideline for the February Revolution. Juan Stefanich has frequently referred to his indebtedness to Woodrow Wilson as the source of his ideals.

The Fascist wing of the revolution was important during the initial phase, as evidenced by the Proclamation of the Liberating Army, Decree Law 152, and the holding of key governmental positions by Caballero (agriculture) and the Freire Esteves brothers (interior and treasury, respectively). Decree Law 152 probably marks the apex of Fascist influence in *febrerismo's* history. The quick, intense popular reaction to that measure, resulting in the dismissal of the Freire Esteves brothers, put an end to that tendency within the movement. Although writers hostile to the *febreristas* have pointed to Decree Law 152 as being typical of the party's totalitarian leanings, it is more accurate to say that Fascist influence did not survive the first few months of the revolution.

The socialist tradition, as exemplified in the revolutionary government by Anselmo Jover Peralta, has continued to play an important role in the development of the party's ideology. After a brief eclipse following Jover Peralta's dismissal from the cabinet, revolutionary socialism re-emerged in the clandestine youth organizations, especially the club Pedro P. Sarmaniego, during the early 1940's. Since that time the socialist tendency within *febrerismo* seems to have split into moderate and radical wings. The moderates claim the Peruvian A.P.R.A. and the Mexican Revolution as their chief models.[1] They emphasize the multiclass nature of *febrerismo* and reject collaboration with the Communist party to achieve the revolution. The radicals, on the other hand, have had less hesitation about accepting aid from the communists. For instance, the Bloque de Defensa de la Revolución, which flour-

---

1. Partido Revolucionario Febrerista, Departamento de Cultura, *Semblanza histórica e ideológica del febrerismo*, 1958, pp. 1-5.

ished briefly in the late 1940's, openly declared its adhesion to the Soviet bloc. This group was expelled from the party in 1951.

The Paraguayan Communist party was founded in the early 1920's and is still led by Oscar Creydt and Obdulio Barthe—both sons of wealthy families. Since the February Revolution the *febreristas* and the Communists have competed for the allegiance of students, peasants, and labor unions. While it is true that *febreristas* and Communists have collaborated at times (for instance, during the civil war of 1947 and afterwards, briefly, in the Resistance Committee), these have been short-lived marriages of convenience. Communist influence during *febrerismo*'s formative period was minimal. The opposition of the Communists to the Chaco War ran counter to the nationalistic sentiments of the February Revolution. However, the coincidence of the Cold War with the bitter aftermath of the post-1947 period in Paraguay, together with a tendency to blame the United States for the Stroessner dictatorship, has made the Communist appeal for a united front attractive to some of the more radical *febreristas*. After the expulsion of the Bloque de Defensa de la Revolución, some of its members actually joined the Communist party. As recently as 1960 the *febrerista* CEN ordered some of the party members to cease participation in the United National Liberation Front (FULNA) because it was a Communist-dominated popular front group for exiles. In short, the bulk of the Febrerista party, both leaders and the rank and file, have taken a hostile attitude towards the Communist party, and all attempts by the Communists to penetrate *febrerismo* eventually have ended in failure.

The over-all trend within *febrerismo* has been a fusion of the nationalistic, democratic, and socialist tendencies. Exile seems to have had little effect in the way of introducing new ideological concepts into the party. Exile has meant, usually, residence in Argentina, but such Argentine movements as *peronismo* have never found any discernible bloc of sympathizers within the party.

The party's Declaration of Principles identifies it as

strongly nationalist.[2] It is asserted that Paraguay was "the first American country to build its organization on a firm policy of economic independence and national sovereignty." However, "progress towards organizing an independent existence was stunted in the year 1870 as a consequence of the extortive intervention of foreign economic forces in the national life." After this date, it is alleged, the country fell into the hands of a political oligarchy that acted in the "obsequious service" of those foreign interests, with the result that "the basic national resources were alienated and exploited indiscriminately for the exclusive benefit of privileged minorities."

The Declaration of Principles then offers a philosophy of action to confront this situation: "The state must always be at the service of men, and not men at the service of the state." The sort of state advocated by *febrerismo* is democratic and is "founded in the respect for human personality considered as the supreme value, and in the work which dignifies it." The party subscribes to the Universal Declaration of Principles of the United Nations and makes special mention of the freedoms of thought, speech, and press as fundamental rights. In keeping with this, it emphatically rejects all types of authoritarianism.

The theory of class struggle is accepted as a "fact inherent in society," but it rejects the idea that any one class should dominate another. Its appeal, however, is directed to the underprivileged. Workers should be free to organize and to have a share in profits. Everyone had the right to a standard of living that would assure them of proper food, clothing, shelter, medical assistance, and insurance against loss of income. Special attention is given to the situation of rural workers. Peasants without land, says the declaration, constitute "an economic and social absurdity, and a political

2. For the party's Declaration of Principles and Program of Government, see Partido Revolucionario Febrerista, Comité Político, *Qué es el febrerismo*, 1953. The authorship of this booklet is usually attributed to Arnaldo Valdovinos. A more recent edition has been issued under the title of, *Ideario, declaración de principios y programa de gobierno*, 1959.

crime." Every agricultural worker should be given his own plot of land.

In its Program of Government the party is more specific as to the manner in which an agrarian reform should be carried out, but this does not depart in any important way from the Agrarian Reform Law passed during the February Revolution. The state is authorized to expropriate and divide all unproductive *latifundios,* designating certain lands to be exploited privately, other lands to be worked by families, and still others to be held as public domain. No land is to be expropriated until it has been studied and its expropriation deemed to be in the public interest. That is to say, there is to be no general policy of total nationalization. All lands rationally exploited by their owners are to remain in private hands.

Those lands which are redistributed are to be sold, not given, to their new owners. The price will be set at the cost of the compensation paid to the original owners, and the terms of payment will be based on low installments paid over long terms. The new proprietors must work the land themselves and live on it at least nine months out of the year, in order to prevent absentee landlordism and land speculaton. Such lands will also be exempt from being attached through lawsuits. Plots of land larger than ten hectares but smaller than twenty-five hectares will be subject to special laws prohibiting their division upon the owner's death, in order to prevent *minifundios.* The program also foresees that a simple redistribution of the land is not enough. Regional agricultural schools and extension divisions to provide technical aid must be set up, and rural credit and insurance must also supplement the agrarian reform.

In short, the state has the power of eminent domain, and while private property should be respected it must also fulfill a social function. As for foreigners, they should enjoy "juridical and political treatment that will guarantee them the protection and security of their persons and property." Capital, whether national or foreign, "should enjoy sufficient guarantees for its useful employment": "The Partido Revolucionario Febrerista postulates the application of an economic system which, while respecting and stimulating private initiative, proposes the nationalization or socialization of the public services and national wealth of the country."[3]

The Popular Party Front | One other event is noteworthy in order to round out this description of the Febrerista party's ideological position. In August, 1960, it joined with the Peruvian Aprista party, Venezuela's Acción Democratica party, the Partido Liberación Nacional of Costa Rica, and the Movimiento Nacionalista Revolucionario of Bolivia to hold a Conference of Latin American Popular Parties. The motive for this meeting was to promote co-operation based on ideological similarity across national lines. The "Declaration of Lima" that resulted from this conference emphasized their nationalist, anti-imperialist, and democratic-socialist orientation.[4] It pointed to the "existence in the Western Hemisphere of two clearly-defined zones. On one side, the United States, industrialized and capitalistic. On the other, Latin America, economically underdeveloped." The declaration went on to say that the United States practices "almost uncontrolled exploitation" of Latin America and charged the United States with systematically maintaining tyrannies and oligarchies.

To rectify this, the parties proposed the general mobilization of the Latin American peoples and democratic governments against the remaining dictatorships and stressed the promotion of economic development—principally agrarian reform. Such development, it was held, should be based on state planning through a policy of the progressive nationalization of those businesses in control of the essential services and means of production. Also, the economic development of each country should be carried on with an eye towards the eventual economic integration of Latin America as the most efficient and constructive way to counter imperialism.

The declaration is also strong on regionalism, suggesting

---

3. P.R.F., *Qué es el febrerismo*, pp. 20-21.
4. See Primera Conferencia de Partidos Populares de America Latina, *Documentos* (Lima: Oficina de Coordinación, 1960).

not only Latin American economic integration but also an eventual political federation. The parties also assert the "genuinely Latin American" nature of their doctrines and programs, rejecting the importation of foreign systems as not being applicable to Latin American realities. Such an attitude is opposed not only to intervention by the United States in Latin American political and economic affairs but to Communist penetration as well.

The parties "reiterate their unwavering rejection of totalitarian Communist penetration in Latin America, against which our parties have always fought, because of the unbridgeable difference in social and political philosophy, and because of the prejudicial deviationist action and frequent complicity with dictators and reactionary forces that has been typical of communism in Latin America."[5]

These, then, are the doctrinal and programmatic positions of the Febrerista party. Whether, given the backwardness of Paraguay, they could be applied realistically should it come to power is a separate question. The experience of the February Revolution suggests that the *febreristas* might exercise a strong hand in pushing through their program. Although they reject in retrospect the notorious Decree Law 152 that outlawed political opposition, their critics have not forgotten it. Indeed, Liberal writers such as Policarpo Artaza accuse the *febreristas* of setting a precedent for the allegedly totalitarian dictatorships that have followed the February Revolution up through the present. On the other hand, the party did show a firm commitment to democratic fair play when, as a prerequisite to participating in Morínigo's coalition government, it demanded the lifting of the stage of seige; guarantees for freedom of speech, press, and assembly; and the legalization of all political parties, including their old enemies, the Liberals.

Febrerista ideology plays a central role in the party's life, as we shall see in the chapters that follow. As Paraguay's social revolutionary "left" and youngest of the three major parties, *febrerismo's* chief source of vitality, its members often claim, is its appeal to those who feel dissatisfied with Paraguay's present economic, social, and political situation and wish to

5. *Ibid.*, p. 5.

change this without joining movements of an "antinational" character, i.e., the Communist party. *Febrerista* ideology is vague enough to permit debate within the party over the ramifications of its socialist principles. Such subjects as the class struggle, the precise nature of the projected social revolutions, and the proper position for the party to take within the international scheme are open to various interpretations among *febreristas*. Nonetheless, there is no dispute over the party's nationalistic stand, which is fundamental in differentiating it from the Communist party. Also, all factions within *febrerismo* have always given at least lip service to such democratic principles as free elections, the rights of opposition parties, free speech, and free press.

In the personal opinion of this writer, one of the main reasons for the continuing existence of the Febrerista party, despite some twenty-nine years of almost constant exile and persecution, is the vitality and flexibility of its ideology. Moreover, when it is noted that every Paraguayan government since the February Revolution has had to pretend, at least, to promote agrarian reform, the rights of labor, and planned economic development, it becomes clear that *febrerismo* has had an impact upon Paraguayan politics of far-reaching consequences. It has created—through the February Revolution in the original instance, and through its continued propaganda—new political demands. Nearly all of the main tenets of *febrerismo* have found their way into the programs and platforms of the older, traditional parties. In this respect, *febrerismo* has been an educational as well as a political movement. Indeed, its ideological impact on the other parties may be, in the long run, of greater significance to Paraguay's political, social, and economic development than the Febrerista party itself. However, as long as the Febrerista party pre-empts the position of the country's secular, nationalist, democratic-socialist party, as it has since 1936, it will probably continue to exist as an important factor in Paraguayan politics.

Party Membership

It is impossible to say with any certainty how many people belong to the Febrerista party. Such information is not made public by the party, and this is understandable for an organization that is, in part, clandestine. Estimates vary greatly. Some *febreristas* claim over 100,000 party members, basing this on the former membership of the Asociación Nacional de Ex-Combatientes. Antonio E. González, a Colorado, estimated in 1947 that, in an honest election, the Febrerista party could count on probably 12,500 votes, not all of which would be cast by actual party members.[6] *Febreristas,* on the other hand, claim that, if they were given adequate time to campaign in the countryside, their party would win at least a plurality in any given election. Manuel J. Cibils cites Benigno Perrotta's *Seis meses en el medio rural paraguayo* to show that, in the campaign before the scheduled 1947 elections, Dr. Perrotta was able to put *febrerismo* on an equal numerical footing with the traditional parties in the province of Misiones in only six months.[7] At the same time, it is probable that many marginal members discreetly disassociated themselves in fear of the "terror" after the civil war of 1947. In any case, there has been no opportunity until now to see a clear demonstration of *febrerismo's* electoral strength.

One way of reaching a very rough approximation of the party's membership is to base it on representation in the National Party Convention. In 1962 (the year for which we have complete figures), seventy credentials were expedited by the Central Electoral Committee. Also, we must add to this another five credentials from the town of Posados, Argentina, which were not given to either list because both were held to be guilty of fraudulent practices during the elections. Since each delegate supposedly represents between 100 and 199 members, we might estimate the party's total membership to be in the range of 7,500 to 15,000.

The Febrerista party is a mass party, not a cadre of notables, and recruitment of new members is a central concern of the party leaders. According to Article 115 of the constitution, a candidate for membership must meet the following qualifications: (1) he must be a Paraguayan citizen, (2) he must not

---

6. Antonio E. González, *La rebelión de Concepción*, (Buenos Aires: Editorial Guanaría, 1947), pp. 101-2.

7. Manuel J. Cibils, *Anarquía y revolución en el Paraguay* (Buenos Aires: Editorial Americalee, 1957), p. 114.

have incurred any scandal connected with either his public or his private life, and (3) he must subscribe to the party's program. Articles 117 and 118 provide for special membership for foreigners of extra merit: "Non-national members of Indo-American origin will be organized in a special way, with the primary criteria being to increase contact and promote the unity and solidarity of the peoples of our continent." Such special membership can be granted only by the CEN.

Each candidate must be sponsored by a party member in good standing. Recruitment is done usually through the fractions, while petitions for admission are handled either by the regional or the local committees. Only in cases of special membership or when there is some opposition in the party to the admission of a candidate for membership does the CEN involve itself directly in this field. In such cases the CEN decides by majority vote. The application form a candidate must fill out requires little information from him other than his name, the names of his parents, his civil status, the name of his/her spouse, his residence, profession, place of work, and his identification number. He is also asked if he can afford to pay an extra monthly quota to support the party. The sponsor then fills out the back of the form, which calls for the following information: his name, residence, and length of party service.

Once a member is accepted, he is enrolled in one of the fractions where he begins a course of political education that includes instruction in party history, party doctrine, contemporary national and international politics, political theory, and national development. His rights and obligations as a party member are also explained. His rights include: an equal voice and vote in party meetings and assemblies, voting for party officers or holding office himself, and calling upon the party for help in personal circumstances as well as in matters of general party interest. He is obligated to spread the party ideology, to provide assistance to other party members, to obey the party statutes and orders from the CEN, to participate actively in unions or professional groups, and to contribute to the party organization.

Party discipline is carried out by a Tribunal of Conduct, composed of three members and three alternates appointed by the National Party Convention, which hears cases sent to it by the CEN. After a decision is reached, it is referred back to the CEN for enforcement. The range of sanctions that may be applied against a party member are: warning, removal from official duties, suspension of membership, and expulsion from the party. An expelled member may be readmitted after a four year period, if the National Party Convention approves such a recommendation from the Tribunal of Conduct.

Financing the party has been a continual problem. Party members are supposed to contribute monthly, according to their ability, but many peasant, worker, and student members cannot meet this obligation. Moreover, the economic insecurity of many exiles leaves the party treasury in a constantly desperate situation. As a result, many activities, such as publishing a party newspaper, mutual financial aid to members, and the maintenance of a staff of full-time party workers, are often interrupted or just not undertaken at all. One of the party's main weaknesses is that very few of its members, from the CEN on down, can afford to devote their full time to party work. It may be said with great accuracy that the Febrerista party is a party of militant political amateurs.

The methods of financing the party, then, are mostly informal. Regional and local committees often supplement their treasuries by holding dances, parties, or other social events at which a small entrance fee is charged. The committee that sponsors this event usually keeps a percentage of the proceeds for itself and sends the rest to the next highest committee. Members may also be asked for special donations or loans. In Buenos Aires the party's regional monthly newspaper is distributed free of charge to all members, but those who can afford to do so are asked to subscribe.[8]

Electors (voters), supporters (sympathizers), and militants —according to Maurice Duverger's nomenclature—can be

8. This writer has relied here in large part on a "Boletín Informativo" of the Buenos Aires regional committee, July-August, 1958.

found in the Febrerista party. It is not necessary to deal with electors, but there seem to be many Paraguayans who might be described as supporters of *febrerismo* without actually having become members of the party. In fact, the political education or indoctrination of a new member often begins before he has actually been received into the party. Those sympathizers who show an interest in affiliating are often invited to attend party meetings to hear discussions on ideology or national problems and to fraternize with the other members. An especially apt candidate may have an interview arranged for him with some high party leader in order to demonstrate the organization's democratic nature and to rid him of any reservations.

Some idea of how recruitment is carried on under the difficult conditions prevailing in Paraguay, may be gained from the experience of Dr. Manuel Cibils, as related in his book, *Anarquía y revolución en el Paraguay: Vórtice y asíntota.*[9] Dr. Cibils, a physician, was employed at the hospital in the small town of Coronel Bogado, in the southern interior, from June, 1953, to May, 1956. While he was there, he began the work of rebuilding the local committees and fractions that had been demoralized by the Colorado repression. Cibils started by visiting each of the town's precincts and talking with some nineteen local *febrerista* leaders. His position as one of the town's doctors must certainly have aided him in this, for it would have appeared as though he were simply making house calls. By repeated visits, says Cibils, "little by little we managed to break the climate of terror that had prevailed since the civil war of 1947."

Once the inertia was overcome, it was possible to find eight or nine *febreristas* who agreed to use their homes for classes in political education. Such classes were held simultaneously in different parts of town, with only three or four members attending at the time, so as not to arouse the suspicions of the police.

This was rather boring for the teachers who, week after week, had to repeat tediously the same concepts, but it per-

9. The account that follows is from Cibils, *Anarquía y revolución*, pp. 88-117.

mitted them to explore some of the great revolutionary themes.
. . .

Furthermore . . . since after a couple of months there were some thirty *compañeros* familiar with the party's basic concepts, these automatically converted themselves into other foci of mass recruitment.

Petitions for membership began to flow in, and with this there was created, little by little, an atmosphere favorable to *febrerismo*.

One interesting aspect of Cibils' experiences with party recruitment is the resistance he met on the part of the peasants towards changing their party affiliation. Some recalcitrants felt that *febrerismo* was synonymous with communism. This argument, says Cibils, was relatively easy to refute. It was pointed out that the party's president, Rafael Franco, was a Chaco War hero. The listener was also reminded that on Franco's return to Paraguay in August, 1946, he had been greeted at the docks by Monsigneur Bogarín, the country's most venerated prelate. Far more difficult to deal with were the fatalism and traditionalism of the peasants. A frequent answer from the peasants was, "I am the son of poor people and I will have to die poor." This inability to perceive any hope of betterment was, according to Cibils, a major barrier to recruitment. Another problem was the strong party identification of many peasants, based on their families' traditional loyalty to either the Colorado or Liberal parties. This made changing their affiliation seem something like treason. To quote Cibils:

One of the most serious obstacles that we encountered in the task of enlarging our contingent of members was a simple word: *Yeré,* which literally translated from Guaraní means "turn," make a change, or turn oneself around and—in our case—to change parties. Invented by God knows what *caudillo* of satanic wisdom, it possesses a tremendous force of inhibition in the spirit of the simple Paraguayan, whose culture is reduced to that rudimentary idea of life that comes from direct contact with a nature not yet dominated. This nature is that of a wandering orphan because of the scantiness of the learning— little, very little or none—that he is able to assimilate in the first two or three grades that he managed to attend at the rural school. This work is, without a doubt, one of the most powerful factors of cohesion and coercion that Paraguay's traditional parties can count on, along with the blue [Liberal] or red [Colorado] scarf. . . . It has aspects of a tabu. . . .[10]

By the first part of 1955, the *febreristas* felt strong enough to advance beyond the classroom stage and take an active stand on local issues, hoping to gain new members and sympathizers. One campaign dealt with helping local farmers secure a better price for their cotton by putting their harvest in common storage and holding off on selling until prices went up. Although the plan failed because of the unstable economic situation that forced the farmers to sell before they could obtain maximum prices, the attempt, Cibils claims, helped the party's popularity. The other issue was a drive to have a high school opened for the adult public. According to Cibil's, the *febreristas* were able to secure the backing of the town's public school teachers and were also able to get seventy prospective pupils to sign up for courses. Nonetheless, the local Colorado authorities refused to approve the plan, despite popular protests at night in front of the locked schoolhouse.

As the local movement began to grow, however, some of the members became incautious. On May 1, 1956, some *febreristas* publicly celebrated this international labor day with denunciations of the government's exploitation of the workers, and

10. The argument used by Cibils to confront this resistance by the peasants is entertaining in itself. He told them: "Yeré means to turn, something like a weathervane, while standing in the same place. There is good reason for this . . . when it is used to refer to changing from the Colorado Party to the Liberal Party, or vice versa, because they are essentially the same in their basic ideas, their methods and their objectives, so that passing from one to the other incurs no change of position other than a simple turn, staying, nevertheless, in the same place. It is evident that the Colorado Party and the Liberal Party are static organs . . . that represent the stagnation of outworn ways of the past. *Febrerismo,* on the other hand, with its eyes on the future and its modern doctrine, is a new, young powerful impulse forward, so that to pass from the traditional parties to the Partido Revolucionario Febrerista is not to 'turn' but 'to take ten steps forward.' Now then, since in a society those who remain stationary with relation to progress . . . stay behind, that is, fall back, the truth is that those who remain with the traditional parties, refusing to join *febrerismo,* certainly don't turn, but fall behind."

the local Colorado authorities immediately cracked down. Homes of suspected *febreristas* were invaded and their occupants arrested. Cibils himself was taken into custody and held for two weeks before being sent into exile.

As a postscript to this account, we might quote again from Cibils. In his explanation of why the party organization failed to extend itself, he touches upon the question of strategy:

> We tried repeatedly to extend our operative technique to the national scale, which would have been a great step towards converting the PRF into the overwhelmingly majority party . . . but—in fact—we invariably clashed with the inertia and the inveterate illusion of those who think and act exclusively on the basis of the law of the least effort. We would be tending, of course, towards a change of political method in Paraguay, where almost all of us are devoted to the immediatist mirage. It is known already how difficult it is, historically, to rectify directions in whose determinations the sociological character of our community, painfully formed throughout more than four centuries of unbroken violence, has entered as a factor of the first importance . . .

In short, there was a clash of methods arising out of the Febrerista party's dual character as both a mass party and a clandestine party.

It is difficult to ascertain from which classes *febrerismo* recruits most of its members, because so little information about its membership has been made public. A few facts concerning the social background of some of its leaders are available, however, and from these we may get a rough idea of the leadership's social characteristics. Party elections were held in 1961 to send delegates to the Third National Convention. Two lists presented candidates: a radical list (List 17 Febrero) and a conservative one (Institutionalists). This writer was able to obtain information concerning the occupations of twenty-five leaders from each list. It must be remembered that the party has no professional politician class, which means that these categories represent the actual occupations of the individuals studied.

Breaking down each of these lists by occupation, we find:

	Institutionalists		List 17 Febrero	
	number	%	number	%
Lawyers or solicitors	11	44	12	48
Doctors	2	8	6	24
Economists	4	16	3	12
Workers (manual and white collar)	1	4	2	8
Business and commercial	3	12	1	4
Military	2	8	0	0
Journalists	1	4	0	0
Students	1	4	1	4
TOTALS	25	100	25	100

There is little difference, then, between the two sets of leaders with respect to their occupations. The lawyer-solicitor group is the largest by far in both lists. If we combine the two lists we get the following ranking of occupations in the *febrerista* leadership:

	number	%
Lawyers or solicitors	23	46
Doctors	8	16
Economists	7	14
Businessmen and merchants	4	8
Workers (manual and white collar)	3	6
Military	2	4
Students	2	4
Journalists	1	2
TOTALS	50	100

The three most common occupations found among *febrerista* leaders are law, followed at some distance by medicine and economics. All of these are high status occupations—although economists perhaps do not enjoy quite the same prestige in Paraguay as the more traditional professions of law and medicine. At the same time, workers—both manual and white collar—represent only a small fraction of the party leadership. The *febrerista* businessmen and merchants, all of whom are small entrepreneurs, are also a relatively small group. No peasant leaders are found in this list of top party leaders.

Lack of information on party membership prevents any firm conclusion as to whether the Febrerista party is mainly urban or rural based. Many *febrerista* leaders have admitted to this writer, however, that the party is weak in the peasantry. One rough indicator of the party's relative strength in urban and rural areas is the number of credentials expedited by the Central Electoral Committee in the party elections of 1961. Of the 70 credentials issued, 31 were to delegates from Asunción or urban areas with over 100,000 population in the exterior. Since the delegates were elected on the basis of one for each 100 members in their local or regional committee, this would seem to indicate that roughly 44 per cent of the party members reside in urban areas. Given the fact that only about 11 per cent of Paraguay's total population—those living in Asunción—can be classified as urban, it might be said that there is a significant over-representation of the urban element in the Febrerista party.

In conclusion, we might say that *febrerista* leadership comes mainly from the Paraguayan upper-middle class (see Introduction) and that the party is largely an urban-based party. Such tentative conclusions are founded on somewhat tenuous evidence, however, and should be regarded cautiously.

Party Organization

The *febrerista* Constitutional Convention of 1951 decided the question of the party's formal structure. According to the constitution, the supreme party authority is the National Convention, which is elected by the regional and local committees. It is supposed to meet every three years, although the last two conventions have been held four years apart. It may also be called into extraordinary session by the CEN on its own initiative or on the request of a number of regional committees representing a majority of the party's members. The National Convention has the power to modify the constitution, to fix the party's ideological position, to decide on broad questions of political strategy, to proclaim the

winners of the elections to the convention in case of a dispute, and to name the new National Executive Committee.
Because of the three- or four-year lapse between National
Conventions, this usually provides occasion for a general review of the party's situation. Therefore, the convention delegates are appointed to special committees to study and then
report on particular issue areas of general party interest.
There are at least three regular committees: the Committee
on Party Affairs, the Committee on National Politics, and the
Committee on International Politics. Half of the delegates
plus one must be present for the convention to begin its
sessions, and all resolutions of the convention must be
adopted by a simple majority of those present and voting.[11]

Elections to the National Convention are of paramount
importance in the Febrerista party, for there are always two
or more factions representing distinct opinions on party
ideology and/or tactics. Such differences may not seem surprising when we remember that the Febrerista party was
formed through a gradual process of building coalitions
among several, and often disparate, revolutionary groups and
that ideological heterogeneity has characterized *febrerismo*
since the days of the February Revolution. This characteristic
was probably augmented during the period of decentralization, from the fall of the revolutionary government in 1937 to
the founding of the Concentración Revolutionaria Febrerista
in 1945. In that period each revolutionary group was independent. Such heterogeneity was reflected in the federative
nature of the Concentración, and even though the Partido
Revolucionario Febrerista is a more centralized organization
than the *Concentración,* it is still the product of many separate groups welded into one. Moreover, the *febrerista* ideology is broad enough to permit many different interpretations.
As a result, opposing factions or tendencies exist within the
party and attempt to gain control of its apparatus by winning
a majority of delegates to the National Convention, thus
earning the right to form the new National Executive Committee.

11. Partido Revolucionario Febrerista, Comité Ejecutivo Nacional,
Carta Orgánica, 1962, Articles 6-21.

The electoral process is begun by the National Executive Committee, which informs the party members through their regional and local committees that elections are to be held. It also determines the date on which these are to take place. Each regional and local committee then appoints an electoral committee for the purpose of registering their members to vote, and these lists are sent to the Central Electroral Committee, whose task is to supervise the entire electoral process. Electoral lists must register with the Central Electoral Committee at least three months before the election date in order to be recognized officially.[12]

Each precinct in Asunción and each town in the interior and in exile may elect one delegate for each one hundred members. A candidate may stand for election in a place where he is not a resident, and he may run for election in more than one local committee, but he may not represent more than one place. If he wins in more than one place, he must choose which he wants to represent. Then the runner-up in the other race is declared elected. Voting is direct and secret. A plurality is sufficient to win.[13]

Each list is allowed to appoint observers to the Central Electoral Committee and to the local electoral committees. This is especially important because it must be remembered that these elections are often held during periods when the party is outlawed. Therefore, the polling place must be kept secret from the police and, since voting usually takes place over three or more days, the urn may be shifted from place to place. Voters do not appear in large groups. As a result of such clandestine procedures, it is relatively easy for electoral irregularities to arise. The Central Electoral Committee often receives petitions for an investigation of alleged electoral frauds. In such cases the Central Electoral Committee may withhold credentials from challenged delegates pending an investigation. Should such accusations be verified, it may award the credentials to the injured party. Whatever the decision of the Central Electoral College may be, such disputes may be carried on to the National Convention, which is the final arbiter.

---

12. *Ibid.*, Articles 92-99.
13. *Ibid.*, Articles 7-9, 97.

The National Executive Committee (Comité Ejecutivo Nacional, CEN) / The CEN is appointed by the National Convention, is composed of a president, a first and a second vice-president, and twenty-two members. The powers of the president include convoking and presiding over meetings, dispatching CEN resolutions to appropriate committees, presiding over the Political Committee, creating special commissions, and directing the work of the executive departments indirectly through the secretary general. The first and second vice-presidents exercise the duties of the president during his absence. Their roles take on a special importance because the party operates both within and outside Paraguay, and the exiles are scattered over much of southern South America. Consequently, the vice-presidents are often called upon to exercise presidential powers.[14]

The secretary general has the important task of directly coordinating the executive departments: foreign relations, peasant affairs, labor affairs, student and youth affairs, finance, press and propaganda, education and culture, census and statistics, social assistance, aid to veterans, and the women's organization. Each of these has its own secretary, who is a member of the CEN and is directly responsible to the secretary general. The secretary general must prepare an annual report on the progress of each department and present a three-year report to the National Convention.[15]

Another key post is the secretary of organization, who is in charge of supervising the regional and local committees. Such close contact with the party's "grassroots" make the secretary of organization a powerful figure. It can, as happened in one instance, allow him to build a large personal following from which to launch an attempt to seize control of the entire apparatus. In any case, it is probably true that no other individual is more familiar with the day-to-day operations of the party.[16]

The Political Committee is an advisory body of five members, headed by the party president, whose primary function

14. *Ibid.,* Articles 30-32.
15. *Ibid.,* Article 34.
16. *Ibid.,* Article 41.

is to maintain contact with the government and with other Paraguayan parties or political groups. Contacts with other Latin American parties are to be promoted by the Department of Foreign Relations.[17]

There are four other party organs that are dependent on the CEN. The first, whose existence is quite tenuous, is the Commission for Assistance to Indigeneous Populations—a consultative body for the purpose of drawing up plans to aid Paraguay's Indian tribes. Although it is of little importance now, presumably it could become important should the party come to power. A second body is the Superior Council of Scientific and Technical Research, whose task is to make specialized studies on national problems, especially economic problems. It is relatively active and has published some economic studies that are worthy of attention. A third advisory organ is the Workers' Congress, whose sole purpose is to carry out studies of specific labor problems and forward its recommendations to the CEN. Finally, there is the National Party Conference, convoked by the CEN, which is composed of the members of the CEN, the presidents of the regional committees, and the general secretaries of the local committees. National Party Conferences are called when extraordinary circumstances warrant a discussion among all party leaders and a pronouncement by the party as a whole to lend it special force. All participants have an equal voice and vote. National Conferences are not frequently held and their decisions are not binding on the CEN. When they are called, however, their pronouncements can be considered as reliable indices of general party opinion and, as such, carry great weight with the CEN.[18]

Regional Committees, Local Committees, and Fractions / There are four regional committees at the present, corresponding to the following geographical areas: (1) the Paraguayan interior, (2) Formosa, the principle city on the Argentine frontier, (3) Buenos Aires, and (4) Montevideo. The precinct committees of Asunción fall directly under the

---

17. *Ibid.*, Articles 42, 62-64.
18. *Ibid.*, Articles 100-11.

supervision of the secretary of organization of the CEN. Each regional committee is organized in a manner similar to the National Executive Committee, having a president, a secretary general, and various executive departments. Its members are to be elected every two years and are eligible for re-election. Each regional committee is required to send periodic reports to the secretary of organization on party activities within its zone.[19]

The local, or town, committees are immediately below the regional committees in the party hierarchy, with an organization similar to that of the CEN and the regional committees, except that they are headed by a secretary general rather than a president. Their officers are elected for two years and may be re-elected. The local committees meet once a week in regular session and call a general meeting of all members at least once every three months, in order to co-ordinate the work of the fractions. The locals are required to furnish reports to the appropriate regional committee every three months, but the CEN and/or the regional committee may demand information from a local committee at any time. The locals are somewhat similar to Maurice Duverger's "branches" designed to appeal to the masses, enroll new members, hold classes in political education, and thereby increase the size and *esprit de corps* of the party. The *febrerista* locals are supposed to propagandize, organize cultural activities, collaborate in community sports and social events, and participate in community projects of a progressive type.[20]

The locals' most important task is to supervise the work of the fractions or subcommittees. These are party cells, organized either as work-place cells or neighborhood cells, and participation in them is obligatory for all party members. Each fraction is headed by a "chief" (*jefe*) and a secretary, elected by the cell members. They meet each week to receive information from and transmit information to the local committee. The fractions have the task of spreading propaganda, politically educating their members, gaining new converts,

---

19. *Ibid.*, Articles 69-75, 83-86.
20. *Ibid.*, Articles 76-82.

and engaging in whatever militant action the circumstances require.[21]

This use of both the branch and the cell in the same party is a phenomenon apparently not foreseen by Duverger, who states that: "In contrast with the branch, the cell has not been the subject of imitation, at least of successful imitation. Several non-Socialist parties have succeeded in organizing themselves on the basis of the branch: Communist parties alone have the cell as their basis."[22]

The reason for this characteristic of the Febrerista party is suggested by Duverger himself: " . . . The choice of the cell as the basis of organization entails a profound change in the concept of a political party. Instead of a body intended for the winning of votes . . . the party becomes an instrument of agitation, of propaganda, of discipline, and, if necessary, of clandestine action. . . ."[23]

In other words, the most plausible explanation of the Febrerista party's peculiar structure lies in the conflict between the democratic ideals it professes and the restrictive political environment in which it must operate. Ideologically, the party falls into the democratic-socialist category. It is concerned with recruitment and makes its appeal to peasants, workers, and dissatisfied members of the middle class. Its goal is to become a mass party, not an elitist party. Therefore, it utilizes the "branch" as one of its "basic elements."

On the other hand, the use of cells is a logical response to the realities of the Paraguayan political environment. The repression and violence that have marked the country's politics in recent times require the *febreristas* to adopt a type of organization that facilitates clandestine action. Barred from acting openly, the party turns to subversion—which in turn, no doubt, gives its opponents further cause to continue persecuting it. Thus, the political environment—the *anti-febrerista* policies pursued by the various governments since 1937—have

---

21. *Ibid.*, Articles 87-91.

22. Maurice Duverger, *Political Parties: Their Organization and Activity in the Modern State* (New York: John Wiley and Sons, Inc., 1963), p. 31.

23. *Ibid.*, p. 35.

had an impact upon that party's internal organization. Its structure provides for both mass politics and underground activities.

In Duverger's terms, the Febrerista party employs "vertical linkage" in its organization. As we have seen, the local committee supervises the fractions, is in turn controlled by the regional committee, and both are responsible to the CEN. As Duverger points out, this type of linkage facilitates the transformation of a public group into a secret movement.

Centralization and Communication: The Case of the Resistance Committee / The problem of communication within the Febrerista party, both across geographical areas and among the different levels of the party hierarchy, sheds some light on the related question of centralization. Samuel Eldersveld's concept of political parties as task groups, communications subsystems, and decisional groups is especially helpful as an ordering device in studying this area of party life.[24] As far as this particular study is concerned, this writer has decided to emphasize the direction of the flow of communications within the Febrerista party. The content of such communication has been ignored and identified only as either "information" (about the political situation in Paraguay) or "commands."

In beginning this description, we might note once again that the party's organization is spread over four more or less distinct zones: (1) Asunción, the Paraguayan capital, (2) the Paraguayan interior, (3) the Argentine frontier, and (4) Buenos Aires and Montevideo, both of which are more than six hundred miles from Paraguay. The party's president, General Rafael Franco, lives in Montevideo. The other members of the CEN are dispersed among Asunción, Buenos Aires, and the Argentine frontier. The six-hundred-mile trip between the frontier and Buenos Aires is more than a full day's journey by train or highway, and it is at least three days by riverboat. Moreover, in traveling across national bounda-

---

24. Samuel J. Eldersveld, *Political Parties: A Behavioral Analysis* (Chicago: Rand McNally and Co., 1964), pp. 333–40.

ries, there is the problem of presenting proper documents. Understandably enough, this is often made more difficult by the Paraguayan government through diplomatic pressure on neighboring countries or by its failing to provide exiles with such documents.

Communication between Asunción and the interior is no less difficult, for within Paraguay the *febreristas* have had to cope with the police. The interior is sparsely settled, with no town larger than 35,000 in populaton. This makes it relatively easy for government officials to watch for the arrival of "outsiders." Therefore, contacts between Asunción and the interior are usually maintained by *febreristas* from the interior traveling to the capital.

These difficulties often result in lapses of unanimity between party leaders, especially between the CEN members in Asunción and those in exile. Generally speaking, the latter, viewing the situation from a distance and experiencing the frustrations of exile, often tend to favor less discreet action. One example of this was the series of guerrilla invasions in 1959-60, which were strongly opposed by most *febreristas* in Paraguay since they were the ones who had to bear the brunt of the government's retaliation.

The leaders in Asunción are in a complicated position. They are kept under surveillance by the government but are tolerated as long as they are not discovered to be engaging in subversion and as long as they do not publicly challenge the regime. Consequently, in order not to endanger the party's foothold within the country, they must act with great caution. Sometimes activist exiles accuse them of being "conservative" or of compromising themselves with the government. On the other hand, the leaders in Asunción enjoy a certain prestige by virtue of the fact that they are thought to be taking greater risks and that they have real first-hand knowledge of the true situation there. Their reply to their accusers —that they should "come back up here and see what the situation is really like," or "it is easy to be so brave when you are so far away from the fire"—are fairly effective in undermining criticism. After all, most of the exiles have left Paraguay voluntarily, and in many cases it is lack of work and a low standard of living rather than government action which influenced their decision.

At this writing, both the first and second vice-presidents of the party live in Asunción and exercise the powers of the presidency. Geographically, then, intraparty communication tends to follow the following complex pattern: Information is carried from the interior to Asunción, from Asunción to the Argentine frontier, and from there to Buenos Aires and Montevideo; commands are carried from Asunción to the interior, while a two-way flow exists between Asunción and the exiles, the primary channel tending to be from Asunción to the exterior and the secondary being from the exterior to Asunción. Such communication is often carried on by personal contact, through agents ostensibly on business trips, in order to avoid the risks involved in using the mails.

The description given above must be qualified immediately. That pattern is apparently true for the party at the time of this writer's research in 1964, when many members of the CEN were living in Asunción. However, in the period just after the civil war of 1947 all of the Concentración's leaders and almost all of its members were in exile, leaving behind only the Resistance Committee to maintain a precarious underground movement. Although the men who came to head this committee proved themselves to be capable, they were not from the upper echelons of the party hierarchy. Their lack of personal prestige—even though the committee itself was esteemed as a symbol of party valor—eventually resulted in a serious dispute with the CEN.[25]

Friction between the Resistance Committee and the CEN first developed over the feeling on the part of the former that

---

25. Although this case study concerns events during the period of the Concentración Revolucionaria Febrerista, there is no reason to assume that inferior party organs have enjoyed any greater autonomy since 1951. First, the party is more centralized today than it was from 1947 to 1951, when its federative structure was actually recognized in the constitution of the Concentración. Second, the relatively relaxed political situation in Paraguay today permits most of the members of the CEN to be located in Paraguay, where they can exert more direct control than was possible before. Therefore, conclusions about party centralization based on this case study should be, if anything, even more applicable today.

it was being left to fight alone by the rest of the party. The report from the secretary of organization of the Resistance Committee to General Franco, to which we have already referred in the previous chapter, remonstrates with the CEN for its failure to give support:

> From the first moment the Resistance Committee has focused its activity in conjunction with the objectives laid down by the party (CEN), taking the initiative on doubtful points not foreseen in the general orientation. . . .
>
> From the beginning the Resistance Committee sought contact through correspondence and has sent special reports through agents for the purpose of regularizing relations with all the constituted organs, and especially with the CEN. These repeated attempts by the Resistance Committee have proven fruitless;
>
> It [the Resistance Committee] has applied the party's political line in *motu propio,* due to the lack of instructions from the CEN, which at no time has paid attention to the Committee.
>
> The activity of this Committee is completely clandestine, and it confronts daily problems connected with changing situations of the moment, usually unforeseen and coming in rapid succession. In these highly special circumstances it is permissible, or should be permissible to take quick action. . . . If the Resistance Committee had to await instructions from the CEN in each instance, the following inconveniences might arise:
>
> (1) Instructions might be inopportune or tardy, due to distance and difficulty in communication;
>
> (2) The problems might not be well interpreted [by the CEN] for lack of contact with the actual situation;
>
> (3) It would remove from the Resistance Committee sufficient flexibility for taking initiative.
>
> We believe, therefore, that the Resistance Committee should operate WITH FULL AUTONOMY, always within the general lines determined by the CEN. . . .
>
> Neither harmony nor co-ordination in leadership and revolutionary tasks can exist if responsible organs, the CEN and the Resistance Committee, live isolated and unconnected. It is indispensable, therefore, that the CEN aid our organization in every way: aid in leaders, financial aid, and aid in propaganda materials. Only thereby can we avoid misunderstandings and give vigor and dynamism to our revolutionary work.[26]

---

26. Concentración Revolucionaria Febrerista, Comité de Resistencia, *Construyendo el febrerismo* (Buenos Aires: Alea, 1951), pp. 47-48.

Such aid never came. In fairness to the exiles, it should be pointed out that, as in the case of many exile groups recently uprooted, they were probably too disorganized and demoralized to render significant aid in money or materials. It is harder to justify the failure to send the party leaders requested. Since at this time—1947 to 1948—the country was in the climactic stages of the "Colorado Terror," it is probable that most exiles were understandably unwilling to return and to run the great risks involved. Nevertheless, one group did return about this time, a pro-Communist faction of young *febreristas* called the Bloque de Defensa de la Revolución. This faction's activities will be described in more detail later. Let it suffice to say for the present that the Bloque was engaged in a determined attempt to unseat the incumbent party leaders by capturing the Labor Department and the Resistance Committee.

Now the CEN, fearful of a *bloquista* take-over, began to take a more active interest in the Resistance Committee, for the latter represented the only *febrerista* organization left in Paraguay. The Resistance Committee began to receive a stream of commands that its leaders felt to be impractical and restrictive of its right of initiative. With respect to the *bloquistas,* they were soon expelled from the committee by the resistance leaders themselves. But meanwhile the CEN's intervention in the Resistance Committee's operations had led to a near-break between the two. In August, 1950, a general conference of the resistance was held to prepare a slate of delegates to the party's forthcoming constitutional convention. Two events occured at this conference which alarmed the CEN. First, the Resistance Committee drafted a constitutional clause that would require any member of the CEN who succeeded in having proposals adopted with regard to the Resistance Committee to go to Paraguay to help implement them personally. Otherwise such proposals would not be binding on the Resistance Committee. Second, the secretary general of the Resistance Committee, José A. Huidobro, was replaced by Salvador García Melgarejo, who favored a firmer stand against CEN intervention. Ricardo Franco (no relation to General Rafael Franco) the party's secretary of organization, was informed by Huidobro that García Melgarejo and Carlos Chávez del Valle, who had organized Huidobro's ouster, were preparing to separate the Resistance Committee from the rest of the party.[27]

Apparently the precarious situation of the resistance movement in those days, along with the effectiveness with which Garcia Melgarejo and Chávez del Valle had held off the *bloquistas,* convinced the CEN that immediate and direct intervention would not be wise. However, in the elections of 1951 to the Constitutional Convention, the CEN faction in Paraguay, led by Huidobro and Ricardo Franco, cut the ground from under both the Resistance Committee and the *bloquistas.* Their methods were simple; they stuffed the ballot boxes. The charges of fraud brought to the convention by petitioners from the Resistance Committee were later confirmed by an investigating commission headed by Roberto Paniagua. However, the convention had already been held, and it was felt that to officially recognize the fraud would undermine the entire legality of the Constitutional Convention, throwing the party back into an organizational chaos. In fairness to the other party leaders, it should be noted that Ricardo Franco and José Huidobro had acted on their own initiative and not on orders from the CEN.[28]

This example of conflict between a subordinate committee and the CEN suggests certain conclusions that might be made concerning communications and centralization within the Febrerista party. First, there appears to have been a trend towards centralizing decision-making in the CEN whenever circumstances permit, and the fact that the Resistance Committee enjoyed so much freedom for a time could probably be attributed to the general state of party disorganization after the Civil War of 1947. By 1950, however, the party was sufficiently reorganized to be able to call elections and to send the secretary of organization to Paraguay, and the CEN had

27. Interview with Carlos Chávez del Valle (March 12, 1964).

28. *Ibid.* This account was confirmed to this writer's satisfaction during a meeting between rival *febrerista* factions held in Buenos Aires on March 20, 1964. It should be said that even Chávez del Valle, the Resistance leader, considers that Huidobro and Franco acted on their own.

begun to re-establish its authority over the Resistance Committee.

It seems, also, that a two-way flow of commands is acceptable only among members of the CEN. The situation in 1964, in which eighteen members of the CEN, including both vice-presidents, the secretary general, and the secretary of organization, were located in Asunción while only seven remained in exile, allowed communication between those within Paraguay and those in the exterior to be a discourse among equals. Indeed, if anything, the leaders within Paraguay might be said to exert more influence. This was not the case with the Resistance Committee. While it is true that Huidobro and Garcia Melgarejo were members of the CEN, the former was not strong in pressing for more autonomy for the Resistance Committee, and the latter was only one out of twenty-five CEN members. Therefore, the Resistance Committee's demands for autonomy were viewed by the CEN as a challenge to its authority. Despite the Resistance Committee's presumably better acquaintance with the political situation in Paraguay, the CEN insisted that commands could flow only one way in this situation. The demands as well as the informative reports of the Resistance Committee seem to have been ignored for the most part.

This case study also makes it difficult for this writer to accept fully the applicability of the statement by Samuel Eldersveld that:

> It is our position, without questioning directly the validity of other oligarchic phenomena, that the theory of elite control of the organization which the oligarchic model assumes, is empirically incorrect. In lieu of the doctrine of elite control, we suggest that, although authority to speak for the organization may remain in the hands of the top elite nucleus, there is great autonomy in operations at the lower "strata" or echelons of the hierarchy, and that control from the top is minimal and formal.[29]

As far as the Febrerista party is concerned, it would seem that while unusual circumstances may allow lower echelons to exercise considerable autonomy, the over-all tendency is to-

---

29. Eldersveld, *Political Parties*, pp. 99-100.

ward centralization. It is true, on the other hand, that the difficulties in communication, attributable largely to the prevailing political situation in Paraguay, necessitate initiative on the part of the locals and that the party's constitution grants the regional and local committees the power to take the initiative in such matters as recruitment. Nevertheless, the constitution calls for close supervision of those subordinate bodies by the secretary of organization, and the CEN has the right to intervene an inferior committee and remove its officials. Therefore, unless one wishes to state the obvious—that no elite group can possibly control each and every act, down to the most inconsequential, of an inferior body—it is probably dangerous to generalize on the subject of party elite control only on the basis of the relatively loose structures of American parties.

4. Febrerismo Divided

The Febrerista party has been divided into factions since the February Revolution. It will be recalled that the revolutionary government of that time was divided into a right faction directed by Bernardino Caballero and the Freire Esteves brothers, a left faction represented by Jover Peralta, and a center group whose chief figures were Juan Stefanich and Elpidio Yegros.

By 1945, w h e n the Concentración Revolucionaria Febrerista was founded, a new influx of militants had entered *febrerismo*. These were the students who had been too young to play active roles in the February Revolution. They became the nuclei of the clubs Pedro P. Sarmaniego and Fermin Franco Delgado. Younger than the men of 1936, and coming to active politics under different conditions than had their predecessors, these new *febreristas* viewed national politics in their own terms. While they admired and respected the older revolutionaries—especially Rafael Franco—it was still true that it was they who were fighting against the Morínigo dictatorship from within Paraguay. They were taking daily risks while the older *febreristas* remained, for the most part, inactive and ineffective in their exile. It was only natural that this younger generation of *febreristas* should feel an especial *esprit de corps* about their revolutionary clubs and also feel that they were entitled to be treated as equals by the men of

121

the February Revolution. Lastly, perhaps because of their youth, their university origins, or their more direct participation in the revolutionary struggle, their political beliefs tended to be more radical than those of most of the older leaders. The club Pedro P. Sarmaniego proclaimed the organization of a "socialist democracy" as its goal. Where left revolutionaries of 1936, such as Jover Peralta, had identified with the Peruvian Aprista Movement, the left revolutionaries of this new generation, such as the Bloque de Defensa de la Revolución, went beyond that and declared their support for the Soviet Union. For this reason, Antonio E. González, in *La rebelión de Concepción,* identifies two distinct tendencies within *febrerismo.*[1] The first he calls *febrerismo neto,* "pure" *febrerismo,* the beliefs of the men of the Liga Nacional Independiente, the dissident Liberals, and the military men who staged the February 17 coup. *Febrerismo neto,* says González, is really nothing more than old liberalism under a revolutionary disguise. It is more or less personified by Juan Stefanich, the founder of the Liga Nacional Independiente. It will be recalled that the Liga was a nationalistic group organized primarily to pressure the government into taking a stronger stand in the Chaco, and had relatively little to say about domestic, social, or economic questions. While Stefanich did display some concern over the control of vast tracts of Paraguayan territory by foreign *latifundio* owners, this could be attributed at least as much to national pride as to concern about the peasants' welfare. During the February Revolution, Stefanich struggled successfully to keep the government on a middle-of-the-road course, first purging the Freire Esteves brothers and then Jover Peralta. Next to the truce talks, Stefanich's chief worry seemed to be the leftward drift of the revolution. Radical critics were expelled from the country, and labor agitation was suppressed by putting the unions under the control of the Ministry of Labor, headed by Germán Soler, another Liga member.

From the fall of the revolutionary government to the founding of the Concentración Revolucionaria Febrerista,

1. Antonio E. González, *La rebelión de Concepción* (Buenos Aires: Editorial Guanaría, 1947) pp. 37-42.

febrerismo experienced a period of decentralization. This was the time during which the younger men formed their underground clubs and began to build a tradition of revolutionary *febrerismo*. Under the Concentración, however, leadership was placed back in the hands of the older generation. The triumph of *febrerismo neto* was amply demonstrated by the fact that the Concentración's charter called for *two* presidents, a concession to Stefanich, who then shared the leadership with General Franco. Just as Stefanich had been the "strong man" of the revolutionary government, so he also became the "strong man" of the Concentración's National Executive Committee, and he proved to be no more mellow towards socialism than he had been in 1936. In the aftermath of the Civil War of 1947, he led the campaign to expel the left-wing from the party—*febrerismo's* first purge.

The platform that Stefanich tried to impose on *febrerismo* was based on liberal democracy, with social reformist leanings —a sort of Paraguayan New Deal-ism. That is, *febrerismo neto* adheres to the old liberal beliefs of representative government and individual liberties, while at the same time it accepts modern ideas to the effect that labor must be protected, that social equality should be fostered, and that government must intervene in the economy occasionally for the good of society. *Febrerismo neto* would accept the doctrine that the right to own property is not absolute and that private property must also fulfill a social function. "Institutionalist" *febreristas,* as those who subscribe to *febrerismo neto* are sometimes called (and we shall call them that), would accept the legitimacy of agrarian reform.

Under Stefanich's leadership, the Concentración began to take on more definite shape. The extreme decentralization of the previous period slowly gave way to a more coherent movement, as the revolutionary clubs began to lose their autonomy, but this process was not free from friction. Sometimes rather arbitrary methods were used to impose party discipline on the lower echelons, as in the case of the Resistance Committee. Many of the younger dissidents who rebelled against increasing centralization were read out of the ranks. Stefanich, himself, became the party's most controversial figure. Accused by the radicals of having previously emasculated the February Revolution by making it a monopoly of the too-conservative Liga Nacional Independiente, he was now said to be stunting *febrerismo's* growth by driving away its younger, more vigorous elements. In the end, these party battles centering around Stefanich's leadership led to a compromise of sorts. In 1951 the party's constitutional convention purged the more extremist young radicals, rewrote the charter, and abolished the post of second president. Stefanich was demoted by the delegates to first vice-president. Even this did not satisfy the growing resentment against the incumbent CEN, whose leaders were basically the same as under the Concentración. The anti-institutionalist reaction, directed especially against Stefanich and Soler, led to the radical triumph in the party elections of 1954.

González calls this other *febrerista* tendency, "revolutionary" *febrerismo*. Besides its closer affinity to socialism, "revolutionary" *febrerismo* also tends to favor tactics differing from those of the institutionalists. The latter have usually pursued what their radical critics disparagingly term "high level diplomacy": the institutionalists have preferred to negotiate with military officers, in order to attempt a coup, or with the government, in order to secure an amnesty for the party so that it can operate openly. The institutionalists are so called because of this emphasis on negotiating for the party's legalization and their belief that, if permitted to operate publicly, *febrerismo* can achieve power ultimately through peaceful, institutional methods. In contrast to this, the radical *febreristas* tend to emphasize "revolution from the bottom"; they believe in an intensive campaign of propaganda and recruitment to prepare the masses for some future general uprising. Only by these means, they argue, would a revolution acquire a secure base. To support their thesis they point to *febrerismo's* failures in 1937 and 1947, claiming that these were because of a lack of firm mass support. Despite these attitudes, however, the radicals have not shunned direct, violent action by small groups, such as guerrillas. Nor have the institutionalists ignored political education and mass recruitment as tactics.

The institutionalists, as we have seen, have been in command of the party throughout most of its history. The radicals succeeded in gaining control of the CEN only at the First National Convention, in 1954. This happened when Benigno Perrota, the leader of a radical group called Democracia y Revolución, negotiated a pact with Ricardo Franco. Franco, a rising party leader, headed a group of rather moderate young *febreristas* who looked upon him as the party's future *caudillo.* This group had supported the institutionalist old guard in the 1951 crisis but now deserted that coalition in order to join with Perrota in a revolt of the younger generation. No sooner was the triumph achieved, however, than the two groups began to quarrel over the division of seats on the CEN. In the end, Ricardo Franco withdrew his support, and Perrota's radicals were left with a minority government in the party. Four years of relative stagnation followed, which caused disillusionment among many members who had hoped for more vigorous leadership from the radicals.

Disappointment with radical leadership led to a crushing victory for the institutionalists in 1958, as they carried more votes than all three of the opposing lists combined. Much of the credit for the institutionalist revival was due to Elpidio Yegros, who took over the leadership of this sector after Juan Stefanich retired in 1954. In Yegros, the institutionalists had Stefanich's logical successor—indeed, his protégé, since Yegros had once been Stefanich's student in law school. Yegros' *febrerista* background stretched back to the February Revolution, when he headed the Chaco War Veterans' Association. After the Colorados had been edged out of the revolutionary government, he had taken over as mayor of Asunción. In the post-revolutionary period he had been the chief architect of the Committee of Revolutionary Organization, which had brought the scattered *febrerista* groups together. Later, as the secretary-general of the Concentración, and then of the Febrerista party from 1951 to 1954, he was considered to be Stefanich's capable right-hand man. Like Stefanich, Yegros was considered to be an unemotional, pragmatic leader— "almost like a *gringo,*" as one respondent described him to this writer. Although he lacked Stefanich's intellectual background and interest in political philosophy, Yegros had been the veteran of many party battles and had proven himself to be a formidable politician. Perhaps no other *febrerista* has such a complete archive of documents on Paraguayan politics, nor such a total grasp of party affairs with respect to its activities, personnel and relations with other political groups.

Standing behind Yegros in 1958 were two other old guard institutionalists: Carlos Caballero Gatti and Roque Gaona. Caballero Gatti had been the secretary-general of the Chaco War Veterans' Association during the February Revolution and had worked closely with Yegros. During the period from 1958 to 1964, before the party was granted its present amnesty, Yegros headed the exile organization, while Caballero Gatti and Gaona—who were permitted by Stroessner to reside in Paraguay—managed the party's affairs inside the country. Yegros held the post of first vice-president, as had Stefanich, while Gaona and Caballero Gatti were second vice-president and secretary-general respectively. Elpidio Yegros also represented the Febrerista party at the 1960 Lima Conference of Popular Parties, along with Dr. Galo Achar, who had prepared the ground for *febrerismo's* participation through his extensive correspondence with other Latin American leaders of the democratic left.

By 1962 Yegros had created a host of enemies within the party. Like Stefanich, he had become the principal target for radical attacks on the institutionalist leadership. Also, like Stefanich, he headed a campaign to expel his detractors from the party. First, Arnaldo Valdovinos and his Vanguardia Febrerista sector were purged. This was followed by a revolt led by Ricardo Franco, which resulted in several more expulsions. Finally, these party convulsions were capped by a particularly vicious battle in 1962, during the elections to the Third National Convention. Once again the radicals lost, but in the process the party became so badly divided that a change in leadership was obviously needed. Indeed, it was uncertain whether the institutionalists still enjoyed majority support, or whether they had managed to hang on to the party apparatus only by using improper tactics. In any case, Caballero Gatti took over as the first vice-president, and Yegros stepped down to an ordinary seat on the CEN, although he still retained control over the Buenos Aires regional committee and continued to represent the party in its foreign relations. The substitution of Caballero Gatti for Elpidio Yegros represents no split in the party leadership. The institutionalists have proven to be a highly cohesive group; they have worked together closely over the past three decades. Indeed, this may be the secret of their success in beating back radical attacks. Therefore, such shifting of personnel within their ranks probably does not constitute any real change in outlook but rather tends to underscore the degree to which there has been continuity in party leadership since 1936. The line of succession from Stefanich to Yegros to Caballero Gatti is straight and clear.

A similar continuity exists, as we shall see, among the "revolutionary" *febrerista* dissident movements that have challenged the institutionalists over the years. Having briefly mentioned some of the more notable factional struggles, let us now describe them in greater detail. In doing so, we may reveal some of the major causes of the factionalism that has plagued the party in exile.

The Bloque de Defensa de la Revolución

The Bloque was founded in Buenos Aires in December, 1947, by a group of young *febreristas*. Its purposes, as stated in its Act of Founding were: (1) to gather, organize, and discipline the leaders of the party; (2) to direct the forces of the left within the party; (3) to maintain a consistently revolutionary position in party dealings with other political groups, both national and international; (4) to defend the anti-imperialistic principles of *febrerismo;* (5) to demand the holding of a Febrerista Constitutional Convention; (6) to work for the Bloque's eventual control of the party; and (7) to spread propaganda for the Bloque and to indoctrinate other *febreristas* with its principles. Among the original signers of this act were Raimundo Careaga and Domingo Bañuelos, who had recently worked with the Resistance Committee inside Paraguay; Agustín Loncharich, the party's secretary general; and Ricardo Franco, the secretary of organization.[2] Considering the importance of these men as party leaders, it can be seen that the Bloque began with considerable strength on its side.

Unity was short-lived within the Bloque, however. On the one hand there were the true Marxist radicals, led by Miguel Angel Soler (hijo), Victor Ojeda, and Badri Yampey, who wished to bring the party over to a pro-Soviet position. The other group, led by Ricardo Franco, Agustín Loncharich, Carlos Zelada, and Arevalo Paris, were simply party dissidents who wished to supplant the institutionalist old guard—Stefanich, Yegros, and other first generation *febreristas*. The split between these two groups, only a few weeks after the Bloque's formation, came at a meeting in which working papers presented by Zelada were attacked by Soler and Ojeda as "not corresponding to an organization of leftist *febreristas*." Elections to name a directorate for the Bloque resulted in defeat for Ricardo Franco and his group, whereupon they withdrew from participation.[3]

This left the party divided into three groups: the institutionalists, the bloquistas, and Ricardo Franco's sizeable personal following. It would probably be true to say that the institutionalists represented a plurality of the party's membership. Moreover, they could count upon the crucial support of General Rafael Franco, the party's most prestigious figure by far.[4] Ricardo Franco's group, however, included the party's secretary of organization (himself) and the secretary general. By controlling these two key posts, it had the probable advantage of being able to mobilize its support, through the close contacts of the secretary of the organization with the lower party committees. Consequently, this group sent a note to General Franco in November, 1948, demanding that the CEN comply with its duty to call a constitutional convention. By striking early it might win the elections and dominate the convention. General Franco countered this by appointing a commission to "study" the question and to make

2. Concentración Revolucionaria Febrerista, Comité de Resistencia, *Construyendo el febrerismo*, p. 16.

3. *Ibid.*, p. 17.

4. Rafael Franco received his title of "General" from the Revolutionary Army in 1947.

recommendations. Several months later this commission reported that October 23, 1949, might be considered as election day, but October passed without action from the CEN. Finally, in December, General Franco made a declaration to the effect that to allow elections at that time would mean "the usurpation of the sovereignty of the revolutionary citizenry by a regimented, antidemocratic and fraudulent party convention." He also directly attacked Ricardo Franco and his group for attempting to hold elections before it could be ascertained by the Resistance Committee whether the great majority of the party's members in Paraguay could even vote or send delegates to a convention. Ten days later a meeting of the CEN agreed to postpone the elections until June 15, 1950.[5] In this way the institutionalists had outmaneuvered Ricardo Franco who, after the general's declaration, had lost all possibility of winning an election.

During these months the *Bloque* had been busy organizing. Its first step was to set up a Labor Secretariat in Exile to coordinate labor groups, receive information from them and either use such information directly "for the party's benefit" or transmit it to the proper party organ.[6] Active campaigning by the Bloque among exiled workers resulted in the secretariat's growth until it eventually stood as a challenge to the importance of the Labor Department of the CEN. This again brought the Bloque into conflict with Ricardo Franco, who in addition to being the secretary of organization was also the secretary of labor. This conflict became an open struggle at a Labor Assembly held in Buenos Aires on February 13, 1949. The assembly had been prepared by the *bloquistas,* but they had asked permission to hold it from Ricardo Franco in order that it might be recognized as an official party assembly. Franco's conditions were that he preside at the meeting and prepare the agenda. These were agreed to by the bloquistas,

---

5. C.R.F., *Construyendo el febrerismo,* pp. 53-55.

6. *Ibid.,* p. 29. Such activities were hardly compatible with Article 47 of the constitution, which read: "The CEN will be connected directly with all the party's organizations, within the country and in exile, through its authorized agencies. Correspondence will be exchanged directly with the Presidents of the Committees and will be signed by the corresponding authorities of the CEN. No other form of contact will have official validity nor should be taken into consideration by the party."

but once the meeting had started a motion from the floor demanded that the presiding officer be elected by the assembly. Despite Franco's protests, the motion was carried and he was replaced by a *bloquista*. Next, the agenda was changed, again over the protests of Ricardo Franco and his group. The meeting was dissolved finally in the midst of chaotic personal abuse and threats.[7] Nonetheless, the *bloquistas* had scored a victory and proven themselves capable of gaining ground within the labor sector of the party.

Towards the end of 1949, Badri Yampey, Domingo Bañuelos, and other *bloquistas* began to re-enter Paraguay for the purpose of organizing in Asunción and, by this route, eventually taking over the leadership of the Resistance Committee, then headed by José A. Huidobro and Carlos Chávez del Valle. It had weathered the worst of the "Colorado Terror" but was still living an uneasy existence. Since Huidobro and Chávez del Valle were largely out of touch with the party in exile, they welcomed the new arrivals as additional strength for the resistance. The feud that was to wrack the committee came only a few months later when the *bloquistas*, sensing Chávez del Valle's animosity towards the CEN, attempted to win him over to their group. At his request, they presented him with a copy of their booklet, "Minimal Program of Struggle and Work for the Labor Department of the Concentracion Revolucionaria Febrerista."[8] The main points of this program were:

1. Adhesion to the CTAL (Confederación de Trabajadores de America Latina), the pro-Communist labor movement headed by Lombardo Toledano of Mexico.

2. Emphasis on class struggle. According to the Bloque, "Modern unionism is Marxist and therefore revolutionary and class-based . . . By definition, structured action in workers' organizations should be leftist, and leftism, in order to be revolutionary, is based on Marxist principles in the struggle against capitalist exploitation." The *bloquistas* could point to the "Declaration of Principles of the Club Pedro P. Sarmaniego" to defend the legitimacy of this view within the

---

7. *Ibid.,* pp. 93-96.
8. *Ibid.,* pp. 97-101.

Concentración. Nevertheless, the multi-class character of the party was a major given, as the *bloquistas* themselves admitted further on: "The Concentración Revolucionaria is a multi-class movement [and therefore] it seems logical that disparate interpretations should exist among its members with respect to this question . . . [But] within the CRF we are not, and cannot be, ideologically identical. Different social classes can defend common interests and be integrated by a program of struggle only in certain stages. These stages cannot be permanent. They are only a certain step in the revolutionary process."

3. Rejection of the so-called "third position" in the struggle between the United States and the Soviet Union as being dishonest. Although the *bloquistas* did not accept the Soviet model as "ideal" for the economic development of Paraguay, "considering the necessity of defining our position in the case of the present [international] struggle, *we are decidedly with Russia.*"

Chávez del Valle flatly rejected this program and told the *bloquistas* that he considered them Communists, not *febreristas*. From that point on the Resistance Committee was divided.

Meanwhile, in Buenos Aires the institutionalists and Ricardo Franco were reaching a *rapproachement* based on the need to close party ranks against the *bloquistas*. Instead of calling the Constitutional Convention scheduled for June, 1950, Juan Stefanich, the acting president of the party, called for a National Party Conference for April 15, 1950. Its object was to discuss the *Bloque,* but attendance was by personal invitation only. This kept the *bloquistas* from being represented. The conference fixed December, 1951, as the date for convoking the Constitutional Convention and, needless to say, recommended to the CEN that the *bloquistas* be expelled from the party for "subversion and indiscipline."

The only avenue now left to the Bloque was to capture the Resistance Committee and turn the fight into one between the organization within Paraguay and the exiles. Therefore, the *bloquistas* in Asunción organized the Second Workers' Congress, held on March 5, 1950. Although Huidobro and

Chávez del Valle could not prevent the holding of this congress, they were determined to prevent it from exercising any control over the resistance. As was expected, despite the protests of the resistance leaders as to the legality of the congress, the *bloquistas* got the endorsement of the majority of the participants for their program. They also elected a labor secretary of the resistance, but when the *bloquistas* moved to vote on the incorporation of the labor secretary as part of the directorate of the Resistance Committee, Huidobro and Chávez del Valle flatly announced in advance to the congress that, no matter what the outcome of the vote, they would not collaborate with the labor secretary. This time it was the *bloquistas'* protests that were ignored, for they were powerless to overrule this decision legally. Article 33 of the constitution of the Concentración stated that the secretary general of the resistance—in this case, Huidobro—had the sole authority to direct and control the party organization within Paraguay.

Chávez and Huidobro then called upon the resistance leaders in the interior for support. On April 15, some seven weeks after the Second Workers' Congress, the assembled leaders of the resistance voted to expel the *bloquistas*. With this move the *bloquistas* had been outmaneuvered a second time. Although a Third Workers' Congress was held in late 1950 to repudiate both the National Party Conference and the conference of resistance leaders, the bulk of the party's apparatus now stood against the Bloque. The final move came at the Constitutional Convention. Fifteen of the *bloquista* leaders were expelled from the party, and another twenty-five were suspended for an indefinite period.

This was the first major "purge" in the Febrerista party. The defeat of the Bloque had important ramifications. First, it defined the ideological boundaries somewhat more clearly by rejecting the concept of class struggle and emphasizing the multi-class character of the party. Moreover, it placed the party squarely within the democratic-socialist camp and specifically with the West. Second, the expulsions marked a climax in the trend towards centralization and integration. Most of those disciplined had formerly been members of the Club Pedro P. Sarmaniego and as such had participated in the founding of the Concentración Revolucionaria Febrerista. These men were, then, the victims of a process that had begun with autonomous groups—each with its own statutes and directorate—being integrated first into the COR, then into the Concentración, and finally merged entirely into the Partido Revolucionaria Febrerista. From a loose confederation of disparate groups, *febrerismo* had become a relatively disciplined, integrated hierarchy.

The Vanguardia Febrerista

Unlike the Bloque, the Vanguardia's differences with the CEN were not ideological, nor was this an attempt by its leader, Arnaldo Valdovinos, to form a new party. This dispute arose, chiefly, over the question of tactics. A related issue was whether *febreristas* could appeal to moral considerations to justify political activities in contradiction to orders from the CEN. Valdovinos claimed that in 1958, at the time the Vanguardia was founded, over half a million Paraguayans —about one-third of the country's population—were living in exile. He also accused the party leadership of doing nothing significant to promote the revolution that would allow these people to return.[9]

Arnaldo Valdovinos had a well-established reputation as a thorny critic of institutionalist leadership. He had begun his career in *febrerismo* as the second vice-president of the Chaco War Veterans' Association, just under Elpidio Yegros in command. He broke with Yegros and Stefanich early in the February Revolution over what he considered were the government's too-cautious policies with respect to labor and social reform. Never one to hold his opinions quietly, he kept up a blistering attack against the government in his newspaper, *El Diario*. Eventually his denunciations of the revolutionary cabinet became so violent and personal that he was exiled.

Nevertheless, when the various *febrerista* sectors met in Montevideo, in October, 1945, Arnaldo Valdovinos was there to participate in the founding of the Concentración Revolucionaria Febrerista. Moreover, since he enjoyed great re-

---

9. Speech by Dr. Arnaldo Valdovinos (Montevideo, Uruguay, February 17, 1959).

spect, both among the Chaco War veterans and the younger generation of the revolutionary clubs, he was elected the Concentración's second vice-president and was also put on the Political Committee, whose function was to keep in contact with other Paraguayan political groups. The coalition government with Morínigo and the Colorados was his project. Not only did he negotiate the pact, but he had to fight against strong opposition from a majority of the CEN in order to get the party to eventually ratify it.

Under the coalition government, Valdovinos held the posts of minister of agriculture and minister of industry and commerce. Hardly a "radical" with respect to tactics, he bitterly fought the CEN's resolution to withdraw *febrerista* representation from the cabinet and walked out of the meeting in disgust when the vote went against him. Nor was he a "radical" in his ideology. As second vice-president of the party at the 1951 Constitutional Convention, he voted to expel the *bloquistas.* In sum, Arnaldo Valdovinos was a leader of unquestioned brilliance and forcefulness, who had repeatedly clashed with Stefanich and Yegros over questions of strategy and tactics. Impatient and irascible, he posed a serious threat to the CEN's control over the rank and file. His charismatic character, wedded to a program of direct, violent action, appealed to those exiles who could wait no longer for "the return."

The Vanguardia Febrerista described itself as "a movement of opinion" within the party. It disclaimed any intention to speak for the party as a whole, to represent it officially, or "to supplant . . . the present authorities."[10] It might be termed a pressure group formed inside the party, demanding action from what it considered a slow-moving CEN. It was resolved to pursue, in any case, what it considered its moral imperatives: (1) an open declaration of war against the Stroessner dictatorship, (2) direct, violent action—guerrilla warfare, (3) the moving of the party's seat of command from Buenos Aires to "some secret place within the country [Paraguay] or the

10. Jefatura de Coordinación del Comando de la Vanguardia Febrerista, *Posición del Comando de la Vanguardia Febrerista en la lucha contra la dictadura del Paraguay.* (Buenos Aires: January 30, 1959).

Exterior," and (4) the formation of a "national revolutionary front" with other parties or groups. The Vanguardia offered to put all of its resources, its members, and its accumulated arms and munitions at the disposal of the CEN if it would pursue those tactics. If the CEN should refuse, the Vanguardia members considered it their right and duty as Paraguayan citizens to act on their own initiative.[11]

The Vanguardia might be seen as a result of several factors related to the pressures of exile. In the first place, the *febreristas* had been exiled some twelve years, since the civil war of 1947. For many of them, especially the uneducated or poorly educated, these were years of economic hardship. They lived either in the slums that ring Buenos Aires or in the Argentine frontier towns, from which they could see their country just across the river. Exile also creates many psychological pressures. According to Dr. Roberto Doria Medina, a Bolivian psychologist, in a report to the Eighth Argentine Congress on Mental Health:

> The impact of these hardships on their minds results in pathological symptoms that make them bad mixers and lead them to self-ostracism.
> They find it difficult to get work owing to lack of personal papers, lack of license to exercise their careers and also mistrust of employers.
> Thus, the exile's difficulties push him down in the social scale and he is compelled to take jobs that are below his capacity and cultural standard. He feels underestimated, humiliated and undervalued.
> The fact that the frontiers of his country are closed to him and the loss of contact with the problems of his people and family lead to anguish and loneliness and to an overpowering urge to return.[12]

Dr. Doria Medina goes on to describe the exile as a person constantly waiting for an amnesty or the success of "his revolution." He works and longs, "often in a mere wishful-thinking mood, because the very intensity of his day-dreaming distorts the real facts for him."

Twelve years of exile have additional pressures of a more

---

11. *Ibid.*
12. *New York Times,* January 10, 1965.

rational sort. For instance, there is the experience of many parents who view with alarm the "foreignization" of their children; many of these children who were born in exile or were very young when their parents left Paraguay grow up without much attachment to their parents' homeland. They often do not learn Guaraní, feel little interest in Paraguayan culture or history, have little desire to live there, and do not consider themselves Paraguayans.

Other factors can be added to such considerations to explain why violent action became a popular tactic in the years 1958 to 1960. The failure of the party's leaders, both radical and institutionalist, to give effective direction caused frustration among the party members. Moreover, the political scene in Argentina had changed and seemed more favorable, since the fall of Perón had deprived Stroessner of a valuable ally. Lastly, in Venezuela the Acción Democrática party had just overthrown the dictator, Pérez Jiménez. Acción Democrática's triumph seemed like a perfect model to many *febreristas,* and the two parties' similarity of principles made Acción Democrática a likely source of support, now that it was in power.

It is not entirely certain what source armed the Vanguardia. It is strongly alleged, however, that these supplies came from the Argentine military government, which, since it was so strongly anti-Perón, would look with favor upon Stroessner's downfall. The first important guerrilla strike was at a military post in the town of Colonel Bogado, on April 1, 1958. The invaders managed to secure a few arms and munitions but lost several of their own men in the attack. Although Stroessner protested to the Argentine authorities, guerrilla activity now became more frequent along the border.

Meanwhile, the Febrerista party held its Second National Convention in July, 1958. Although the institutionalists had won a sweeping victory in the elections, the platform adopted by the convention seemed very similar to that of the Vanguardia: "struggle without pause against the Dictatorship" and the formation of a national front. The convention then went on to note that certain sectors within the party were pursuing a parallel course of action that was "weakening the "party's vitality and creating a climate of internal confusion." The new CEN promised to integrate all sectors of the party and impose discipline: "Without discipline, the party's progress is made impossible. Through lack of it, action is dispersed into marginal activities, led by different groups, each one of which pretends to interpret better the party's postulates and objectives and the way to secure them. This system menaces the party's unity, strength and hierarchy, and carries within itself the germ of anarchy.[13]

Nevertheless, the Vanguardia continued to operate independently. Its leaders were unconvinced, apparently, that the institutionalists really meant to support guerrilla action. General Franco attempted conciliation with Vanguardia leaders in Buenos Aires at a meeting held in their headquarters on January 30, 1959, but he failed to achieve the Vanguardia's subordination to the CEN. Franco issued a report of this meeting to all party members on the following day, calling the Vanguardia, "the fullest, most categorical and arrogant insurrection against the norms and authorities that govern the party's life." He said that he would submit a fuller report to the CEN so that that body might adopt the necessary measures to deal with the Vanguardia, and made a final appeal to the Vanguardia to reincorporate itself voluntarily into the regular party organization.[14]

The Vanguardia continued to ignore the CEN. Perhaps this was because, while its own guerrillas were active along the border, the regular party leaders had so far taken no direct action of this sort. Perhaps the murder of Raul Ferrari Valdovinos, the Vanguardia leader's brother, allegedly by Stroessner's agents in the Argentine frontier town of Pirané, increased the guerrilla's determination. On February 18 the CEN, acting on Franco's report, informed the party that no unofficial group of *febreristas* could pretend to plan and to execute party strategy. It disavowed the activities of the Van-

---

13. Partido Revolucionario Febrerista, Segunda Convención Ordinaria, *Linea politica* (Exile, 1958).

14. From the text of a note received by the Buenos Aires Regional Committee from General Rafael Franco, dated January 31, 1959, and published by the Regional Committee on February 6.

guardia and instructed all regional and local committees to give that organization no support. A copy of this declaration was sent to the party's Tribunal of Conduct, along with disciplinary recommendations. The Tribunal of Conduct convened on April 24 and, in a report issued the following day, decided unanimously that the Vanguardia's leaders be suspended from the party.[15]

In May, 1959, President Stroessner lifted the state of siege. The chief reason for this was probably the serious split within the Colorado party. By this time the "democratic" Colorados had gained the upper hand within the party and were demanding a liberalization of the regime. It is impossible to say with any certainty that this could be attributed to pressure brought on by the guerrilla invasions, but it might be remembered that Fidel Castro's revolution had triumphed in Cuba only five months before. In any case, many Liberal and *febrerista* exile leaders returned to Paraguay, and public meetings of the opposition parties were held for the first time since 1946. Unfortunately, this respite lasted only thirty-three days, when student demonstrations against an increase in bus fares led to clashes with the police and finally to antigovernment riots. The state of siege was reinstated, and the opposition leaders were sent back to exile. This time they were joined by the "democratic" Colorado leaders, who became the victims of a sweeping party purge. The result of this turmoil was to bring together the Liberal and Febrerista parties. On August 27, 1959, they signed a pact establishing the Unión Nacional Paraguaya (Paraguayan National Union), a national front against Stroessner.

Soon after the founding of the Unión Nacional Paraguaya, the Vanguardia entered into a similar agreement with the "renovating" Liberals, led by Benjamin Vargas Peña, to form the "14th of May Movement." This group disclaimed any intentions of forming a new party. Its only stated purposes were to overthrow the present government, to abrogate the Constitution of 1940, and to establish a revolutionary government that would guarantee free elections within twelve

---

15. "Informative Bulletin" of the Buenos Aires Regional Committee, November, 1961.

months and a National Constitutional Assembly within four years. The "14th of May Movement" was soon split, however, by a struggle for leadership between Arnaldo Valdovinos and Dr. Vargas Peña. Valdovinos apparently made a trip abroad, allegedly to Venezuela, where he secured a large sum of money to finance the movement's activities, but upon his return he found Vargas Peña in control of the movement. Valdovinos then withdrew, taking the money. The "14th of May" became even further divided over a feud between Vargas Peña and Juan José Rotela, who led an invasion on the port of Encarnación which was quickly crushed by the army and the *py nandí*. Most of the guerrillas were rounded up and executed. By the end of 1960, the "14th of May Movement" had become demoralized. As for the Vanguardia, it had broken up over the question of whether to continue in the "14th of May" or retire with Valdovinos. From that point on, guerrilla activity became sporadic and was carried on only in small, isolated groups. This rejection of guerrilla tactics by all but a few exiles reflected an awareness that, in the first place, the Paraguayan terrain is not well suited to such activity. Also, after Rotela's invasion, it was discovered that such ventures only brought harsh government reprisals against known party members in Paraguay, who might otherwise be tolerated. Lastly, unlike the military government that preceded it, Arturo Frondizi's administration in Argentina was promoting friendlier relations with Paraguay. Military aid to the exiles was cut off, and their activities became restricted.

The Movimiento Revolucionario Paraguayo

This organization was more or less the personal vehicle of Ricardo Franco, the former secretary of organization (1946-54). A *caudillo* with a long history of struggles against both radicals and institutionalists within *febrerismo*, it is difficult to say whether his revolt was based on ideological, tactical, or personal grounds. Whatever the case may have been, his following was attracted mainly by his charismatic personality, and it was he and no one else who was the driving force behind the MRP.

Ricardo Franco's political career began in high school

when, during the period just after the fall of the February Revolution, he was the president of the Febrerista Union of Secondary Students. He became one of the original members of the club Pedro P. Sarmaniego, and in 1945 he was the club's delegate to the convention in Montevideo to found the Concentración Revolucionaria Febrerista. In 1946 he was made the representative of the Association of Commercial and Industrial Employees to the Consejo Obrero Paraguayo (Paraguayan Workers' Council), the national labor confederation during the days of the coalition government. Even today many older *febrerista* leaders admit to having been impressed by Ricardo Franco's capabilities. He has been described as highly intelligent and seemingly tireless, spending almost all of his time in party work, often taking on the tasks of other, less motivated members. As a result, his rise was rapid in the party. He became the secretary of organization in the Concentración Revolucionaria—a key post as we have seen—while only in his late twenties, and it was in this capacity that he built up his following.

It seems, however, that for this young *caudillo* the party's old guard—the first generation leaders of the February Revolution era—presented a frustrating barrier to his desire to rise to the very top of the party hierarchy. Respected as he was, it seems likely that he felt over-shadowed by such leaders as General Franco, Juan Stefanich, Elpidio Yegros, Arnaldo Valdovinos, and Roque Gaona, whose long revolutionary careers gave them still more prestige. This might explain why later the Movimiento Revolucionario Paraguayo claimed March 7, 1947—the date of the revolt in Concepción—instead of February 7, 1936, as its birthdate.

Ricardo Franco's history as a *febrerista* follows an apparently erratic course. He was one of the founders of the Bloque de Defensa de la Revolución, which had been formed to oust the institutionalists from control of the party. When he failed to become its leader, he joined forces with the institutionalists to expel the Bloque from the party. During the same period, he was one of the chief critics of the CEN for its failure to give more active support to the Resistance Committee. However, when the Resistance Committee removed his friend, Huidobro, as its secretary general, he undermined it. In 1954 he joined the Benigno Perrota to defeat the institutionalists at the First National Convention in 1954 but soon split with Perrota over the parceling out of seats on the CEN. After withdrawing from this pact, he joined the institutionalists in opposition to the CEN. He headed his own electoral list in 1958 but was decisively defeated by the institutionalists' landslide victory. Nevertheless, the institutionalists, respecting his large following in Buenos Aires, appointed him president of the Regional Committee there. Later he was made one of the *febrerista* representatives on the Executive Committee of the Unión Nacional Paraguaya. In 1959 he supported the CEN's suspension of the Vanguardia Febrerista leaders for their pursuit of guerrilla activities in contradiction to party orders. In the following year, he also began to form his own corps of guerrillas.

It was the way in which Franco financed these guerrillas which, more than anything, led to his expulsion from the party. In May, 1959, he was commissioned by the CEN to travel abroad—allegedly to Venezuela—as an official representative of the Febrerista party in order to obtain aid from a "sister party." He was given the necessary credentials and letters of presentation by the CEN to make his contacts. The mission was successful in securing an apparently large sum of money, but on his return Ricardo Franco made no move to deliver the money to the CEN and instead deposited it in his personal account. All attempts by CEN representatives to obtain the transfer of this money were unsuccessful. In fact, General Rafael Franco, the party's president, was unable to obtain even an interview with him during a visit to Buenos Aires in September, 1960. The general finally sent Ricardo Franco a letter, dated September 8, 1960, in which he demanded an accounting. Ricardo Franco's reply of September 12 left no doubt as to his position and intentions. He accused the CEN of failing to take any decisive action against Stroessner and of "living in legality [in Paraguay] while modest guerrillas are being killed and mutilated in our jungles." The money, he said, would remain in his possession in order to buy arms for guerrilla squads. Such arms would belong to him and his troops, not to the party. In conclusion, he said that he was following in the "heroic tradition" of the Nicaraguan patriot, Sandino, and the "men of the Sierra Maestra."

General Franco's reply the following day informed Ricardo that he would recommend his expulsion from the party to the CEN. He was told that his failure to turn the money over to the party, after having used party credentials to obtain it, would be considered fraud and theft, not only against the Febrerista party, but against those who had given the money. In defending the CEN, General Franco pointed out that many of them had been abused by the Paraguayan police, that others had been exiled, and that some were still prisoners. Concerning the charge of "legalism," the general replied that in May, 1959, the party had taken advantage "of a tactical maneuver of the dictatorship—the lifting of the State of Siege—in order to take to the streets, mobilize the masses . . . and reinforce its internal structure." At the same time, the party's clandestine activities had never been interrupted. General Franco also pointed out that the Second National Convention had pledged to use a variety of tactics, including peaceful ones, such as negotiations with the government to grant political amnesty. Lastly, Ricardo Franco was reminded that only a short while earlier he had stood with the CEN against Arnaldo Valdovinos' Vanguardia Febrerista when the question of guerrilla tactics first arose in the party.[16]

Ricardo Franco's justification of his insubordination can be gathered from a series of pamphlets and circulars that he published throughout 1961. The main thesis of his stand against the regular party organization can be stated in two propositions:

1. There are two main currents in the anti-Stroessner camp. First, there are the institutionalists: "conservatives," "electoralists," "legalists," or "continuists." The terms are interchangeable. These include the leaders of the Febrerista and Liberal parties, united in the Unión Nacional Paraguaya, as well as the Christian Democrats and "democratic" Colorados (Movimiento Popular Colorado). This "opposition" seeks no

---

16. Comité Regional de Emergéncia de la Regional Buenos Aires, *Boletín interno*, October, 1960.

greater changes in the present situation than a political amnesty and free elections. They simply want to be able to return to Paraguay, engage in business, and have their property protected. They envision no true social revolution—only a periodic change of political parties, all representing the same ruling elite. In short, Paraguayan politics today is nothing but a squabble among different sectors of the same oligarchy. Therefore, this oligarchy rejects the idea of a violent, fundamental change in the society and is interested only in negotiating a pact of reunification. This is why the *febrerista* and Liberal leaders try to prevent guerrilla invasions; they are afraid of repeating the Cuban experience.[17]

2. The revolutionary position, on the other hand, believes in declaring total war against the government and the coalition of oligarchs and foreign imperialists who support it. It seeks a massive insurrection, to be initiated through guerrilla invasions. Once in power, the revolutionaries will achieve a thorough-going change through state ownership of "all land, water resources, subsoil and topsoil wealth, and (will direct) the rational exploitation of these according to a complete plan of economic development."[18] The revolutionary position is to be distinguished from the Communist party, however, in that it is a *national* movement and owes no allegiance to the Soviet Union.

Ricardo Franco's rebellion was short-lived; he was formally removed from his post as president of the Buenos Aires Regional Committee on September 15, 1960. This move was countered by a note from that committee informing General Franco that as of September 17 the Buenos Aires regional would sever all relations with the CEN and that it was declaring its independence from the party. This rebellion was met by a CEN-ordered intervention of the Buenos Aires regional. Cecilio Recalde and Julio Oscar Appleyard were appointed the party's interventors to set up an emergency committee in Buenos Aires. By December of the same year, the

17. Movimiento Revolucionario Paraguayo, *La revolución nacional y el problema de las "izquierdas" en el Paraguay* (Buenos Aires, 1961).

18. Movimiento Revolucionario Paraguayo, *Nuevo ideario nacional: Documento fundamental del Movimiento Revolucionario Paraguayo,* (Buenos Aires, 1961), p. 12.

new committee reported to the CEN that it had consolidated its position and was in control of the party apparatus. Ricardo Franco's Movimiento Revolucionario Paraguayo continued to operate as a parallel committee, publishing a stream of pamphlets and manifestos, but by the end of 1961 his following had dwindled to a handful. It appears that, despite trips to the Argentine frontier, he was unable to win over any of the local committees there, and it is doubtful that his guerrilla forces ever functioned. Confined for the most part to Buenos Aires, the Movimiento Revolucionario Paraguayo has dissipated itself almost entirely in a futile war of pamphlets.

The Final Split

The sanctions applied against the Bloque, the Vanguardia, and the Movimiento Revolucionario Paraguayo did not put an end to the issues that those groups had publicized. Although each of these dissident groups had represented a minority within the party, it was not clear what might result if they should ever combine their forces. This coalition of dissident forces finally did occur in 1961, as the time drew near for the Third National Convention. This time the opposition to the institutionalists was headed by Dr. Benigno Perrota, a physician who had led the radicals to victory in 1954 and had served as secretary general of the party from 1954 to 1958. Perrota had been involved in the guerrilla invasions of 1959, during which he was captured, and he had spent three years in the prison camp at Peña Hermosa before escaping. In Perrota, then, the radicals had a party notable, a "martyr," and a man committed to armed action. The radical faction, called "Democracia y Revolución," also had other well-known leaders, such as Arturo Acosta Mena, a young lawyer who also had spent time in Stroessner's prisons, and Raimundo Careaga, a former resistance leader and *bloquista*.

Perrota's electoral campaign began during the later stages of Ricardo Franco's revolt. Although Ricardo Franco and Perrota were cool towards each other after their dispute in 1954, many of Ricardo's supporters—most notably Manuel Cibils and Ignacio Iramain—joined Perrota's movement in order to oppose the institutionalists *en bloc.* Similarly, the remnants of Arnaldo Valdovinos' Vanguardia Febrerista, now almost totally defunct, threw their support to Perrota in protest against the incumbent CEN. On September 11, 1961, some three months before the elections, a pact was signed among several dissident factions to support Perrota for the presidency. This was the first time in the party's history that an electoral list had failed to nominate General Franco for that post! These groups also agreed upon a platform, which was published in a manifesto entitled *Bases de integración política del sector revolucionario del Partido Revolucionario Febrerista.* Of the twenty-one people who signed this document, ten had actively participated in previous dissident movements. Two had been expelled and two others suspended from the party by the 1951 convention for their participation in the Bloque. Two others were under suspension as Vanguardia leaders. Of the other four, one was in the Vanguardia but had escaped being suspended; and the other three had been supporters of Ricardo Franco.

The platform of this electoral list, which was called "List 17 Febrero," was also an amalgam of previous dissident programs. In order to clarify fully the differences between this list and that of the institutionalists relative to the campaign issues in 1961, their platforms will be presented and contrasted.

THE REVOLUTION

List 17 Febrero: If what oppresses us is a structure (and evidently it is), there can be no revolution until this structure collapses. The large *latifundios* were created to hold and maintain a monopoly over extractive resources. If they are not destroyed, there will be no revolution. . . . Precisely to prevent this inevitable process, imperialism is hurrying to provide a revolution of liberal inspiration for the underdeveloped countries of Latin America. . . . To pretend to escape from underdevelopment by this liberal "revolution" that they offer us from abroad is like trying to escape from a pit by pulling the dirt in.[19]

---

19. Benigno Perrota, *Orientadora y patriotica respuesta del partido revolucionario febrerista a la tirania y a la honda crisis que sufre la nación* (n.p., 1963?), p. 10.

Institutionalists: . . . the first step will be a radical change in the system of land tenure, based today in the *latifundio*, democratizing it to the point of bringing Agrarian Reform to its full achievement. . . . The rhythm and means of accomplishment will, in every case, be in direct and immediate relation to the degree of opposition the reactionaries may present.[20]

CAPITALISM

List 17 Febrero: When we characterize the country's existing regime as a semifeudal and semicolonial structure . . . it is because there is a capitalist mode of production in the exploitation of salaried workers in the cities and factories. . . .[21]

Institutionalists: [Febrerismo] opposes to capitalism as a form of human exploitation . . . the concept that capital should always be at the service of man and society as an instrument of welfare and progress. . . . It recognizes the right of private property, but [it must be] subjected in its exercise to the fulfillment of a social function.[22]

THE UNITED STATES

List 17 Febrero: [Our program is] to make clear constantly to the people's conscience that the present tyranny is nothing but the political manifestation of powerful national and international interests [semifeudalism and imperialism]. . . .[23] [*American imperialism*] dominates Paraguay by seizing the high positions of command and through the dollars it distributes so "generously." It dominates economic centers, politics, universities, and other cultural centers in the country. It tries to dominate the unions and makes a shameful display of its power, to the point where the Department of State becomes the anteroom of the Presidential Palace. The Embassy controls business leaders; the F.B.I. acts as an advisor; the Yankee military missions direct our armed forces, and their command, centered in Panama, repeatedly sends its greetings through the provision of war materials for the defense of successive tyrannies. Its interventionists work in the different ministries and the whole nation falls under their control. It controls commerce, imports, and exports. The country imports the most luxurious automobiles while peasants continue tilling their rented land with

20. General Rafael Franco, *Carta a la ciudadania febrerista* (Montevideo, 1961), p. 3.

21. Perrota, *Orientadora y patriotica respuesta,* p. 9.

22. *Febrero* (Febrerista monthly newspaper), Buenos Aires, May, 1963, p. 3.

23. *Bases de integración política del sector revolucionario del partido revolucionario febrerista,* Part II, Section 4 (Buenos Aires, September 11, 1961).

wooden plows. Small national industries are eliminated in the name of free trade. . . . The present tyranny is nothing but the public and unconcealed expression of American imperialism.[24]

Institutionalists: The anti-imperialism of *febrerismo* is integral and expresses itself against all forms of penetration having the object of subjugation and exploitation, whether from the West or from those countries enslaved by totalitarianism. The Communists and their fellow-travelers only cultivate, clamorously, anti-Yankeeism, responding thus to the demands of Soviet strategy. The erroneous policies of America's Department of State towards Latin America, with its obsessive aid to reactionary dictators . . . has given them, one must admit, their best arguments.[25]

INTERNATIONAL STAND OF FEBRERISMO

List 17 Febrero: . . . an international policy of permanent defense of national interests, of national self-determination, and of independence in relation to the rival blocs of nations.[26]

Institutionalists: [*The party*] ratifies its position of unequivocal support for the democratic world and opposition to all totalitarianism, whether it be from the left or the right.[27]

THE CUBAN REVOLUTION

List 17 Febrero: Expresses its solidarity with the Cuban people, supporting their national revolution of political, economic, and social liberation, and repudiating all foreign interventionist action threatening their self-determination . . . [and] extends its expression of support to the peoples of Algeria, the Congo, Puerto Rico, and other peoples of the world who struggle for the conquest of their independence and self-determination.[28]

Institutionalists: . . . there is an ingredient of pro-Communist penetration that cannot be tolerated, because the ideological purity of the party is then lost. . . . The party has subscribed to a declaration, along with four other revolutionary parties in America, at the Lima Conference, with respect to the Cuban Revolution. In that document our sympathy and support of that revolution as a movement vindicating the legitimate popular and national desires was clearly expressed. But those parties' lines of action were well established in reference

---

24. Perrota, *Orientadora y patriotica respuesta, p. 8.*
25. Elpidio Yegros, *et al., Mensaje a los companeros febreristas* (Buenos Aires, 1961).
26. *Bases de integración política,* Part III, Section 4.
27. *Febrero,* May, 1963, p. 8.
28. *Bases de integración política,* Part III, Sections 5 and 6.

to the present Cuban government's deviation towards communism. In the pact to which you [*List 17 Febrero*] subscribe a position is sustained which is diametrically opposed to that espoused in Lima, plus the aggravating circumstance of limiting yourselves to mentioning your support for the peoples of the Congo, Algeria, and Puerto Rico, leaving in silence the brutal Sino-Soviet actions in subjugating more than seventeen free countries.[29]

PARTY TACTICS

List 17 Febrero: The only way of giving life to the ideals of the nation and the party is by defeating the tyranny. This can be done only by an organized popular struggle along the lines of armed civil insurrection. . . . Any attempt to support the possibility of the tyranny's allowing the country's institutional normalization is contrary to the essence of our struggle, which does not look for the deceitful escape of a formalist democracy.[30]

Institutionalists: There are those who defend exclusively the insurrectional thesis, who cling dogmatically to that position. They admit no alternatives. . . . It must be remembered: both legality and insurrection are valid and viable theses according to the political circumstances.[31]

The problem of party tactics, especially the question of obtaining legalization, is central to the radical-institutionalist split. As we have seen, the radicals reject any attempt to achieve the party's legalization by Stroessner, which would imply its acceptance of the role of "loyal opposition." The institutionalists, on the other hand, claim to be more flexible. Legalization, they argue, would give them more possibilities to "organize our party, regain the broadest possible contacts with the people, and to help them with greater efficiency in the struggle for democracy and the Revolution. This struggle has been carried on in recent years under extremely disadvantageous conditions."[32]

The institutionalists have carried their thesis to temporarily successful conclusion by securing the party's legalization in

---

29. Letter of General Rafael Franco to Drs. Arturo Acosta Mena and Carlos Vásquez, December 9, 1961.

30. Comando de Coordinación del Movimiento Electoral, Lema 17 de Febrero, "Comunicado Interno" (Buenos Aires, October 17, 1961).

31. *Febrero*, September-October, 1964, p. 4.

32. *Ibid.*

August, 1964. The first attempt to reach an agreement with Stroessner was in October, 1963, when they solicited inscription as a legal party before the National Electoral Council. This petition was rejected on the grounds that the Febrerista party is subversive, having promoted the guerrilla invasions of 1958-60. The government also demanded a repudiation of the Unión Nacional Paraguaya. The party's reply of December 2 reminded the government that the guerrilla invasions had been organized outside of the party, contrary to the CEN's orders, and that the instigators had been disciplined. With respect to the Unión Nacional Paraguaya, the party refused to break its agreement with the Liberals. This stalemate was followed during the next few months by a bitter exchange of insults and accusations of bad faith. By August, 1964, however, the Liberal party newspaper, *El Enano,* reported that the government and the *febreristas* had reached an agreement. This was confirmed by an announcement to party members signed by Carlos Caballero Gatti, the first vice-president, and Francisco Sosa Jovellanos, the secretary of organization and acting secretary general.[33] As of this writing the results of legalization are not clear. The party is publishing a weekly newspaper in Paraguay, *El Pueblo,* and is allowed to hold public meetings. Most *febreristas* are eligible to return from exile, including General Rafael Franco. Moreover, it has not been necessary for the party to quit the Unión Nacional Paraguaya, although the Liberal party has not been legalized yet.

The critics of the legalization thesis are not without a strong argument of their own in their belief that "the ruling oligarchy" in Paraguay will never permit *febrerismo* any real freedom to develop. To prove this, they point to the failure of the coalition government from 1946 to 1947 and to the brief period of amnesty granted by Stroessner in May, 1959, which ended in a new wave of political persecution. Real freedom for the Febrerista party, argue these critics, would lead to the overthrow of the present system, for *febrerismo* would dominate Paraguayan politics very quickly if permitted

---

33. *Febrero,* September-October, 1964, pp. 2-3. The party's actual secretary general, Juan Speratti, was still under arrest in Paraguay.

to organize without interference. Since it is absurd, the argument continues, to believe that the "oligarchy" will permit its own destruction willingly, legalization must necessarily be a trap. Either the Febrerista party would have to surrender its principles and accept the role of an ineffective, "tame" opposition, or it would have to act vigorously in demanding its rights. In the latter case the period of legalization would not last.

Party Leadership: A Clash of Generations

The List 17 Febrero leaders carefully attempted to carry out a moderate electoral campaign. A sheet of instructions passed out to its militants warned: "With respect to their [the institutionalists'] insidious campaign: this may tend to make one or several members of our movement adopt an extremist attitude or position. We must show categorically that the movement has an orientation which emanates from the Party's great programmatic principles, which means that it is not linked to any sort of extremism." Nevertheless, the List 17 Febrero leaders left themselves open to institutionalist charges of having Communist sympathies by declaring their support for the Cuban Revolution. With respect to this charge, however, it should be remembered that *Bases de integración política* . . . was drawn up in September, 1961, and Fidel Castro did not declare his adhesion to Marxist-leninism until three months later. After that declaration was made List 17 Febrero dropped the Cuban issue from its propaganda. Nevertheless, the institutionalists drew heavily on List 17 Febrero's uncomfortable position and pointed out that, at the Lima Conference of Popular Parties, the Febrerista party had joined in demanding that the Cuban government pursue its revolution along democratic lines and not become a divisive factor among Latin America's revolutionary forces. This ignored the fact that the signers of the Declaration of Lima had also expressed their solidarity with the Cuban Revolution and had taken a stand against foreign intervention in Cuba in language as strong as that used by List 17 Febrero.

List 17 Febrero made an additional blunder by taking a

position of neutralism in international politics. Since its struggle with the Bloque, the party had been on record as supporting the West against the Communist bloc. Even so, List 17 Febrero's position was more moderate than that which the Bloque had taken. There seems to have been little difference on other issues. In fact, it would seem that tactical rather than ideological questions were at the core of this party struggle.

This campaign might also be seen as a clash between two sets of leaders representing, in general, two different generations in the party. If we examine the party membership we find three more or less distinct generations, or "promotions" —to use the term that the *febreristas* themselves employ. The first promotion refers to those men who were active in the February Revolution of 1936 or in the pre-revolutionary dissident groups, such as the Liga Nacional Independiente, the "dissident" Liberals, or the Asociación Nacional de Ex-Combatientes. The second promotion consists of those *febreristas* who came to play important roles during the period from 1937 to 1951 in the revolt of April 17, 1941, the clubs Pedro P. Sarmaniego or Fermín Franco Delgado, and the Concentración Revolucionaria Febrerista. The third promotion applies to those who joined the party after the Constitutional Convention in 1951.

A simple comparison of the relative degree of representation of each of these three promotions in the institutionalist and List 17 Febrero leadership indicates another important source of cleavage in the party.[34] A list of the National Executive Committee members elected by the institutionalists at the Third Convention in 1962 shows:

Number of Seats on the CEN	25
Members From the First Promotion	11
Members From the Second Promotion	10
Members From the Third Promotion	4

If we add to this the members elected to the Tribunal of Conduct, a sensitive post because of its disciplinary function,

---

34. The following information on "promotions" is based on a number of interviews with *febrerista* leaders of both factions. No official records exist on the topic.

and the Central Electoral Committee, which supervises party elections, we arrive at a total of

Number of Seats	35
First Promotion	17
Second Promotion	14
Third Promotion	4

For the sake of comparison, a list of thirty-seven names of List 17 Febrero . . . was compiled from four sources: (1) the signers of the *Bases de integración política del sector revolucionario del Partido Revolucionario Febrerista,* (2) a booklet published by List 17 Febrero entitled *Tercera Convención Ordinaria: Mensaje a la ciudadania febrerista,* which recounts the events of the Third National Convention, (3) a similar booklet entitled *Informativo y resoluciones de la III Convención Ordinaria al pueblo febrerista,* and (4) the names of List 17 Febrero leaders "expelled from the party by the institutionalists, published in *Boletín Informativo* (Buenos Aires, Regional Committee, June, 1962). It was felt that the names of any List 17 Febrero militants appearing in these documents could be considered as leaders in that movement, although it is not argued that such a list is exhaustive by any means. The representation of the three promotions on this list is in striking contrast to that of the institutionalists:

Number of Leaders	37
First Promotion	6
Second Promotion	28
Third Promotion	3

Such a contrast lends some weight to Dr. Perrota's charge that the institutionalists constitute an "oligarchy of conservatives" who have ruled the party for twenty-six years. However, before we accept this, it is necessary to explore further the composition of the institutionalists, as well as the turnover of leadership within the CEN.

Considering the twenty-five members of the 1962 institutionalist CEN:

1. Eleven had been members of the previous CEN, formed

by the institutionalists in 1958; five of these eleven "repeaters" belong to the second promotion;

2. Six members of the 1962 CEN had been members of the 1951 CEN;

3. Six members of the 1962 CEN had been members of the CEN of the Concentración Revolucionaria Febrerista;

4. Five of the members of the 1962 CEN had been on the CEN of the Unión Nacional Revolucionaria, founded by Juan Stefanich during the February Revolution;

5. Three members of the 1962 CEN had been members of the CEN of the Asociación Nacional de Ex-Combatientes, from 1936 to 1937.

These figures become even more dramatic if we focus just on five key posts in the CEN. These would include the president, both vice-presidents, the secretary general, and the secretary of organization. Concentrating on turn-over in these key posts should result in indications as to (1) the degree to which they are dominated by first-promotion institutionalists, and (2) the degree to which they continue to be held by the same persons. In other words, we wish to see how much control institutionalist "notables" have exercised over key posts throughout the party's history. By "notables" we mean those who have served on one or more of the National Executive Committees, beginning with the Asociación Nacional de Ex-Combatientes or the Unión Nacional Revolucionaria, up to the present. The 1954 CEN has not been included because we are concerned here only with institutionalist notables. It is accepted as fact that Dr. Perrota's victory in 1954 led to a major turnover in the key party posts, and the significance of this will be discussed later.

The Concentración Revolucionaria Febrerista

Post (CRF)	Promotion	Rev. govt. 1936-37	UNR CEN	ANEC CEN	CENs Serving	Key Posts Held
Pres. #1	1	Pres.	Pres.	Pres.	2	2
Pres. #2	1	Minister			2	2
Vice-pres. #1	1	Minister			1	1
Vice-pres. #2	1			Vice-pres.	1	1
Sec. gen.*	1	Mayor	X	Vice-pres.	3	2
Sec. gen.**	1				0	0
Sec. org.	2				0	0

*1945-47. Mayor refers to Asunción, the capital.
**1947-51
X is member of CEN but no key post.

The 1951 CEN

Post (1951)	Promotion	CRF CEN	Rev. govt. 1936-37	UNR CEN	ANEC CEN	CENs Serving	Key Posts Held
Pres.	1	Pres. #1	Pres.	Pres.	Pres.	3	3
Vice-pres. #1	1	Pres. #2	Minister			3	3
Vice-pres. #2	1	Vice-pres. #2	Mayor	X	Vice-pres.	2	2
Sec. gen.		Sec. gen.			Vice-pres.	4	3
Sec. org.	2	Sec. org.				1	1
On CEN		5		4			
Held key post		5		4			

The 1958 CEN

Post (1958)	Promotion	1951 CEN	CRF CEN	Rev. govt. 1936-37	UNR CEN	ANEC CEN	CENs Serving	Key Posts Held
Pres.	1	Pres.	Pres.	Pres.	X	Pres.	4	4
Vice-pres. #1	1	Sec. gen.	Sec. gen.	Mayor	Sec. gen.	Vice-pres.	5	4
Vice-pres. #2	1		X		X		2	1
Sec. gen.	1					Sec. gen.	2	1
Sec. org.	2						0	0
On CEN		2	3		4			
Held key post		2	2		4			

The 1962 Institutionalists CEN

Post (1962)	Promotion	1958 CEN	1951 CEN	CRF CEN	Rev. govt. 1936-37	UNR CEN	ANEC CEN	CENs Serving	Key Posts Held
Pres.	1	Pres.	Pres.	Pres.	Pres.		Pres.	5	5
Vice-pres. #1	1	Sec. gen.				X	Sec. gen.	3	2
Vice-pres. #2	1	Vice-pres. #2		X		Sec. gen.		3	2
Sec. gen.	1	X						1	0
Sec. org.	1	Sec. org.						1	1
On CEN		5	1	2		3			
Held key post		4	1	1		3			

The above tables bring out the following points:

1. In the 1962 CEN, all of the members holding key posts had been *members* of some previous CEN. Four of these five men had held *key posts* in some previous CEN.

2. In the 1958 CEN, four of the five men holding key posts had been members of some previous CEN. The same four had also held key posts in some previous CEN.

3. In the 1951 CEN, all of the men holding key posts had been members of some previous CEN. All had held key posts in some previous CEN.

4. In the CEN of the Concentración Revolucionaria Febrerista, from 1945 to 1947, five of the six men holding key posts had held key posts in some previous CEN or had held key posts in the revolutionary government from 1936 to 1937. From 1947 to 1951 this was reduced to a majority of four out of six.

5. Therefore, in each of these National Executive Committees, a majority—and sometimes all—of the men holding key posts had been members of some previous National Executive Committee. A majority of them also held key posts in some previous National Executive Committee.

6. In 1962 and in 1951 all of the men holding key posts had been members of the immediately preceding CEN. Also, all had held key posts in the immediately preceding CEN, with the exception of the secretary general in 1962.

7. In each of these National Executive Committees, all of the key posts have been controlled by men of the first promotion, with the constant exception of the post of secretary of organization.

8. The man who held the post of secretary of organization has always been of the second promotion. But whenever the institutionalists have won consecutive elections (CRF-1951; 1958-62), the man who held that post in the immediately preceding CEN was reappointed to it.

9. In each of these National Executive Committees, a majority of the men holding key posts had also held one or more key posts in one of the three original institutions of the period of the February Revolution: the revolutionary government, the UNR, or the ANEC.

These facts seem to indicate "oligarchization" within the key posts of the party's National Executive Committee. This might become even clearer through a brief review of the history of factionalism within the party.

The Concentración was designed as a federative party, bringing together both the older revolutionaries and the younger men of the clubs Pedro P. Sarmaniego and Fermín Franco Delgado. Nevertheless, from 1945 to 1947 its key posts were dominated, five to one, by men of the first promotion, all of whom had held key posts in one of the three main institutions of the February Revolution: the government, the UNR, or the ANEC. Only Ricardo Franco, the secretary of organization, represented the second promotion. This relationship was changed with the resignation of Elpidio Yegros as secretary general in 1947 and his replacement by Agustín Loncharich. Although Loncharich belongs to the first promotion, he had served on none of the previous National Executive Committees. Moreover, he was an ally of Ricardo Franco.

The 1951 National Executive Committee reflected a coalition of Ricardo Franco's following and the institutionalists against the *bloquistas*. By this time, however, the institutionalists had become better unified behind the influential figure of General Franco, and their triumph in the party elections gave them a four-to-one majority of key posts. Ricardo Franco was retained as secretary of organization but, with the Bloque defeated, his support was not as crucial as before.

This institutionalist—Ricardo Franco coalition broke up before the 1954 National Party Convention, as Ricardo threw his support behind Benigno Perrota. Perrota's victory overthrew the institutionalist domination of the party, and the radicals became the principal leaders for the first time since the decentralized period from 1937 to 1945. General Franco was retained as president, but the other institutionalist leaders were replaced. Ricardo Franco's subsequent split with Perrota left the latter with an ineffective minority government within the party.

The institutionalists were able to capitalize on this split to win a resounding victory in 1958. Four of the five key posts went to men of the first promotion, all of whom had been members of previous National Executive Committees, and all of whom had held key posts in one of the three main bodies of the February Revolution. Francisco Sosa Jovellanos was appointed secretary of organization but, unlike Ricardo Franco's case, his appointment does not appear to have been a way of appeasing some organized faction. Eight of the twenty-five CEN seats were offered to the opposition, but only four of them were accepted. Perrota continued to serve on the CEN but without a key post.

From the point of view of the List 17 Febrero leaders, then, the party's history might be broken down into certain stages that have ultimately culminated in creating a party oligarchy:

1. *The Pre-Revolutionary Period,* in which the roots of *febrerismo* were laid down by the Liga Nacional Independiente, the "dissident" Liberals, and the Asociación Nacional de Ex-Combatientes.

2. *The February Revolution,* in which the men of the first promotion captured the government. The two main pillars of the revolutionary government were the Asociación Nacional de Ex-Combatientes and the Unión Nacional Revolutionaria. The latter might be seen as a coalition of the Liga Nacional Independiente, the "dissident" Liberals, and other revolutionary groups. The radicals' general view of this period might be summed up in this judgment by Manuel Cibils: "The cabinet was composed almost entirely by members of the Liga Nacional Independiente, whose moderate-center tendency—perhaps too moderate for this revolutionary moment—introduced an excessive slowness in the process of transformation, in disagreement with popular anxiety and demand.[35]

3. *The Period of Decentralization* (1937-45), in which the forces of *febrerismo* were scattered among several autonomous groups. The men of the second promotion acted independently through their revolutionary clubs and formed the vanguard of the fight against Morínigo from within Paraguay. Control by men of the first promotion was minimal; their

---

35. Manuel J. Cibils, *Anarquía y revolución en el Paraguay* (Buenos Aires: Editorial Americalee, 1957), p. 48.

influence was moral rather than organizational. This freedom of action was ended gradually, first by forming the Committee of Revolutionary Organization (COR) and later by the Concentración Revolucionaria Febrerista.

4. *The Institutionalist-Ricardo Franco Coalition,* in which the institutionalists were forced to combine with Ricardo Franco against their common enemy, the Bloque. This resulted in the party's first major purge and began a trend towards the suppression of doctrinal heterogeneity. Also, through this coalition, the men of the first promotion began to re-establish their control over *febrerismo.* The institutionalist—Ricardo Franco coalition was unstable, however, because once the common enemy was defeated the two groups began to compete with each other.

5. *The Radical CEN* (1954-58) came into being when Ricardo Franco left his coalition with the institutionalists and supported Perrota. When this support was withdrawn, Perrota found himself blocked by the combined opposition of Ricardo Franco and the institutionalists. As a result, he was unable to carry on an effective administration of the party.

6. *The Institutionalist Hegemony* (1958-62), in which the institutionalists profited from the reaction to the party's stagnation to defeat both Perrota and Ricardo Franco, who ran on separate lists. Twenty-one of the twenty-five CEN seats were held by institutionalists, and all of the key posts were held by men known to be loyal to that faction. This was the most complete control ever held over the CEN by the institutionalists. Although some of their old leaders were missing, especially Juan Stefanich and Germán Soler, their places had been taken by other notables of the first promotion: Elpidio Yegros; Roque Gaona, the second vice-president; and Carlos Caballero Gatti, the secretary general. All had held posts in the Unión Nacional Revolucionaria during the February Revolution, and Caballero Gatti had been the secretary general of the ANEC. Nevertheless, the slow passing of the first promotion notables can be seen by comparing the above tables as to the number of key figures who had also held important posts in one of the three chief institutions of the February Revolution period. Under the Concentración the number

was five; in 1951 and 1958, the number was four; and by 1962, it had been reduced to three.

The years from 1958 to 1962 proved to be a period of further centralization of authority in the CEN and of greater impositions of conformity in doctrinal and tactical matters. This was the period in which disciplinary action was taken against Arnaldo Valdovinos and Ricardo Franco. It may be significant that expulsions and suspensions have occurred only when the institutionalists were in command.

These facts strongly suggest a tendency within the party for the first promotion notables to keep the key posts in their hands. If we may call this "oligarchization," then oligarchization seems to have become accelerated since 1958.

Since General Rafael Franco has been the undisputed leader—until 1962—of the party since its genesis, his role should be discussed with respect to the phenomena of factionalism and oligarchization. As we have noted, no National Executive Committee, with the exception of the UNR, has ever failed to elect Franco its president. From the time that the Liberating Army, on February 17, 1936, referred to Rafael Franco as "our only authentic leader," it has been evident that he is the leading figure—perhaps the hero—of *febrerismo*. Indeed, until the founding of the Concentración Revolucionaria Febrerista, *febrerismo* was known as the *franquista* movement. The general's role is an extremely complex one. He is a Chaco War hero, a political symbol, and a party leader. As a war hero, he, more than any other *febrerista*, lends prestige to the party. As a political symbol he was used as a banner for every faction within the party—until 1962. As party leader, he has been called upon from time to time to lend his support to one side or the other in factional disputes. The result is a conflict in roles between being, on the one hand, the party's "Great Man" and beyond factional squabbles and being, on the other hand, the leader of the institutionalist faction, taking part in the bitter, intraparty feuds. It is possible to get some idea of this role conflict, as perceived by General Franco himself, through some of his letters to opposition leaders during factional struggles.

The first is an open letter to the party which was published

during the Bloque struggle: "Their desire, perhaps legitimate, to raise unjust accusations and charges which affect me
personally does not impel me to write this memorandum. My
only intention is *to call upon all of the soldiers of the February Revolution* to reflect dispassionately about a problem
which cannot be solved without spiritual serenity and con-
sciousness of responsibility . . .[36]

The second letter is to Ricardo Franco, written just before
the latter's expulsion from the party:

> The only point on which I agree with your opinion is in
> reference to my modest qualities and my limited capacity for
> leadership. The fault is not mine. Since 1936 to the present *my
> name has been attached to all the electoral lists, without my
> ever participating in those battles.* I have asked repeatedly to
> be relieved of the high party function that they have always
> invested me with, perhaps undeservedly. . . .
>
> Twenty-five members compose the CEN; *I listen with satis-
> faction to various opinions and respect the decisions of the
> majority,* without reservations or, even less, with any desire to
> sabotage them. I assume the greatest responsibility because of
> the position I occupy, but no one can accuse me of deviation,
> dishonesty, or of imposing my own will. *I am a party man and
> nothing more.* . . .
>
> I have said that all the electoral lists have proposed me for
> the presidency, which was always granted me by unanimous
> vote, despite my pleas to the contrary. I almost forgot that
> when you were an important electoral factor you voted the
> same way.[37]

The third, and last, letter is to two leaders of List 17
Febrero, Arturo Acosta Mena and Carlos Vásquez: "*I have
never participated in electoral battles,* because of thinking—
precisely—that my conduct might help promote internal
cohesion and unity within the party and movement, as long
as those battles stayed strictly on the party level."[38]

The recurring theme in each of these letters is that General
Franco conceives of himself as being above factional battles

---

36. Quoted in Concentración Revolucionaria Febrerista, Comité
de Resistencia, *Construyendo el febrerismo* (Buenos Aires: Alea, 1951), p.
54. Italics added.

37. Letter to Ricardo Franco, September 13, 1960. Italics added.

38. Letter to Arturo Acosta Mena and Carlos Vásquez, December
9, 1961. Italics added.

("I have never participated in electoral battles"), an impartial "party man" ("I listen with satisfaction to various opinions and respect the decisions of the majority"), the leader of all the *febreristas* ("My name has been attached to all the electoral lists"), and one whose chief role is to "help promote internal cohesion." Nevertheless, he is inevitably drawn into the factional battles because of his role as the "Great Leader" whose moral authority can settle a party issue. His pronouncements against the Bloque, the Vanguardia Febrerista, Ricardo Franco, and List 17 Febrero were major efforts to promote the institutionalists' cause. Once he has taken his stand, of course, he becomes a target for criticism by the opposition; he has been described by the Bloque as "authoritarian," by Ricardo Franco as a "do-nothing" and by List 17 Febrero as "a man respected for his moral courage" but lacking the capacity to create a "citizens' army" and lacking any idea of "ideological-doctrinal strategy." Such criticisms naturally clash with the general's self-image. His reaction is to reply by combining a reiteration of his role as he sees it with self-depreciation: their desire to "raise unjust accusations against me may be legitimate"; "the only point on which I agree with your opinion is in reference to my modest qualities and limited capacity for leadership"; "I have asked to be relieved of the high party function that they have invested me with, perhaps undeservedly"; and so on.

Why does Franco allow himself to become involved in party battles, against his own ideas of what his role should be? Why does he identify himself especially with the institutionalists? The most plausible answer would seem to be that, like him, most of the institutionalists are men of the first promotion, the men of the ANEC and the February Revolution. This is supported by the following passages from his letters, the first being from the same letter to Ricardo Franco already quoted above: ". . . only think of the generation which made the Revolution . . . no one, not even the most bitter enemy, can show one single dishonest act in its management of public affairs. If all this is worthless, at least it served to earn respect, which you do not seem to feel, for those who sacrificed the greater part of their lives in the service of the popular cause."[39]

The other letter is the one to Arturo Acosta Mena and Carlos Vásquez, quoted above: "I do not believe that the revolutionaries are only in your sector, especially when I see that the principal figures in the list constituted as a reaction (to yours) are men who made the February Revolution, the glorious Agrarian Reform, the Declaration of Social Rights, and other such achievements."[40]

List 17 Febrero did not include Franco in its list of party "oligarchs"; to these leaders Franco was "a man respected and appreciated by us, a man capable of great deeds when in command of an organized army," but incapable of heading a political party. As in the case of the counterrevolution of August, 1937, the attacks did not come against Franco but against his circle of advisors, who were said to be taking advantage of his naïveté. According to List 17 Febrero, the party oligarchs (Yegros, Gaona, Caballero Gatti, and Sosa Jovellanos being the ones specifically mentioned by List 17 Febrero) were "certain Rasputins who sought to shelter themselves beneath Franco's reputation." This is shown in Duverger's description of one type of "inner circle":

> From the point of view of their formation the classes of leaders and inner circles can be divided into several kinds. No doubt the simplest is to be seen in the *camarilla,* a small group which makes use of close personal solidarity as a means of establishing and maintaining its influence. Sometimes it takes the form of a clique grouped around an influential leader: this leader's retinue has a monopoly of the positions of leadership and takes on the characteristic of an oligarchy.[41]

Another point suggested by Duverger is the problem of renewing this inner circle. The institutionalists have taken important steps to deal with this in a manner also described

---

39. Letter to Ricardo Franco, September 13, 1960.

40. Letter to Arturo Acosta Mena and Carolos Vásquez, December 9, 1961.

41. Maurice Duverger, *Political Parties: Their Organization and Activity in the Modern State* (New York: John Wiley and Sons, Inc., 1963), p. 152.

by Duverger: "Sometimes the bureaucratic oligarchy assumes the form of a technocratic oligarchy. Courses for leaders are set up inside the party which one must attend before being given a post of leadership."[42]

Younger *febreristas* are given two kinds of opportunities to acquire political training for future leadership. First, the party runs its own school in Asunción at which members attend classes and have access to a library on contemporary politics, political theory, economics, and related subjects. Second, the party also participates in the Inter-American Institute of Education for Democracy in San José, Costa Rica, whose purpose is to train future political leaders of Latin American democratic revolutionary parties. This school is especially important in that it is a means of establishing contacts among like-minded parties, which may result in aid by a party in power to another that is struggling to get into power. Since access to both of these schools is controlled by the institutionalists, they have an important advantage over their radical opposition. Not only can they count on external aid, but their capacity to organize and recruit is enhanced.

Although the evidence so far points to a trend towards oligarchy in the Febrerista party, the institutionalists are not without a defense against this charge. In the first place, the establishment of schools of political education might be considered an attempt to rejuvenate the party, rather than simply "recruitment into the inner circle." They undoubtedly serve the useful and important service of providing a more highly trained party leadership. As for the "inner circle" itself, it can be argued that the older leaders, having more experience, are better qualified to hold the more responsible posts. Also, while men of the first promotion are heavily represented in the 1962 CEN, they do not constitute a majority, and the institutionalists can point to their peaceful surrender of the CEN to the radicals in 1954. Such behavior runs counter to what would be expected from a party oligarchy. In fact, the institutionalists might even turn the argument around and claim that their overwhelming victory in 1958 has not been gracefully accepted by the radicals—that the

---

42. *Ibid.*, p. 155.

latter have rejected the institutionalists' legal mandate by going outside of the official party to establish parallel organs. In short, it might be argued that the radicals, not the institutionalists, have acted undemocratically.

The Third National Party Convention

The elections held to send delegates to the Third National Convention were marred by charges of party disloyalty and fraud. The List 17 Febrero leaders were called "Castro-Communists" by the institutionalists who, in turn, were accused of complicity with the Stroessner regime. As for the alleged fraud, the welter of charges and counter-charges make it difficult, if not impossible, to say who really won the elections. List 17 Febrero has published a booklet entitled *Informativo y resoluciones de la III Convención Ordinaria al pueblo febrerista*, which purports to tell the story of the electoral campaign and the events of the Third National Convention. The final election figures published in this booklet state that seventy delegates carried credentials from the Central Electoral Committee to the convention. Of these, it is claimed, thirty-nine corresponded to List 17 Febrero and thirty-one to the institutionalists.[43] According to List 17 Febrero, the results of the local elections to send convention delegates were:

The Capital (Asunción)
by Precinct

List 17 Febrero		Institutionalists	
Sajonia	1	Centrice	1
Hospital	2	*Vista Alegre	1
Tacumbú	2	(two more claimed)	
Barrio Obrero	2	Villa Morra	1
Trinidad	2	Pinoza	3
Ciudad Nueva	3	San Vicente	1
Chacarita	1	Mariscal López	1
Recoleta	1		—
Tablada	1		8
Escalinata	1		
Plaza Italia	1		
	—		
	17		

43. Partido Revolucionario Febrerista, Lema Electoral "17 de Febrero," *Informativo y resoluciones de la III Convención Ordinaria al pueblo febrerista* (Asunción, June, 1962), p. 3.

The Interior

*Puerto Sastre	3	San Pedro	2
*San Ignacio	3	*Pilar	2
*Villarica	4	Coronel Oviedo	2
*Pedro Juan Caballero	2	Encarnación	1
Concepción	1	San Lorenzo	1
Iturbide	1	*Itaguá	1
Luque	1	Ipacaraí	1
*Eusebio Ayala	1	*Areguá	1
*Itacurubi	1	*San Juan	1
San José	1	*Fassardi	1
*Yaguarón	1	*General Artigas	1
*Itá	2	Pirebebuy	1
	21		15

The Exterior

*Clorinda	1	Montevideo	1
	1	*Buenos Aires	4
		Resistencia	1
		Formosa	2
			8

Grand Total	39	**Grand Total**	31

*delegates were challenged by the opposing list before the Central Electoral Committee for fraud.

The local committee of Posadas was entitled to five delegates but was not represented because both lists had committed fraud, and the Central Electoral Committee nullified the elections there entirely.

A brief review of the challenged elections may give some idea of the bitterness with which they were fought. Beginning with List 17 Febrero's challenges, we have:[44]

Buenos Aires (4 delegates)

List 17 Febrero accused the institutionalists of electoral fraud because the Regional Electoral Committee had refused to allow the registration of some 243 members of their list. The institutionalists were accused of other electoral irregularities as well: voting places were located in the homes of institutionalist leaders and List 17 Febrero members were refused admittance.

---

44. All of these from *ibid.*, pp. 18-23.

The institutionalists answered by saying that List 17 Febrero had been given seven months to get its members registered before the elections. Nevertheless, only fifteen days before, Galo Achar, the List 17 Febrero leader in Buenos Aires, brought a list of 243 names to be registered. Many of these lived far out of town, and the list was not accepted because there was not enough time to check it. Moreover, the institutionalists pointed to the party electoral law stating that the registration list shall be formed on the basis of past lists, plus new members from a census made by the Regional Electoral Committee. The 243 disputed names had been censused not by the Regional Committee but by List 17 Febrero itself. They were therefore unauthorized and unacceptable. "This [the registration of the names] could not be done," argued the Regional Electoral Committee, "because it would establish a regimen of uncontrollable disorder, distortion, and permanent fraud. It would supplant the legitimate and natural authority of the committees, who alone are able to grant status to those members who apply for it."

List 17 Febrero claimed that it was necessary for it to census its members because the old list had been taken by Ricardo Franco, the former president of the Buenos Aires Regional Committee, when he was expelled from the party. They also claimed that in making the new census the Regional Committee leaders had purposely neglected to inscribe known List 17 Febrero supporters. In view of the Regional Electoral Committee's refusal to accept these 243 names, List 17 Febrero abstained from the elections in Buenos Aires and filed a petition with the Central Electoral Committee to intervene, but this request was turned down. The Central Electoral Committee upheld the results in Buenos Aires, which forced List 17 Febrero to appeal its case to the National Convention.

Posadas (five delegates)

List 17 Febrero also claimed to be the victim of fraud in Posadas, a border town in Argentina just across the Paraná River from the Paraguayan port of Encarnación. Again, the Regional Electoral Committee, it is claimed, refused to permit the registration of over six hundred List 17 Febrero supporters. The institutionalists claim that, as in the case of Buenos Aires, the list was fraudulent. List 17 Febrero also claims that the Regional Electoral Committee even refused to allow it to present official candidates on the basis that List 17 Febrero had not presented itself for legal recognition on time. List 17 Febrero points out that it is necessary only to register with the Central Electoral Committee. The Central Electoral Committee did intervene in Posadas and nullified the elections entirely, permitting neither list to send delegates to the convention. Again, this dispute would have to be resolved by the convention.

Vista Alegre (1 or 3 delegates—number disputed)

The institutionalists claimed three delegates from this precinct of Asunción. List 17 Febrero recognized one of these but argued that the other two were invalid because Vista Alegre lacked a sufficient number of *febreristas* to be entitled to three delegates. The Central Electoral Committee upheld List 17 Febrero's argument and granted the institutionalists only one credential. This was one more dispute that was taken to the convention as the court of last resort.

Pilar (2 delegates)

List 17 Febrero gives the following figures: as of April 30, 1961, Pilar had 146 *febreristas,* according to the Regional Committee's official records; however, 305 people were registered to vote for the 1962 elections. This, says List 17 Febrero, "gives one the impression of being in the presence of a dynamic regional, a virile and herculean *febrerismo,* a *febrerismo* in full growth, a *febrerismo* in agile, all-powerful expansion. But . . . such optimism falls to the earth when . . . no more than 165 *febreristas* voted." In short, it was claimed that the registration list had been packed by the institutionalists. Moreover, List 17 Febrero claimed that Pilar did not have enough members to be entitled to two delegates, and the election of Elpidio Yegros from Pilar was contested on the basis that he was not a resident there but lived in Buenos Aires, over 1,200 kilometers away. (However, the constitution does say that a candidate may run in a district in which he is not a resident.)

Areguá (1 delegate)

List 17 Febrero claimed that Juan A. Monges, the institutionalist delegate, appointed himself without holding elections. Also, it was claimed that Areguá did not have the necessary one hundred members to elect a convention delegate in the first place.

San Juan Bautista (1 delegate)

Francisco Sosa Jovellanos, the secretary of organization, lost to List 17 Febrero in the Asunción precinct of Plaza Italia. Some days later he was presented suddenly as the institutionalist candidate in the town of San Juan Bautista, where he won. List 17 Febrero claimed that Sosa Jovellanos had violated Article 53 of the electoral code that states elections shall be simultaneous. If this article had been respected, argued List 17 Febrero, it would have made it impossible for Sosa Jovellanos to be elected in San Juan, for he posited his candidacy only after losing in Plaza Italia. In short, the elections had not been held at the proper time, Sosa Jovellanos had not been registered as a candidate at the proper time, and the local electoral committee had provided no voting tables, ballots, or poll watchers.

Artigas (1 delegate)

List 17 Febrero claimed that no elections had been held. The delegate had simply been appointed by the institutionalists.

Itaguá (1 delegate)

List 17 Febrero claimed that no more than twenty *febreristas* were registered here and that this local had no right to a delegate. Moreover, the delegate had been appointed not elected.

Fassardi (1 delegate)

List 17 Febrero claimed that the institutionalists, who headed the Local Electoral Committee, had juggled the registration list to give themselves a majority.

The institutionalists pointed out similar cases involving alleged List 17 Febrero fraud.[45] For instance:

Puerto Sastre (3 delegates)

The institutionalists claim that Arturo Acosta Mena, a leading List 17 Febrero figure, flew to this Chaco port on the Upper Paraguay River and organized a local committee entirely outside of the party's regular, official organization. Since this committee was simply a vehicle to fabricate members, votes, and delegates, the entire matter represents high fraud. While it is admitted that some *febreristas* are in Puerto Sastre, it is claimed that there are not enough to be entitled to even one delegate, let alone three.

Yaguarón (1 delegate)

The institutionalists claim that elections were never held here. The local committee simply sent false results to the Central Electoral Committee.

Villarica (4 delegates)

The institutionalists cite an alleged violation of Article 15 of the electoral code, which states that there must be as many electoral committees as there are local or precinct committees. According to the accusation, the Regional Committee of Villarica forced nearby local committees—in Yataytý, Tebicuarý, and Coronel Martínez—to come to Villarica to vote. In this way, List 17 Febrero, which controlled the Villarica Regional Committee, gained more delegates than it deserved, for Villarica does not have enough members to claim four delegates.

---

45. All of these from a letter by Silvio Rios to Dr. Manuel Dejesus Carvallo, president of the Central Electoral Committee, May 2, 1962.

Itacurubí (1 delegate)

The institutionalists claim that this local lacked the necessary 100 members to elect a delegate and so used votes from the town of Santa Helena to make up the difference. However, Santa Helena not only has its own local committee, but it is located nowhere near Itacurubí.

Itá (2 delegates)

It was alleged that the List 17 Febrero-controlled local committee refused to allow institutionalists representation on the electoral committee and the right to vote.

Pedro Juan Caballero (2 delegates)

The institutionalists claim that the local committee held no elections but simply appointed two delegates from List 17 Febrero.

San Ignacio (3 delegates)

The institutionalists claim that they, not List 17 Febrero, elected three delegates from here. However, List 17 Febrero got possession of the list of the elected delegates to be sent to the Central Electoral Committee and changed the names.

Eusebio Ayala (1 delegate)

The institutionalists claimed unspecified electoral irregularities.

Clorinda (1 delegate)

The institutionalists claim that these elections were held after the proper date and were invalid. List 17 Febrero claims that there was only a delay in sending the electoral results to the Central Electoral Committee. This delegate first arrived at the convention without credentials, and these were procured for him later from the Central Electoral Committee. However, this was done after the Central Electoral Committee had already closed the electoral process and announced the final results. Consequently, there was a dispute over the legality of his credentials.

The Third National Convention was held in Corrientes, Argentina, from June 9 through June 12. Twenty-four hours before the sessions began, a Commission of Powers was appointed by the CEN, as required by the constitution. The following articles of the constitution are crucial for an understanding of the issues that arose in the Commission of Powers, which in turn led to the party's division into two hostile conventions:

> *Article 13:* The National Executive Committee shall designate a Commission of Powers, composed of five members, for the purpose of considering the credentials of accredited delegates to the Convention.
>
> *Article 14:* The Commission of Powers shall convene within twenty-four hours before the date set for the opening of the Convention for the purpose of declaring itself on the validity of the credentials of the elected delegates.
>
> *Article 15:* Those delegates whose credentials are not objected to by the Commission of Powers shall form the Party Convention at the day and hour set for the convocation.
>
> *Article 16:* The Convention shall be the only judge of the validity of the credentials observed by the Commission of Powers.

The language used in the articles is somewhat confusing, making it appear that Articles 14 and 16 are contradictory by giving both the convention and the Commission of Powers the right to pass judgment on the validity of credentials, but there is a difference in the type of decision that each body is empowered to make. The Commission of Powers is a limited body, whose sole task is to examine the credentials of arriving delegates to check their authenticity—that is, to verify that they have not been falsified or altered and that they were duly authorized by the Central Electoral Committee. The jurisdiction of the convention extends to disputes over whether a delegate was legally elected, and it has the final decision over claims of fraud. It is true, however, that these articles were badly written, leaving room for varying interpretations. It was just such a difference in interpretation that divided the Febrerista party.

To begin with, seventy credentials in all were issued by the Central Electoral Committee, in the same proportions as given above: thirty-nine to List 17 Febrero, thirty-one to the institutionalists. On June 5, 1962, the Central Electoral Committee sent a letter to the CEN, officially terminating the electoral process, nullifying the elections in Posadas, and turning over the Vista Alegre issue to the consideration of the convention. At this time, seventeen of List 17 Febrero's thirty-nine delegates had been officially challenged by the institutionalists, which meant that a decision from the convention would be called for. As for the institutionalists, only their four delegates from Buenos Aires were challenged.

On June 8, twenty-four hours before the convention was scheduled to open, the CEN appointed the five members of the Commission of Powers: Juan Silvano Díaz Pérez, David Monges, and Bartolomé Ortiz, from the institutionalist list; and Carlos Alfieri and Atilio Garcete from List 17 Febrero. As List 17 Febrero saw it, this put them in a dangerous position. Since List 17 Febrero was outnumbered three-to-two on the Commission of Powers, there existed the possibility that the commission would not recognize the credentials of the seventeen challenged List 17 Febrero delegates, leaving those delegates without a vote in the convention until or unless the convention validated them. This would leave List 17 Febrero in a minority of twenty-seven to twenty-two—assuming that the Commission of Powers might decide to act "fairly" and not recognize *any* challenged credentials. If this should happen, there would be little likelihood that their seventeen challenged delegates would ever be incorporated in the convention. This possibility was countered beforehand by a series of strategic maneuvers.

First, arriving List 17 Febrero delegates were instructed to hand over their credentials to Carlos Alfieri, so as to prevent them from falling into the hands of the opposition. Now these delegates could not be pressured into surrendering their credentials to the Commission of Powers, for all of them were in Alfieri's possession. The other maneuver was to send Alfieri to Asunción to present a list of challenges against seven of the institutionalist delegates elected from the interior, and this list was received by the Central Electoral Committee on June 7. On the following day, that committee authorized credentials for the List 17 Febrero candidates in each of those elections, invalidating the credentials already issued to the institutionalists. What is surprising about this decision is that it was taken three days after the Central Electoral Committee had officially terminated the electoral process, and it is equally surprising that the Central Electoral Committee accepted this list. After all, List 17 Febrero had over two months after the elections in those places to present its challenges, but it had kept silent until the last hour.

Nevertheless, because of the unfathomable reasoning of the Central Electoral Committee—which has never been explained—Alfieri flew back to Corrientes on June 8 with seven new credentials in his pocket. Now if the institutionalists wanted to allow only unchallenged delegates onto the convention floor, List 17 Febrero had whittled down the number of unchallenged institutionalists to twenty delegates—two fewer than the number of unchallenged List 17 Febrero delegates.

Alfieri presented the seven new credentials to the Commission of Powers when it convened, pointing out that they invalidated those previously given to the institutionalists. Since these new credentials had been granted after the closing date, a serious argument developed over which set of credentials was truly valid. Alfieri suggested the following by way of compromise: (1) All delegates whose credentials had not been challenged by either list should be incorporated into the convention immediately—twenty-two List 17 Febrero delegates, as opposed to twenty institutionalists. The question of the validity of the new credentials would be left to the convention to decide. (2) The Commission of Powers should declare its lack of jurisdiction to examine in any way the cases of Posadas and Vista Alegre, because those delegates had not exhibited any credentials from the Central Electoral Committee. (3) It should be recognized that only the convention had the right to decide upon challenged credentials, according to Article 16 of the constitution.[46] In short, Alfieri was hoping to throw the credentials fight onto the floor of the convention,

46. From P.R.F., *Informativo y resoluciones de la III Convención Ordinaria*, p. 3; and the institutionalists' *Boletín Informativo* (Buenos Aires, June, 1962), p. 3. The text is the same in both.

where List 17 Febrero would have a majority, rather than battle the issue in the Commission of Powers, where the institutionalists had a majority.

Alfieri's proposal drew the anger of Bartolomé Ortiz, who accused Garcete and him of trying to prevent the Commission of Powers from carrying out its constitutional duties by injecting arguments of a "political character" into the discussion. Alfieri's demand that the Commission of Powers should accept the seven new credentials of List 17 Febrero rather than those previously granted to the institutionalists was an attempt, he argued, to have the commission exercise discretionary powers beyond its constitutional limits. The compromise was no better, either, because the commission had no power to admit the unchallenged delegates to the convention while at the same time refusing to allow the challenged ones to enter. Only the convention could declare which delegates were legally elected.

Since a stalemate had been reached at this point, a brief adjournment was called, during which Dr. Ortiz withdrew from the commission "for reasons of health," and his place was taken by Dr. Dario González Vera. The second meeting also proved fruitless. Dr. Monges suggested that the commission take up the question of the validity of the credentials and decide on each by a majority vote. This was totally unacceptable to List 17 Febrero. Alfieri announced that if such a proposal were sustained, he and Garcete would walk out. After further discussion of Dr. Monges' proposal, Alfieri reiterated his intention to withdraw. The commission then admitted its unreconcilable deadlock and agreed to dissolve. Before doing so, however, it drew up a brief memorandum of its proceedings, with the following conclusions: (1) that the opinions expressed by Dr. Ortiz constituted a poor interpretation of the position adopted by Drs. Alfieri and Garcete and that they were his personal opinions only; (2) that Drs. Alfieri and Garcete had attempted in every way, and in good faith, to allow the Commission of Powers to fulfill its functions but that no action could be taken on matters specifically reserved to the Central Electoral Committee in the first instance and the National Convention in the final instance; (3)

that the motion of Dr. Monges to submit the examination of credentials to a majority vote was not based on any norms of jurisprudence in the party; and (4) that the position taken by Drs. Alfieri and Garcete should be interpreted as a vehement desire to better the party through a strict respect of the law. (!)[47]

This declaration was signed at 11:30 A.M. on June 10 by Drs. Díaz Pérez, Monges, Alfieri, and Garcete. Amazingly enough, it seems that the institutionalists went out of their way to flatter Alfieri and Garcete while deprecating themselves. The obvious question is, why, if these institutionalists were so eager to declare Alfieri and Garcete justified in their position, did they not agree to adopt their position? The most plausible answer is that the institutionalists wanted to dissolve the commission in a hurry and were willing to sign any declaration Alfieri and Garcete wished, as long as it did not mean that they would have to change their vote. This seems verified by the fact that just two and a half hours after the commission dissolved itself, the institutionalists met again and formed a "rump" Commission of Powers composed of Drs. Juan Silvano Díaz Pérez, David Monges, and Bartolomé Ortiz. A new agenda was drawn up. The cases of Posadas and Vista Alegre were sent to the convention for its decision, and then the new commission went on to examine the credentials before it. However, only thirty of the seventy-seven credentials issued, including the seven new ones, were in its possession. The other forty-seven either belonged to List 17 Febrero delegates or to neutral delegates who, for reasons unclear in the commission's report, had turned them over to List 17 Febrero leaders and were unable to get them back.[48]

According to List 17 Febrero, after the first Commission of Powers had been dissolved, its leaders had appointed a delegation to talk with Elpidio Yegros, acting-president of the CEN. Their objective was to reach some agreement on forming a new Commission of Powers, unaware that the institutionalists had already done so. Upon arriving at the hotel

---

47. *Ibid.*
48. *Boletín informativo,* p. 3.

where the convention was to take place, they found that the institutionalists had already begun the convention, and the List 17 Febrero committee was refused admission. In view of this, the List 17 Febrero delegates convened at their own hotel, quickly appointed their own Commission of Powers—which validated all of their credentials and issued credentials to the Posadas delegation and began their own convention.[49]

List 17 Febrero's convention elected Benigno Perrota president of the party, in place of General Franco, and lifted all of the sanctions against any former member of the Bloque, the Vanguardia, or the M.R.P. who had not joined another party after being disciplined. It reaffirmed its allegiance to the party's Declaration of Principles and Program of Government but firmly declared its opposition to any negotiations with Stroessner and restated its thesis of armed insurrection as the only acceptable strategy. No mention was made of the Cuban Revolution.

The institutionalist convention re-elected General Franco to the presidency and reaffirmed the party's participation in the *Unión Nacional Paraguaya.* Moreover, it agreed to expel sixteen of the top List 17 Febrero leaders from the party.

The Fourth National Convention

The Febrerista party remained divided and weakened until the institutionalists achieved legalization in August, 1964. Upon returning to Paraguay, they established a weekly newspaper, *El Pueblo,* and began to take part openly in their country's politics. Their position with respect to the government has been that of a controlled opposition; they are permitted to criticize the authorities and even campaign for office, but they have little hope of winning power through elections in the near future. For example, while the Febrerista party participated in the municipal elections of October, 1965, the result was a predictable victory for President Stroessner and the Colorado party. In fairness to Stroessner, one must admit that he probably would have won anyway be-

---

49. P.R.F., *Informativa y resoluciones de la III Convención Ordinaria,* pp. 7-9.

cause of his popularity with the Colorado *py nandí*, but his margin of victory was certainly amplified by considerable electoral fraud.

Febrerista radical intransigents—unregenerate List 17 Febrero supporters and Ricardo Franco's small sect—pointed to the election results as proof that legalization could result only in deception and defeat. Nonetheless, other *febreristas* took a longer view of the results. The ultimate victory of *febrerismo,* they argue, will not be achieved quickly. The romantic idea that the Paraguayan people are ready to rise up and follow the *febrerista* banner at any given moment must be discarded in favor of a more realistic acceptance of the fact that the party is small and has little peasant backing. It could not win a majority even in a free election. The only remedy for this situation is for the party to patiently build up its backing in the countryside and to wean the peasants away from their traditional party loyalties. This, in turn, requires a political environment that permits *febrerismo* to propagandize and organize legally with relatively more freedom than it has enjoyed in the past. Therefore, temporary defeats such as the municipal elections count for little.

By the time of the Fourth National Party Convention, in February, 1966, the institutionalists appeared to have won over all but a small fraction of the party. Besides having the advantages of publicity, organization, and open recruitment afforded them by being legalized, they also profited from an atmosphere of optimism among the exiles, who seemed to sense a gradual democratization in the political situation. Institutionalists were capitalizing on their affiliations with other Latin American "popular" parties in recruiting young adherents. Student party leaders were being sent to schools for political education in Costa Rica and Caracas to strengthen ties with other parties and to provide the coming generation of leaders with a broader political background.

By 1966 the List 17 Febrero wing had disappeared almost entirely. It had organized no guerrilla bands to carry out its insurrectional thesis, launched no invasions, and apparently had disintegrated quietly. Some members had returned to the main body of the party, while others, such as Carlos Vásquez, who had been elected vice-president by List 17 Febrero, simply withdrew from politics altogether.

Two lists presented themselves for election to the Fourth National Convention, both subscribing to the institutionalist position. List 17 Febrero neither presented a slate of candidates nor held a parallel convention. The chief difference between the two active lists seemed, again, to be generational. Opposing the old guard, headed by Carlos Caballero Gatti, Elpidio Yegros, and Roque Gaona, was the *Coincidencia* or neo-reformist list. This was led by Francisco Sosa Jovellanos and Humberto Pérez Caceres, both of the second promotion. Both lists nominated General Franco for the party presidency. Rather than split the party over their rather marginal ideological and tactical differences, they settled these peacefully at the convention. The new CEN was composed of leaders from both lists and included a far larger proportion of second promotion *febreristas*. The fact that a few former List 17 Febrero sympathizers were given seats as well seemed to emphasize the party's desire to restore cohesion. The extent to which the leadership was being rejuvenated can be seen from the following table:

Representation on the CEN by Promotion

	1958	1962	1966
First promotion	15	11	8
Second promotion	10	10	14
Third promotion	0	4	3

There is even a slight let-up in the first promotion's hold over the key posts, as the next table shows. However, at the same time it appears as though the old leaders are being careful to promote only "safe" candidates. All five of the holders of key posts have held seats on the two previous Executive Committees and so have already proven their loyalty in battle against the radical opposition.

The 1966 CEN

Post (1966)	Promotion	1962 CEN	1958 CEN	1951 CEN	CRF CEN	Rev. govt. 1936-37	UNR CEN	ANEC CEN	CENs Serving	Key Posts Held
Pres.	1	Pres.	Pres.	Pres.	Pres.	Pres.		Pres.	6	6
Vice-pres. #1	1	Vice-pres. #1	Sec. gen.	X			X	Sec. gen.	4	3
Vice-pres. #2	2	X	X						3	0
Sec. gen.	2	Sec. org.	Sec. org.						2	2
Sec. org.	1	X	X						2	0
On CEN		5	5	2	1		2			
Held key post		3	3	1	1		2			

X is member of CEN but no key post.

Whether the new CEN represents a truly reunified party is an open question, of course. Perhaps consensus has been achieved only at the cost of purging the party down to a small faction of like-minded conservatives, as the radicals allege. On the other hand, the new burst of party activity since legalization was achieved seems to indicate the contrary. The establishing of a new weekly newspaper, *El Pueblo,* the holding of public meetings, and the return of General Franco to Paraguay seem to reflect new strength in *febrerismo.* If the Stroessner government is serious about its stated desire to take the first steps toward democracy, and if the *febreristas* are wise enough to have abandoned "immediatism," Paraguay may have entered its long-awaited era of civic peace and progress.

5. The Politics of Exile

At the beginning of this study, we stated our belief that exile parties do not constitute a genre of political organization different from other parties. Exile parties, too, are organized to achieve control of the government. To this purpose the behavior of their members is channeled through an organizational structure with different levels of authority. Cohesion and morale are important. An efficient working relationship must be achieved between the leaders and the rank and file. New members must be recruited. These problems are common in all parties. What differentiates the exiles is that they must confront these problems under abnormal conditions.

To begin with, there is their illegal and clandestine status, which creates serious organizational problems. Recruitment may suffer if the risks of joining are too high. Indeed, prolonged persecution may cause a party to lose many of the members it already has, especially if they can see little hope of eventual success. We might recall at this point the memorandum sent to the CEN by the Resistance Committee, describing the shattered state of the party organization caused by the Colorado "Terror." As a result of that "Terror," the Febrerista party has never fully recovered its pre-1947 strength in the labor unions and student organizations.

The Febrerista party structure is highly adaptable. We

have already noted its use of both the "branch" and the cell as basic elements of organization—a possibility not foreseen by Maurice Duverger in his classification of party structures. The uniqueness has been explained by showing that the use of local committees (branches) corresponds to the party's desire to build a mass base, while its "fractions," or cells, are a logical response to the persecution it faces. In other words, the Febrerista party structure is designed to respond to the challenges of its peculiar environment. Despite the democratic program of *febrerismo* and its interest in mass recruitment, electoral activity has been eliminated for it as a choice of tactics by the parade of dictators who have proscribed it since 1937. This has driven the party underground and necessitated clandestine, subversive tactics, rather than those of a public character.

This underscores the necessity of placing the party within the context of its political environment in order to fully understand its operations. An especially pertinent quote from Samuel Eldersveld follows:

> In attempting to delineate the properties of the party, we assume that our knowledge of its tasks and roles in the larger political system will be enhanced. Parties came into existence to perform certain critical functions for the system, and derived their basic form in the process of implementing these functions. If one is interested in understanding the tasks presumably fulfilled by parties, it is necessary to analyze the party as a functioning structural subsystem. This is not to say that all party groups perform the same functions and possess identical structural properties. Social and political environmental conditions vary from one culture to the next. The same is true of "functional priorities." Parties are merely a particular structural response, therefore, to the needs of a social and political system in a particular milieu.[1]

Nevertheless, one suspects that the Febrerista party cannot operate indefinitely in an illegal fashion. There must be some real hope of eventually coming to the power. Moreover, we have already seen in our case study of relations between the CEN and the Resistance Committee how the pressures of a hostile political environment cause serious difficulties in in-

1. Samuel J. Eldersveld, *Political Parties: A Behavioral Analysis* (Chicago: Rand McNally and Co., 1964), p. 2.

traparty communications. This, in turn, may lead to factional splits in the organization. Moreover, while switching from "branches" to cells may be necessary for a party's self-defense, the cell system is not efficient for securing financing for party activities or for broadening its base through recruitment.

Another abnormality affecting the exiles' political organization is their removal from direct contact with the nation's political life. Again, we may point to the case of the CEN's relations with the Resistance Committee as an example of how the exiles' lack of knowledge of the day-to-day realities back home may cause misunderstandings over policy. We have noted a tendency for exiles to be more radical in their tactics than their colleagues working within the country. It is significant, for instance, that most of the support for the insurrectionalist thesis came from (and still comes from) exile groups. Party members working within the country tend to take a dim view of what they call "immediatist" tactics. After all, they are usually the first ones to suffer when the government clamps down.

One explanation for this difference in perspective concerning tactics is the exile's longing to return to his homeland. Some would go back at almost any price; others dream of returning in triumph and imposing a terrible revenge on their persecutors. We have already noted that exiles often have difficulty in finding work and therefore frequently sink to a lower socioeconomic status. Such downward mobility might in itself be sufficient to explain the acute sense of frustration and impatience. Beyond that, however, there is the difficult and sometimes impossible problem of adjusting to a new culture. In this respect, the *febreristas,* most of whom live in Argentina, are fortunate. The language is the same, and the customs are not radically different.[2]

---

2. An important ramification of this is that intellectuals such as lawyers and journalists are able to work at their trades. This is not always the case. The German, Italian, and East European intelligentsia in exile often have found themselves to be the most difficult class to integrate into a new culture because their skills no longer are in demand. For a discussion of the problem with respect to exiles other than the Paraguayans, see Donald Peterson Kent, *The Refugee Intellectual* (New York: Columbia University Press, 1953), and Harold Fields, *The Refugee in the United States,* (New York: Oxford University Press, 1938).

Nevertheless, even under favorable conditions the exile's social position is never fully secure. He tends to be declassed, or at least he feels that this is so. There is the added psychological pressure, too, of exiled parents who watch their children growing up without any attachment to the old homeland. This is an especially serious problem for the highly nationalistic Paraguayans, who try to keep this attachment alive in their young through Paraguayan cultural centers and by teaching them Guaraní.

All of these factors tend to contribute to a feeling on the part of many exiles that the hour of retribution must be soon at hand. Consider, for instance, this speech made at the time when the Vanguardia Febrerista was being launched in early 1959: "Paraguayans—the four hundred thousand of you who now live outside the Fatherland, having found no legal or economic security there. Look! A Crusade is beginning, blessed by Our Lady of Paraguay. Look! Now we are embarked upon our return to the Homeland—our Homeland so worthy of a better fate than it has had. We must all unite in a common program, in a national front for justice and liberty."[3]

The guerrilla bands who invaded Paraguay, such as the one led by Juan José Rotela, all promised their followers that their presence there in defiance of the dictatorship would touch off mass uprisings. Many of them began poorly equipped, expecting support from the peasants, and it is ironic that they were hunted down not only by Stroessner's army but also by machete wielding peasants—the very people they had come to liberate. Despite this, the apocalyptic vision of a mass uprising dies hard. Even after Rotela's tragic failure, we find List 17 Febrero proclaiming: "The only way of revitalizing the ideals of the nation and of our party is to defeat the tyranny. And this can be done only by an organized popular struggle along the lines of armed civil insurrection."[4]

However, not even the entire List 17 Febrero was prepared

---

3. Speech by Father Ramón Talavera, Montevideo, February 20, 1959.

4. Comando de Coordinación del Movimiento Electoral Lema 17 de Febrero, "Comunicado Interno" (Buenos Aires, October 17, 1961).

to subscribe to this position. The Ateneo Cultural—a group that formerly published the party's cultural paper and directed List 17 Febrero's campaign in Buenos Aires—came out strongly against the insurrectionalist thesis. In a paper entitled "Febrerismo en su hora decisiva" ("Febrerismo in its Hour of Decision"), the Ateneo attacked with sarcasm the notion that *febrerista* guerrilla leaders could repeat the Cuban experience: "We lack leadership; we lack people; we lack an organization; we don't influence even one sergeant; we don't have even one rifle; we have no money. That is to say, we haven't any of the means necessary to wage a victorious armed action." Those who subscribe to the insurrectional thesis and talk of imitating Fidel Castro do so from their secure position in exile, "talking of war to the death against the dictatorship, but keeping themselves hundreds of kilometers from the theatre of battle." Moreover, such would-be generals forget that

> The Paraguayan social, economic, political, cultural, and geographic realities are distinct from those of Cuba. Castro had, at the beginning of his campaign, one million dollars inherited from his father. *Febrerismo* has no money. . . . Castro put himself at the head of his guerrillas. . . . Our leaders send brave freedom fighters to their death but keep themselves on the other side of the Paraná River. Castro knew how to act with the political intelligence necessary to gain the support of democratic sectors in his country and in the United States. Our leaders say such extremist things that they repel Paraguayan democratic sectors and provoke the opposition of powerful groups in neighboring countries. . . . Batista's army was an army of corrupt mercenaries, without roots or historical tradition. . . . The Paraguayan army has deep national roots, and a glorious and heroic tradition.[5]

Of course it is also possible to argue, as do the *febrerista* radicals, that it is the institutionalist thesis that really represents wishful thinking and that it is adhered to by people whose desire to return to Paraguay outweighs their committment to *febrerista* principles. For the radicals, the idea that democracy can be nurtured gradually under a right-wing military dictatorship is nothing less than a rationalization for

---

5. El Ateneo Cultural Febrerista, *Febrerismo en su hora decisiva* (Buenos Aires, [1963?]), p. 7.

"selling out." Whatever the case may be, there is little doubt that the institutionalist leaders have strengthened their hold over the party since achieving legalization. One good reason for this is that they have procured for their followers the right to return under an amnesty.

The politics of exile is, then, politics carried on under abnormal conditions, and the resulting pressure threatens the internal cohesion of exile parties. The old leaders, having lost in the national political struggle, must either bring the party back to power or be discredited. Unless they can achieve a quick reversal of the party fortunes, their authority may be challenged by other, would-be leaders, who articulate the growing impatience of the rank and file. Factionalism is the bane of exile parties.

In our study of factionalism within *febrerismo,* we presented four case studies, each suggesting different factors that might weaken party cohesion. The Bloque de Defensa de la Revolución was the most serious ideological split that the party has experienced, and we have suggested elsewhere (see Introduction) that ideology may have certain psychological functions in exile politics. Among these are: the maintenance of morale under difficult conditions, the justification of one's position despite defeat, and a means to challenge the old leadership. All of these were present to some degree in the *bloquistas'* fight against the CEN, although their primary stated purpose was to challenge the incumbent leaders. The usual purpose of ideology is not to divide a party, but to induce a feeling of solidarity. Exile organizations, however, frequently disintegrate over petty quibbles over ideology. The frustrations of the situation tend to creat a desire to rectify things through a change of leaders. The old leaders, on their part, try to use ideology to smother criticism and read the dissidents out of the party. A pertinent quotation from a proclamation issued by the institutionalists expelling List 17 Febrero from the party in 1962 follows:

> A prolonged and painful process has just reached its culmi-
> nation in this present emergency. Anarchistic factions within
> the party have long disrupted its development, seriously affect-
> ing its efficiency in combating the dictatorship. These factions

are those groups which call themselves "Vanguardia Febrerista," "Democracia y Revolución," "Febrerismo Rebelde," "Bloque de Liberación," and some of the leaders of the so-called "Ateneo Cultural Febrerista." . . . They are frankly Castro-Communist, some of them. Others are simply ungovernable groups who lend themselves very nicely to extremist plots.[6]

In giving their version of the story, the radicals were no less adept at ideological name-calling:

> Young *compañeros,* you who have always been the thought and action of *febrerismo* . . . you will understand that this clique of conservative oligarchs not only rebelled against the majority of the representatives at the Corrientes Convention, but also broke the democratic laws and norms of the party. In the last analysis there is [within the party] a revolutionary ideology and a conservative one. The latter, because it is comprised with national and international oligarchies, was obliged to set itself against the majority of party representatives, who belonged to the triumphant "List 17 de Febrero."[7]

At times, of course, the "ideological" question is simply glitter to distract attention from a real battle over some narrower concern—such as a dispute over tactics or a personal feud. We have used the Vanguardia Febrerista as an example of a factional split over tactics. Having interviewed many of the former participants in this movement, this writer is of the opinion that, unlike the case of the Bloque, this split was nonideological. Nevertheless, like the *bloquistas,* the Vanguardia posed a serious threat to the CEN's hold over the party. The social and psychological pressures are even more apparent as motivating factors in this case. As Dr. Arnaldo Valdovinos put it: "There is no other alternative. The crimes committed by the various dictators who have followed one another to power these past twelve years show us that our only salvation lies in direct action by the people." After twelve years, a new generation was beginning to grow up in Paraguay without any knowledge of the Febrerista party, and also a new generation was beginning to grow up in exile with

6. Partido Revolucionario Febrerista Comité Regional de Buenos Aires, "Definiciones Claras: Comunicado de la Tercera Convencion Ordinaria," *Boletín Informativo,* June, 1962, p. 4.

7. Benigno Perrota, "Mensaje a la juventud febrerista" (m.p., m.d.).

no memory of the homeland. In the end, prolonged exile could only mean the gradual extinction of *febrerismo*.

The impatience of the *febrerista* rank and file was registered in the 1958 party elections. Fortunately for the institutionalists, the radicals were the incumbents and so had to bear the brunt of the widespread discontent.[8] Thus, the institutionalists won by a landslide: although there were four electoral lists in the running, the institutionalists won an *absolute majority* of the seats in the convention.

The institutionalists were trapped, however, by their own electoral triumph. Despite the popularity of the insurrectionalist thesis, they were unwilling to subscribe to it. Instead, they tried to placate the rank and file by seeking to form a national front of parties—also one of the Vanguardia's main points. The Unión Nacional Paraguaya was an attempt (at least in this writer's opinion) by conservative *febrerista* and Liberal party leaders to give the impression that plans were being laid for a massive co-ordinated effort against the dictatorship. Beyond the printing of a few pamphlets, the UNP did nothing during the next four years. Then the institutionalists had to face, in their turn, disapproval from the party members. The strong showing of List 17 Febrero in the 1962 elections indicates the degree to which the institutionalists' support had deteriorated.

In the meantime, Ricardo Franco's revolt had further split the party. The cause of Franco's dissension cannot be termed ideological. During the period of the coalition government he had been one of the *febrerista* representatives to the Paraguayan Workers' Council, the Communist-dominated labor confederation. In this capacity, he had distinguished himself as one of the Communists' most bitter enemies, proposing that the *febreristas* break away and form their own union. Superficially, his revolt appeared to be based on a dispute over tactics, since he claimed to be forming a guerrilla army. Not only was this army never formed, but one must doubt his sincerity when it is remembered that only a few months be-

8. The reader will recall that a Perrota-Ricardo Franco coalition won control of the CEN in 1954 but split immediately afterward. As a result, the CEN was without a workable majority.

fore he had helped condemn Valdovinos and the Vanguardia for pursuing precisely the same policy. We mention this primarily as an example of a personalist revolt by an overly ambitious young leader.

The challenge of List 17 Febrero points to still another important factor weakening party cohesion: the failure of old leaders to periodically renovate the party by promoting younger people to responsible positions. Permitting a party to stagnate in its upper echelons may be dangerous enough in a stable, open party system, but under the intense pressures of exile, it is suicidal. We do not mean to imply that ideological and tactical considerations played no role in List 17 Febrero's challenge to the institutionalists, but we do want to emphasize that this was definitely a generational conflict as well. The relative inaccessibility of important party posts to younger men not approved by the first promotion leaders tended to exacerbate other differences.

The politics of exile, then, seems to revolve largely around the question of leadership—its quality and effectiveness. In their struggles to retain control, the incumbent leaders are almost always on the defensive, since they lack the usual weapons of patronage and prestige. Using disciplinary methods such as sanctions or expulsions simply reduces the size of the party. While it is in exile and thus lacks the ability to materially reward loyalty, there is nothing to induce members to remain in the party other than their voluntary commitment to its principles. One of the ironies of exile seems to be that, as the party dwindles in size, the struggles for leadership become more intense struggles that are often rationalized by violent quibbles over petty ideological points.[9]

Febrerismo is a movement that has been in existence for more than thirty years, and all but a few of those years have been spent in exile. Having just described the formidable pressures of exile and the tendency towards disintegration

---

9. Again, this seems to fit the *febrerista* experience. When this writer carried on his interviews among the Buenos Aires exiles in 1964, the atmosphere was one of widespread bitterness and apathy. The 1962 Convention had left deep wounds. Many *febreristas* had become inactive in party affairs. In Paraguay one *febrerista* leader said that unless the party achieved legalization soon it was in danger of becoming extinct.

these produce, we must then ask ourselves: how has *feb-rerismo* been able to survive? Several possible factors tending to promote cohesion suggest themselves. To begin with, there has been both quality and continuity in the leadership. It is a paradox that this should also be a cause of factionalism. Nevertheless, having such well-known figures as General Franco, Juan Stefanich, and Elpidio Yegros at its head has earned the party more respect than its small size would normally command. General Franco, one of the nation's great military heroes, is probably *febrerismo's* strongest single asset. Moreover, the institutionalists tend to exploit him and their own past deeds in a manner reminiscent of Roberto Michels' descriptions of oligarchy:

> The leaders acquire fame as defenders and advisers of the people; and while the mass, economically indispensable, goes about its daily work, the leaders, for the love of the cause, must often suffer persecution, imprisonment and exile.
>
> These men, who have often acquired, as it were, an aureole of sanctity and martyrdom, ask only one reward for their services. Gratitude is displayed in the continual re-election of the leaders who have deserved well of the party, so that leadership commonly becomes perpetual.[10]

This sentiment was played upon by the institutionalists in their electoral propaganda. When List 17 Febrero broke with the party tradition and failed to nominate General Franco for the presidency, the institutionalists proclaimed in shocked tones:

> We follow our Chief because of his civic honor, demonstrated in his struggle throughout more than thirty years of public action free of any sort of dishonesty or compromise. General don Rafael Franco, in his long political career, has suffered and continues to suffer with high dignity the fate of our people, and has always placed himself at the service of the cause. . . . To attack Franco is to attack *febrerismo*. Therefore, we condemn with all our energy the attitude of some *compañeros* who, blinded by hate and political passion, try to sully the brilliant record of our Chief.[11]

---

10. Roberto Michels, *Political Parties* (New York: Dover Publications, Inc., 1959), pp. 60-61.

11. Partido Revolucionario Febrerista, Corrientes Local Committee, *Por la liberación integral del pueblo paraguayo*, (Corrientes, Argentina: October, 1961).

Although the general's image has been tarnished somewhat by the factional battles of recent years, he apparently still has the admiration of most *febreristas*. Even the List 17 Febrero leaders exempted him from their attacks on the institutionalist "oligarchs."

Michels' "iron law of oligarchy" suggests that there is a natural tendency within parties for the leaders to perpetuate themselves. According to this theory, turnover in the top positions will be low. Not only will power become centralized in the upper echelons, but the leaders will extend their control to all parts of the apparatus. With respect to turnover in *febrerismo*, we have described a definite trend among the institutionalists towards keeping key leadership positions in the hands of first promotion men. However, channels of leadership recruitment from the second and third promotions have been opened to some extent in recent years. This is true especially with respect to the most recent (1966) CEN. Whether such change constitutes a real desire to rejuvenate the party leadership is an open question. It may simply represent the natural attrition of the first promotion ranks because of old age. Also, the use of leadership courses in Asunción and in Costa Rica for young party members seems to show a concern about the future replenishment of the party's top posts. These may be, as Duverger suggests, a conservative device to promote only "safe" men from the younger generation. However, it also provides for more continuity in leadership, a smoother transfer of power from one generation to the next, and valuable training and contacts for younger *febreristas*.

Concerning the centralization of power, there is reason to feel that the "iron law" applies to the *febrerista* case. Our study of the Resistance Committee's relations with the CEN indicates a clear tendency of the leaders to insist on strict party discipline. The expulsions of the *bloquistas*, the Vanguardia Febrerista, the Movimiento Revolucionario Paraguayo, and the List 17 Febrero leaders support that conclusion. Indeed, it is enough to compare the party today with *febrerismo* during the 1937-44 period, when it consisted of autonomous clubs—or even with the relatively loose organization of the Concentración Febrerista—to show the degree to which centralization has taken place.

At the same time, one may question whether the leaders in the CEN really control the party apparatus. If they command more effectively now than they did before the 1962 purge, there is also reason to believe that they control a severely weakened organization. Continued purges could leave them like generals without any army. Moreover, the extent of their control can be questioned on other grounds. For Michels, oligarchy grows out of organization: "It is organization which gives birth to the dominion of the elected over the electors, of the mandataries over the mandators, of the delegates over the delegators. Who says organization, says oligarchy."[12]

In *febrerismo's* case, exile has prevented the growth of an efficient party organization. Few, if any, *febreristas* are able to devote their full time to party work. Instead, they must give their primary attention to the economic and social problems created by their exile status. The party, in turn, lacks the funds to support a permanent staff, and this absence of a party bureaucracy has made difficult, if not impossible, the CEN's effective control of the entire apparatus. Lack of control may be attributed to the fact that apparatus is so dispersed, making intraparty communication a serious problem.

This discussion of the limits on party oligarchization suggests an opposing hypothesis, expressed by Samuel Eldersveld:

> In lieu of the doctrine of elite control, we suggest that, although the authority to speak for the organization may remain in the hands of the top elite nucleus, there is great autonomy in operations at the lower "strata" or echelons of the hierarchy, and that control from the top is minimal and formal. . . .
>
> Furthermore, we hypothesize differently the character of "circulation" of the party elite, as well as the basis for the structural stability of the party in the face of such circulation. There is indeed a high turnover in party leadership at all levels of the hierarchy, just as individual mobility for the determined careerist can occur at unbelievable rates. But this is not a *pro forma* turnover, as the oligarchic theorists would contend, a circulation resulting from the "amalgamation" by the old elite

---

12. Michels, *Political Parties*, p. 401.

of "new elite" elements which are considered "safe." This is not primarily a process of absorption. It is often a process of genuine renovation, adaptation, and reconstitution of the sub-coalitional balance of power within the party structure. Or it is often genuine evidence of loss of power.[13]

The experience of the Febrerista party does not support this position. While the fact of exile places important checks on the leaders' power, in some cases making it "minimal and formal," it is also true that turnover in leadership is not high. We have noted a definite tendency for key party positions to remain in the hands of first-promotion men. Moreover, when renovation does take place, there are strong indications that it is directed by the older leaders, achieved through co-operation from above, and is limited to "safe" elements.

The difficulty here seems to be that Eldersveld is trying to generalize too broadly from his study of parties in Wayne County, Michigan. There is no reason to suppose that American political parties, with their highly decentralized structures, must constitute an organizational norm. By the same token, the German Social Democratic party, upon which Michels based his "iron law," may represent an opposite, oligarchical, pole from Eldersveld's "stratarchical" parties. Writers such as Richard N. Hunt have confirmed its monolithic character.[14] As with *febrerismo*, most parties will probably fall somewhere between these two extreme examples, exhibiting some characteristics of each.

In trying to single out the factors promoting cohesion in the Febrerista party, we should not forget that it has never been totally cut off from the nation's political life. Even in the worst days of the Colorado "Terror," the party had its Resistance Committee. At other times, some *febrerista* leaders have actually been permitted to reside in Paraguay. This is a paradox of Paraguayan politics; it is often violent, yet political groups seldom wage total war on their opponents. In this context we might observe about factionalism that it does not

13. Eldersveld, *Political Parties*, pp. 2, 90-100.
14. Richard N. Hunt, *German Social Democracy, 1918-1933*, (New Haven: Yale University Press, 1964). See also, Lewis J. Edinger, *German Exile Politics: The Social Democratic Executive Committee in the Nazi Era* (Berkeley: University of California Press, 1956).

seem to reach such serious proportions among those working within Paraguay as it does among the exiles.[15]

Another important factor in promoting party cohesion is the sharing of past experience among the members. There is, for instance, a considerable *esprit de corps* among men of the first promotion who went through the Chaco War and the February Revolution together. Many second-promotion men have in common the clandestine clubs of the 1940-46 period, as well as the Civil War of 1947. There is probably no *febrerista* who has not shared some risk for the party. Out of such shared experiences come symbols whose emotional value knits the party together. Dates such as October 23 (1931), February 17 (1936), and March 7 (1947) act as reminders of the party's dramatic past. Slogans and phrases, coined at key historical junctures, invoke a feeling of solidarity. *Febrerismo* also has its martyrs, such as Joel Estigarribia and Humberto Garcete, to hold up as models of the true revolutionary spirit.

Luis Alberto Sánchez, the *aprista* writer, once described *febrerismo* as a mood.[16] In doing so he indicated still another source of cohesion. There *is* a mood common to *febreristas* which emphasizes strong dissatisfaction with the *status quo* and with the traditional parties. The Febrerista party has established itself in Paraguayan politics as the movement that gives expression to that mood. It stands for modernization through socialism. This general orientation takes in a broad slice of the political spectrum—hence the frequent disputes over its application to specific problems. The party's doctrinal heterogeneity is, then, both its strength and its weakness, but in the balance, it is probably an advantage. Because it is flexible it proves, in the long run, to be tolerant. The fac-

---

15. This is based on the writer's observations. When he visited Asunción in July, 1964, he was impressed with the degree of co-operation that existed between the institutionalist and List 17 Febrero factions there. Not only were the leaders already negotiating for the party's reunification at the next convention, but the youth groups were already meeting together. This was in marked contrast to the almost total lack of communication between the factions in exile. The explanation offered by the *febreristas* in Paraguay was that having to confront the dictatorship daily made co-operation a pragmatic necessity.

16. Luis Alberto Sánchez, *Reportaje al Paraguay* (Asunción: Editorial Guarania, 1947).

tional fights do not always end in the permanent alienation of the losers; many former *bloquistas* and Vanguardia members have returned to the party. Three members of the present CEN supported List 17 Febrero in 1962.

For the present, it can be said that the factors promoting cohesion have proven to be stronger in *febrerismo* than those which weaken it. There is no intention here, however, to paint a rosy picture of the party's future. The intraparty struggles of the past fifteen years have left *febrerismo* considerably weakened, and prolonged exile has hurt the recruitment of new members. Before 1947, *febreristas* won most university student elections, and today there are signs that the party may be regaining its strength, as it ran well in the faculties of medicine and mathematics in 1965. However, much rebuilding will be necessary before the party reaches its pre-1947 strength, and it suffers from a serious lack of peasant support. Unless it can wean away the rural masses from their attachment to the Liberals and Colorados, there is little hope that *febrerismo* will come to power. The building of such support will come about only through a relatively slow process of education and recruitment, and this will require in turn, that the present period of legality continue.

It is always unwise to predict the future in such an unstable environment as that existing in Paraguayan politics. Let us be satisfied, then, with saying only that as long as the Febrerista party continues to offer to concerned Paraguayans a program of social and economic betterment along democratic socialist lines, as long as it differentiates itself from its traditionalistic rivals by presenting itself as the party of modernization, it will probably continue to play an important role in the nation's politics, either in legality or in exile.

Bibliography

Principal Books Consulted

Alberdi, Juan Bautista. *História de la guerra del Paraguay.* Buenos Aires: Ediciones de la Patria Grande, 1962.

Artaza, Policarpo. *Ayala, Estigarribia y el Partido Liberal.* Buenos Aires: Editorial Ayacucho, 1946.

————. *Que hizo el Partido Liberal n la oposición y en el gobierno.* Buenos Aires: Lucania, 1961.

Ayala, Eligio. *Migraciones.* Santiago de Chile: La Sud America, 1941.

Bárcena Echeveste, O. *Concepción, 1947.* Buenos Aires: Juan Pelligrini, 1948.

Benítez, Justo Pastor. *La vida solitaria del Dr. José Gaspar Rodríguez de Francia, dictador del Paraguay.* Buenos Aires: El Ateneo, 1937.

Bordón, J. Rodolfo. *La revolución del Paraguay del 17 de febrero.* Buenos Aires: Editorial Claridad, 1937.

Cardozo, Efraím. *23 de octubre: una página de história contemporánea del Paraguay.* Buenos Aires: Editorial Guayrá, 1956.

Caroni, Carlos A. *Longitud, latitud y dinámica del movimiento febrerista,* and *Sintesis histórica del problema agrario en le Paraguay* (two essays in one volume). Buenos Aires: Editorial Tupä, 1948.

Cháves, Julio César. *El supremo dictador.* Buenos Aires: Ediciones Nizza, 1958.

Cibils, Manuel J. *Anarquia y revolución en el Paraguay: Vórtice y asíntota.* Buenos Aires: Editorial Americalee, 1957.

Codas Papaluca, Alcides. *Cuestiones rurales del Paraguay.* Buenos Aires: Editorial Tupä, 1949.

199

Duverger, Maurice. *Political Parties: Their Organization and Activity in the Modern State.* New York: John Wiley and Sons, Inc., 1963.

Eckstein, Harry, and David Apter. *Comparative Politics: A Reader.* New York: Free Press of Glencoe, 1964.

Edinger, Lewis J. *German Exile Politics: The Social Democratic Executive Committee in the Nazi Era.* Berkeley: University of California, 1956.

Eldersveld, Samuel J. *Political Parties: A Behavioral Analysis.* Chicago: Rand McNally and Co., 1964.

Estigarribia, José Felix. *The Epic of the Chaco: Marshall Estigarribia's Memoirs of the Chaco War, 1932-1935.* Edited and translated by Pablo Max Insfran. Austin: University of Texas Press, 1950.

Garcia Mellid, Atilio. *Proceso a los falsificadores de la historia del Paraguay.* Vols. I and II. Buenos Aires: Ediciones Theoria, 1964.

González, Antonio E. *Preparación del Paraguay para la guerra del Chaco.* Vols. I and II. Asunción: Editorial El Grafico, 1957.

———. *La rebelión de Concepción.* Buenos Aires: Editorial Guaranía, 1947.

González, Juan Natalicio. *Como se construye una nación.* Buenos Aires: Editorial Guaranía, 1949.

González, Teodosio. *Infortunios del Paraguay.* Buenos Aires: Talleres Graficos L. J. Rosso, 1931.

González Merzario, Americo. *Politica y ejercito: consideraciones sobre problemas politico-militares del Paraguay.* Buenos Aires: Editorial Yegros, 1955.

Hunt, Richard N. *German Social Democracy, 1918-1933.* New Haven: Yale University Press, 1964.

Jover Peralta, Anselmo. *El Paraguay revolucionario.* Vols. I and II. Buenos Aires: Editorial Tupä, 1946.

Laconich, Marco Antonio. *La paz del Chaco: Un pueblo traicionado.* Montevideo: Editorial Paraguay, 1939.

McDonald, Neil A. *The Study of Political Parties.* New York: Random House, 1963.

Michels, Robert. *Political Parties,* New York: Dover Publications, Inc., 1959.

Neumann, Sigmund. *Modern Political Parties.* New York: John Wiley and Sons, 1956.

Paraguay, República del. *La revolución paraguaya.* Asunción, 1937.

———. Ministerio de Agricultura y Ganadería, *Censo Agropecuario, 1956.* Asunción: Editorial "El Arte," 1961.

Pendle, George. *Paraguay: A Riverside Nation.* London: Royal Institute of International Affairs, 1956.

Pereira, Carlos. *Solano López y su drama.* Buenos Aires: Ediciones de la Patria Grande, 1962.

Pérez Acosta, Juan F. *Carlos Antonio López: "obrero máximo."* Asunción: Editorial Guaranía, 1948.

———. *Migraciones históricas del Paraguay a la Argentina.* Buenos Aires: Talleres Gráficos Optimus, 1952.

Prieto, Justo. *Llénese los claros.* Buenos Aires: Lucania, 1957.

———. *Manual del ciudadano liberal paraguayo.* Buenos Aires: Editorial Asunción, 1953.

Raine, Philip. *Paraguay.* New Brunswick: The Scarecrow Press, 1956.

Rey del Castro, Carlos. *Las clases rurales del Paraguay.* Buenos Aires: Editorial Tupä, 1947.

Servicio Técnico Interamericano de Cooperación Agrícola. *Manual estadístico del Paraguay.* Asunción: S.T.I.C.A., 1963.

Speratti, Juan. *Política militar paraguaya.* Buenos Aires: Abece, 1955.

Stefanich, Juan. *La diplomacia de la revolución.* Buenos Aires: Editorial El Mundo Nuevo, 1945.

———. *El Paraguay en febrero de 1936.* Buenos Aires: Editorial el Mundo Nuevo, 946.

———. *El Paraguay Nuevo.* Buenos Aires: Editorial Claridad, 1943.

———. *Renovación y liberación: La obra del gobierno del febrero.* Buenos Aires: Editorial El Mundo Nuevo, 1946.

———. *La restauración histórica del Paraguay.* Buenos Aires: Editorial El Mundo Nuevo, 1945.

———. *El 23 de octubre de 1931.* Buenos Aires: Editorial Febrero, 1958.

Volta Gaona, Enrique. *23 de octubre: Caireles de sangre en el alma de la patria paraguaya.* Asunción: Editorial El Arte, 1957.

Warren, Harris Gaylord. *Paraguay: An Informal History.* Norman: University of Oklahoma Press, 1949.

———. "Political Aspects of the Paraguayan Revolution, 1936-1940," *The Hispanic American Historical Review,* 30 (Feb., 1950), 2-25.

FEBRERISTA PARTY DOCUMENTS
(A Selected Bibliography)

El Ateneo. Buenos Aires, 1961-62.

El Ateneo Cultural Febrerista. *El febrerismo en su hora decisiva.* Buenos Aires, n.d. [1963?].

Concentración Revolucionaria Febrerista, Departamento de Prensa y Propaganda. *Documentos políticos.* Asunción, 1946.

———, Comité de Resistencia. *Construyendo el febrerismo.* Buenos Aires: Alea, 1951.

Febrero. Buenos Aires, 1955-64.

Franco, Rafael. *Carta a la ciudadanía febrerista.* Montevideo, 1961.

Gaona, Francisco. *La hegemonía argentina en el Paraguay.* Buenos Aires: Continental, 1954.

Gaona, Roque. *Farsa y realidad*. Asunción: Departamento de Cultura del Partido Revolucionario Febrerista, 1961.

Movimiento 14 de Mayo. *Plataforma revolucionaria del Movimiento "14 de Mayo" para la libertad paraguaya*. 1960.

Movimiento Revolucionario Paraguayo. *La integración política antinacional y anti-democrática de las oligarquías de todos los partidos en el regimen de la tiranía*. Buenos Aires, 1964.

——. *Nuevo ideario nacional: Documento fundamental del Movimiento Revolucionario Paraguayo*. 1961.

——. *La revolución nacional y el problema de las "izquierdas" en el Paraguay*. Buenos Aires, 1961.

Partido Revolucionario Febrerista. *Ideario, declaración de principios y programa de gobierno*. 1959.

——. *Para que la ciudadania febrerista sepa*. Buenos Aires, 1960.

——. *Reglamento electoral del Partido Revolucionario Febrerista*. 1961.

——. *Tercera Convención Ordinaria*. Asunción, 1961.

——, Comité Ejecutivo Nacional. *Carta Orgánica*. 1951.

——, Comité Político. *Qué es el febrerismo*. 1953.

——, Comité Regional de Buenos Aires. *Boletín Informativo #2: Finanzas*. Buenos Aires, 1958.

——, Departamento de Asuntos Campesinos. *La realidad del medio rural paraguayo*. n.d.

——, Departamento de Cultura. *Semblanza histórica e idealógica del febrerismo*. 1958.

——, Departamento de Prensa y Propaganda. *Realidad y mentira*. 1955.

——, Lema Electoral "17 de Febrero." *Informativo y resoluciones de la III convención ordinaria al pueblo febrerista*. Asunción, 1962.

——, Movimiento Unidad y Revolución. *Bases para un programa de liberación nacional*. Buenos Aires: Alece, 1957.

——, Segunda Convención Ordinaria. *Linea política*. Exile, 1958.

Perrotta, Benigno. *Orientadora y patriotica respuesta del partido revolucionario febrerista a la tirania y a la honda crisis que sufre la nación*. n.d. [1964?].

Vanguardia Febrerista. *Posición del Comando de la Vanguardia Febrerista en la lucha contra la dictadura del Paraguay*. Buenos Aires, 1959.

Yegros, Elpidio, *et al*. *Mensaje a los companeros febreristas*. Buenos Aires, 1961.

INTERVIEWS

(Much of this work was based on interviews, especially with leaders and members of the Febrerista party. However, since the

writer was in frequent and often informal contact with the persons interviewed, dates have not been included. All interviews took place between February and November, 1964.)

1. Galo Achar Insfran, member of CEN (1951), List 17 Febrero leader
2. Julio A. Acosta, former member of Vanguardia Febrerista, member of CEN (1962)
3. Carlos Alfieri, List 17 Febrero leader in Asunción
4. Gerrardo Banuelos, former *bloquista,* member of Ateneo Cultural
5. Manuel Benítez, member of CEN (1962)
6. Raimundo Careaga, former *bloquista,* List 17 Febrero leader
7. Carlos Chavez del Valle, former secretary of organization of the Resistance Committee
8. Francisco Chavez del Valle, participant in the revolt of February 17, 1936
9. Manuel Dejesus Carvallo, former president of the *febrerista* Central Electoral Committee (1958-62)
10. General Rafael Franco, president of the Febrerista party
11. Francisco Gaona, Paraguayan labor leader, member of the Ateneo Cultural
12. Roque Gaona, vice-president #2 of the Febrerista party
13. Atilio Garcete, List 17 Febrero leader
14. Ignacio Iramain, member CEN (1954, 1958), List 17 Febrero leader
15. Federico Jara Troche, participant in revolt of February 17, 1936
16. Agustin Loncharich, former secretary general (1947-51), former member of Vanguardia Febrerista
17. Epifanio Mendes Fleites, head of the Movimiento Popular Colorado, a dissident Colorado party faction in exile
18. Romain Ortiz Maidana, leader of the *febrerista* youth in Asunción
19. Carlos Pastore, head of the Liberal party
20. Cecilio Recalde, member of the Buenos Aires Regional Executive Committee
21. José Regunega, leader of the *febrerista* youth in Buenos Aires
22. Arnaldo Valdovinos, leader of the Vanguardia Febrerista
23. Federico Varela, secretary general of the Buenos Aires Regional Executive Committee
24. Badri Yampey, former *bloquista,* member of the Ateneo Cultural
25. Elpidio Yegros, member of CEN (1945-47; 1951-54; 1958 to present), acting president of ANEC (1936-37), former mayor of Asunción (1937)
26. Ulpiano Zorrilla, former member of Vanguardia Febrerista

Index